THE BRITI
ECONOMY IN THE 1970s

Edited by
W. P. J. MAUNDER,

Department of Economics, University of Loughborough

Heinemann Educational Books · London

Heinemann Educational Books Ltd

LONDON EDINBURGH MELBOURNE AUCKLAND TORONTO
HONG KONG SINGAPORE KUALA LUMPUR NEW DELHI
NAIROBI JOHANNESBURG IBADAN
KINGSTON

ISBN 0-435-84475-X
ISBN 0-435-84476-8 Pbk

Published by Heinemann Educational Books Ltd
Filmset by Northumberland Press Ltd
Gateshead, Tyne and Wear
Printed in Great Britain by Richard Clay (The Chaucer Press) Ltd
Bungay, Suffolk

Contents

N.B. References are placed at the end of the chapter in which they occur.

Introduction

by Peter Maunder

The continuing growth in the popularity of economics in British schools, colleges and universities since the 1960s has been accompanied by the appearance of many introductory economics textbooks. However, material about the rapidly changing structure and nature of economic institutions has been much less frequently published. Yet those which have been made – such as *The Economist*'s 'Schools Briefs' which first appeared in 1975 – have clearly found a receptive market amongst both teachers and students of economics. In reviewing developments in British economic policy this book tries to offer to a wide variety of readers an account of the influences of government during the 1970s. We hope that teachers of economics will find it of value in the ever-pressing problem of getting a perspective on the recent past. For our undergraduate readers we trust it will at the very least add to their knowledge of contemporary events and the circumstances surrounding them. One may no longer be surprised by the degree of ignorance shown by students of fairly recent events such as the 1967 devaluation of sterling. Yet as teachers we often fail to appreciate that such events occurred when those who were our students in 1980 were only starting primary school! So for our undergraduate readers we hope that the following chapters will be both informative and provide the empirical support to their theory texts.

However, it was not our purpose just to offer a descriptive account. My colleagues have tried to explain the rationale of government policies and assess their effect. Not surprisingly they have found both the identification of policy objectives and the evaluation of the effect of policies not an easy task. We thus strongly echo the comment arising from a similar appraisal exercise, which was undertaken for an earlier period but overlaps with our time span of the 1970s. 'It is not so much a problem of evaluating effects as of deciding what they were. In many cases – indeed perhaps in most cases – the evidence on the effects of particular policies is thin, so that any conclusion about success or failure has to be highly tentative' (Blackaby [1978], p. 1).

Our time span begins in 1970 and covers two complete periods of office of both main political parties – the Heath government of 1970–4 and the Wilson–Callaghan administrations of 1974–9. The decade thus neatly focuses on the changes in policy direction arising from the differing political outlooks of the Conservative and Labour parties. The lack of continuity since 1964 between one government and another in various aspects of economic policy has already prompted one economist to refer to the period as 'the Jekyll and Hyde years' (Stewart [1977]). The early policy decisions of Mrs Thatcher's government in 1979 continued to illustrate this political character of economic policy-making.

Our coverage reflects the shift in the 1970s towards government policies of a more microeconomic, selective character. Inevitably the macro dimension is there at the outset with chapters on monetary and fiscal policy. The constraints on domestic policy-making stemming from the state of the world economy are also necessarily discussed in two further chapters (Chapters 9 and 10). But there are three chapters (Chapters 3, 4 and 5) that encompass the operation of the labour market. The amount of coverage reflects the extent to which recent governments have intervened in the determination of incomes, regulated work patterns and evolved policies on industrial relations. There are also separate accounts of industrial policy (Chapter 6), spatial policy (Chapter 7) and policy towards the nationalised industries (Chapter 8). Chapter 11 assesses the effect that Common Market membership has had on policy-making in Britain.

The reader should appreciate that in putting some perspective on the making and execution of recent economic policies each contributor has necessarily had to sacrifice certain points of detail. Because of the limit on the number of words that each contributor faced none could have hoped to have been encyclopaedic in covering the manifold influences of government within his respective chapter.

Our text follows the style of other economists who have made assessments of government intervention using an instruments of policy approach such as those at the National Institute of Economic and Social Research (Blackaby [1978]). We did consider the alternative of an analysis based on the major objectives of policy. This would have highlighted the issues of inflation, unemployment, the balance of payments, slow economic growth and so on. The merit of this approach would, of course, have been to point out that objectives such as stable prices and full employment involve many government Ministries. However, there were strong opposing arguments. Firstly, these aims are not wholly personalised in the role of Cabinet Ministers. There has never been during the period a Minister for Full Employment, nor one for a Balance of Payments surplus. In practice these broad macroeconomic aspirations are translated into something more tangible at the micro level by the various Ministries. The same is true of the 'newer' issues which came to the fore during the decade (such as 'deindustrialisation'). There is still doubt as to quite what this term really means but in that it indicated concern about the state of Britain's manufacturing industry it has clearly not been just of academic interest. But at the same time there has been no clear policy objective concerning deindustrialisation. Measures taken to improve the health of manufacturing industry such as by slowing down import penetration have been essentially piecemeal. Deindustrialisation is a prime example because it is clear, even without reading the memoirs of one of the decade's prime ministers, that the problems of British industry in the widest sense have been the main preoccupation of recent governments. (Wilson [1979], pp. 116–17). Yet as a former Chief Economic Adviser to the Departments of Trade, Industry, Prices and Consumer Protection has noted it has been difficult to discern 'a clear, consistent and operational set of objectives governing the attempt to improve the performance of manufacturing industry' (Peacock [1977], p. 17). Now we have not lacked diagnoses of the country's poor performance. The White Paper, *An Approach to Industrial Strategy*, indeed offered one succinct analysis which is worth setting out here in full since it is so clearly germane to most of our chapters.

Investment A low rate of investment; inefficient use of capital, which has resulted in a relatively poor return on new investment; poor choice of investment.

Labour Inadequate development of a manpower policy and the consequent regional and sectoral shortages of skilled labour; low labour productivity reflecting poor management, inadequate consultation, restrictive practices, overmanning and disruption by industrial action; attitudes to productivity and labour mobility based on views about appropriate pay and tax structures which reflect long-standing attitudes to relative pay in industry.

Government Sharp and frequent changes of economic regulators to meet the conflicting needs of economic and social priorities, which make it difficult for companies to plan ahead; pre-emption of resources by the public sector and by personal consumption to the detriment of industry's investment and export performance; and Government intervention in the pricing, investment and employment policies of the nationalised industries.

Finance   A decline in rate of industrial profitability: imperfections in the capital market mainly at the medium- and longer-term ends; a capital market which does not give priority to the needs of industry.

(Cmnd 6315 [1975], p. 5)

But when one moves from diagnosis to policy prescription the economist is still in difficulty. Of the 'new industrial strategy' which the above White Paper ushered in it is not surprising that Peacock [1977] has argued that 'with no clear indication which objectives of policy are being maximised and a lack of commitment on the precise nature of the constraints on doing so there can be no assessment of the relative merits of the alternative courses of action to be taken' (p. 20).

Throughout this book it is clear that assessment of the effectiveness of policy is confronted by a number of difficulties relating essentially to the determination of the appropriate criteria to employ. A major difficulty is the fact that the objectives of particular policy measures have been frequently ill-defined and that in particular situations the measures taken have been motivated by political-cum-social and economic considerations at variance with óne another and sometimes with short-term, sometimes with longer-term, considerations in mind. To the extent that the objectives of intervention have been to assist in the achievement of the basic objectives of economic policy – full employment, economic growth, price stability and a balance of payments surplus – then it could be argued that intervention had failed. On the other hand it could be argued that without intervention the economic situation would be worse and that it is in any case too soon to judge the effect of some measures. That debate, therefore, must inevitably remain inconclusive; it is not in any case a fruitful line to pursue for it pays no attention to the appropriate criteria for intervention in particular cases and to the opportunity costs involved.

Given all these problems perhaps the reader will understand why an objectives of policy analysis looked so unattractive to us.

Finally, a note concerning what the book does not contain. ... There is no chapter that attempts to pull together the lessons to be learned from studying different aspects of policy because we intended the text to be used as specialist reading on particular topics. We do not offer a Brookings-style appraisal of Britain's economic prospects

(Caves [1968]). Judgement of the conduct of economic policies in the widest sense is an uneasy task. Moreover given that a dozen economists were involved in the present endeavour unanimity of view in any appraisal would not have been easy to achieve! Nonetheless we hope the value of this text will turn out to be greater than the sum of its component parts.

I am very grateful to my fellow economists at Loughborough for responding to my invitation to contribute to this text. I would never have faced the task of organising the book but for the geographic proximity of enough colleagues willing to participate each one drawing on his own built-up specialist knowledge. The enthusiasm of my colleagues to contribute chapters is particularly notable when one notes that multi-author texts written within just one department of economics are conspicuous by their absence. We did not wish to be exclusive for the sake of it and indeed the participation of Robert Wilson of Warwick University in collaborating with Derek Bosworth on the chapter about the labour market bears testimony to that fact. We were glad to draw on Robert's expertise.

We all owe a real debt to the secretarial staff of the Department of Economics at Loughborough – Mrs Brenda Moore, Mrs Joyce Tuson, Mrs Madge Lowe, Mrs Susan Spencer and also Mrs Gloria Brentnall – and to all we extend our sincere thanks. The pressures imposed on them during the latter part of the autumn term by half the Department simultaneously seeking the typing of successive drafts were real enough for us to point out that this is not the usual routine acknowledgement.

The editorial task proved to be at its most intensive right at the end of 1979. Because of that I wish to record an acknowledgement to Marianne, my wife, for her patience and willingness to prepare for the festive season unaided whilst I was more than usually preoccupied in my study.

References

Blackaby, F. (ed.) [1978], *British Economic Policy 1960–74*. Cambridge: Cambridge University Press, Chapter 1, pp. 1–10.

Caves, R. E. [1968], *Britain's Economic Prospects*. London: Allen and Unwin.

Cmnd 6315 [1975], *An Approach to Industrial Strategy*. London: HMSO.

Peacock, A. [1977], 'Giving economic advice in difficult times', *Three Banks Review*, no. 113, March 1977, pp. 3–23.

Stewart, M. [1977], *The Jekyll and Hyde Years: Politics and Economic Policy since 1964*. London: Dent.

Wilson, Sir Harold [1976], *The Governance of Britain*. London: Weidenfeld and Nicolson.

1 Stabilisation Policy and Fiscal Reform

by Tony Westaway

Introduction

This chapter will concentrate on an examination of the use of fiscal policy to stabilise the macroeconomy in the UK, but it will also introduce the main elements of fiscal reform that were introduced in the budgets presented during the 1970s. In this way all aspects of recent fiscal changes are discussed. It has been common practice in the UK for governments to introduce a major budget in March or April and to announce public expenditure plans in September or October. This practice was supplemented by several mini-budgets and expenditure plans were delayed on several occasions during the 1970s.

The theoretical developments that have been made to allow for the academic and predictive inadequacies of the IS–LM framework are summarised in the final section. During the 1970s the general interpretation of the IS–LM model evolved from the comparative static presentation developed by Hansen to a dynamic model that allows for an external sector, a budget restraint and expectations and other forms of uncertainty. This has partly been a result of the increased acceptance of a monetarist alternative, partly of the increased dissatisfaction with the original model.

Students who wish to examine demand management in the UK economy in greater depth should refer to Posner [1978], Blackaby [1978] and to discussions contained in *Economic Trends* and the *National Institute Economic Review*. A brief summary of budget and public expenditure changes are contained in *Economic Progress Reports* published by the Treasury, and further details can be found in the appropriate White Papers. The theoretical developments are contained within some of the more recent textbooks; for example, Westaway and Weyman-Jones [1977], Turnovsky [1978] and Chrystal [1979]. Finally, a summary of the British fiscal system is presented by Kay

.and King [1978] whilst the most comprehensive examination of the need for fiscal reform has been offered by the Meade Committee (Institute of Fiscal Studies [1978]).

A General Appraisal of the Period as a Whole

Demand management in the 1970s
Chancellors of the Exchequer for both Conservative and Labour administrations repeatedly announced their intention to reduce the amount of fiscal intervention in the long-term control of the economy. In spite of these clearly stated intentions there was an increase in the frequency of the resort to budgetary measures in the 1970s. There are two major reasons why this occurred. On the one hand inflation and unemployment reached levels which were far in excess of anything experienced by the postwar economy. The second major problem was the continual change in major policy target requiring about turns in demand management policy. To some extent these reasons are interrelated, for a policy designed to overcome one macroeconomic problem only resulted in an exaggeration of another and in some cases in the introduction of a further macroeconomic problem. This

Table 1.1 A general survey of policy targets and demand management policy action

	Unemployment	Inflation	Growth	Balance of Payments	PSBR	Policy
1970	low	low	low	surplus	zero	neutral
1971	moderate	rising	low	surplus	rising	go
1972	moderate	falling	moderate	deficit	rising	go (boom)
1973	low	rising	moderate	weakening	rising	neutral
1974	low	high	decline	weakening	rising	go
1975	moderate	peak	decline	crisis	peak	stop
1976	high	falling	low	crisis	large	stop
1977	high	falling	low	strong	moderate	go
1978	high	moderate	moderate	surplus	rising	go
1979	high	rising				stop

is particularly true of the growth throughout the period of the Public Sector Borrowing Requirement (PSBR) which has now become a problem in its own right.

The major targets for government policy control are summarised in Table 1.1 together with a broad summary of the type of demand management employed during each year. Obviously this is a very general treatment, and the precise problems and budgetary policy action will be examined in greater depth in the following sections. The terms used for the policy targets are relative. As an example low levels of unemployment refer to approximately $2\frac{1}{2}$–3% of total employees or a figure of between 500 000 and 600 000 unemployed. In previous decades this would be considered a high level of unemployment. The lowest rate of inflation for the period was 5–6% and the highest in excess of 26%.

A more detailed summary of the changes in the values of policy targets over the period is contained in Figures 1.1 to 1.6.

As can be seen budgetary policy in the first half of the decade was largely reflationary. There were two reasons for this and these too are reasonably obvious. There was seen to be a need to increase the growth of the economy and reduce the level of unemployment. As a result inflation increased rapidly, a phenomenon exaggerated by the rapid rise in the price of oil and other imported goods. This combined with industrial strife led to a decline in the output of the economy.

The reflation was brought to an abrupt halt as inflation peaked, and there was a large deficit on the balance of payments. The PSBR became a major policy target as it exceeded £10 000m in 1975. Even allowing for inflation this was a very large increase from virtually zero in 1970. As the balance of payments improved and inflation fell it was once again considered appropriate to reflate the economy. Unemployment in the last four years of the decade had grown from about 1 million to $1\frac{1}{2}$ million people although there has been a slight decline since the end of 1978.

The decade closed with a major deflation in terms of government expenditure cut-backs. The major change was the newly elected Conservative government's expressed intention to reduce the extent of government fiscal intervention and to rely on a monetarist policy to control the economy. The decade has thus ended as it began with a Conservative government intent on reducing the role of fiscal demand management. Whether this can be maintained will only be-

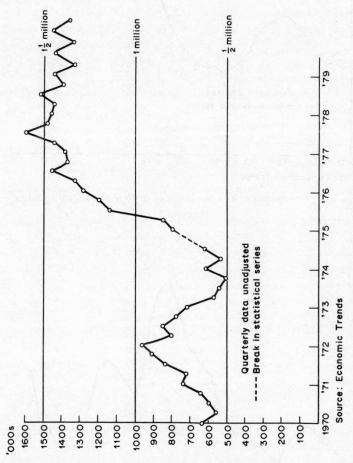

Figure 1.1 *Total numbers unemployed (including school-leavers)*

Source: *Economic Trends*

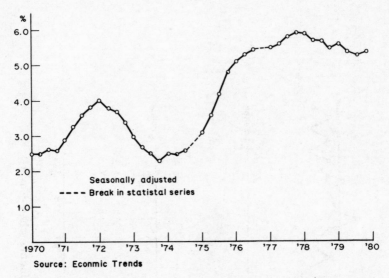

Figure 1.2   *Unemployment as a percentage of employees* (excluding school-leavers)

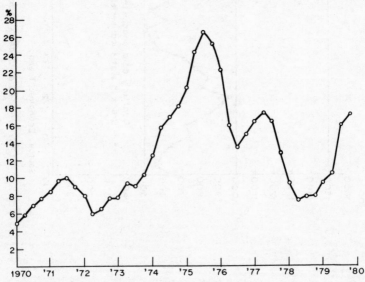

Figure 1.3   *General index of retail prices* (percentage change on same quarter of previous year)

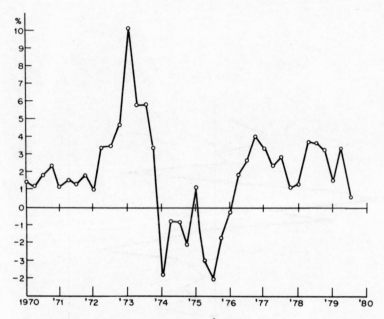

Figure 1.4 Growth: GDP (output based) percentage change on same quarter of previous year

come apparent with experience. The economy appears to be heading for a major recession in 1980 and higher levels of unemployment than those achieved in the 1970s. As the level of inflation is also beginning to rise it will be interesting to see whether the Government can overcome a short-term crisis in order to maintain its long-term monetary strategy.

Fiscal reform in the 1970s
The major items of fiscal reform were introduced during the first three years of the Conservative government's initial period of office. A unified system of personal taxation and VAT were introduced in April 1973, two years after their introduction had been proposed. The chancellor also modified corporation tax in the same budget. Proposals for a more far-reaching reform of direct taxation by the

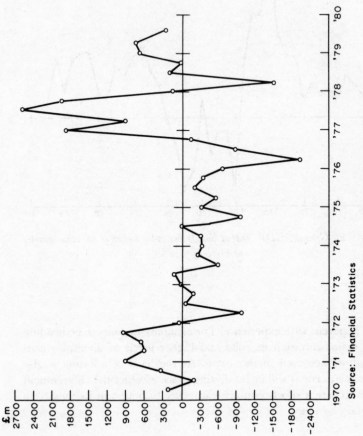

£m

2700
2400
2100
1800
1500
1200
900
600
300
0
-300
-600
-900
-1200
-1500
-1800
-2400

1970 '71 '72 '73 '74 '75 '76 '77 '78 '79 '80

Source: Financial Statistics

Figure 1.5   UK balance of payments: balance for official financing

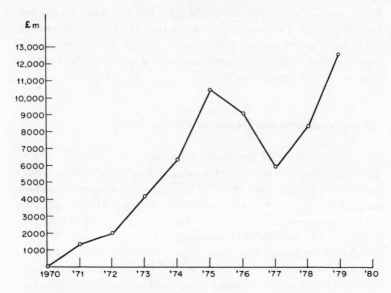

Figure 1.6   Public sector borrowing requirement

introduction of a tax credit scheme were not introduced as was the case for the proposed introduction of an inheritance tax.

The Labour government reformed the taxation of capital transfer on death and during one's lifetime by introducing a capital transfer tax (CTT), but their plans to introduce a wealth tax to supplement CTT were not fulfilled. By the end of the decade there was considerable criticism of a system which taxed some individuals on the one hand whilst paying them social security benefits on the other. This is the so-called 'poverty trap' whereby many low income earners are faced by a marginal rate of tax greater than 100%. This comes about from the loss of means tested benefits coupled with the payments owed for each extra £1 that is earned. (Loss of benefits plus tax owed thus exceeds £1).

This was a problem highlighted by the Meade committee [1978] in its proposals for the reform of the structure of direct taxation. The Meade Committee proposed the introduction of an expenditure tax system to overcome many of the anomolies and inconsistencies that had resulted from the *ad hoc* adjustment of first this tax and then the other combined with the effects of inflation. The structure of direct taxation and social security benefits was also severely criticised, but the Meade Committee did not offer a satisfactory alternative. After less than two years the report is already losing much of its initial impact, and it now seems unlikely that any of the proposed changes will be introduced.

1970–4: Conservative Budgetary Policies

1970–2: Initial period of Conservative government
The Conservatives were elected to office in June 1970 with the precise intention of reducing the extent of government intervention and improving the efficiency of the government machine. There was to be a twofold revision of the role of government management. The ambitious aim was not only to reduce government activity but also to improve the government's cost-effectiveness. These sentiments are very similar to those expressed by the Conservative government that was elected in 1979 and may be assumed to be a general Conservative policy. As with the Labour government that they replaced the Conservatives hoped to break away from the 'stop–go' policies that had characterised the 1960s. This must, however, be judged to have been a failure as the recourse to budgetary action increased as the decade proceeded.

The first announcement of changes in the instruments of demand management was made in October 1970 with the publication of the Government's expenditure plans in a White Paper entitled *New Policies for Public Spending* (Cmnd 4515 [1970]). In this a lower level of growth for public expenditure was announced; approximately £1500m was to be cut from the projected level of public expenditure for 1974/5 at 1970 prices. The broad effect on aggregate demand for 1971/2 was expected to be neutral although the National Institute argued that it was slightly reflationary because the reduction in tax revenue had been slightly smaller than the reduction in government expenditure (Blackaby [1978], p. 54). As Price [1978] points out, these policies were regarded with suspicion because the previous Labour government had completed their switch away from public expenditure by the end of the financial year 1969/70 and had announced that public expenditure would only be allowed to grow as quickly as national resources.

On 30 March 1971 the Chancellor of the Exchequer, Mr Barber, introduced a budget which through a combination of income tax changes, a reduction in the rate of company taxation and the partial abolition of selective employment tax (SET) was mildly reflationary. The overall cut in tax revenue amounted to £680m for a full year, but the effects on the aggregate economy were expected to be slight because of fiscal drag. These measures were followed by changes in purchase tax rates on 19 July 1971 and plans to speed up the public expenditure programme were announced on 25 November 1971. This was to be achieved by bringing forward selective items of capital expenditure. The main aim of these latter measures was to maintain the rate of growth of the domestic economy at about 3%.

The 1971 budget and fiscal reform: personal direct taxation, corporation tax and VAT

The main feature of the 1971 budget was the announcement of a two-year programme of radical fiscal reform. The existing system of personal direct taxation combined income tax, surtax and a system of earned income reliefs. These were unnecessarily complicated in operation and the Government proposed a pattern of reform whereby the current system was to be replaced by a unified system of personal taxation. Details of the proposed reform were given in the 1972 budget and in a White Paper, *Reform of Personal Direct Taxation* (Cmnd 4653 [1972]). The reforms form the basis of the present structure of direct taxation.

The new system had four characteristics. The system of personal allowances was to be retained and a basic rate of tax to cover a broad bank of taxable income was proposed as a replacement for the existing combination of a standard rate of tax with earned income relief. Higher rates of tax were to be applied to higher incomes and investment income was to be subjected to a surcharge over a certain level. Otherwise investment income was to be treated as earnings in order to encourage saving.

The Chancellor had stated in his 1971 budget that corporation tax 'distorts the working of market forces and so tends towards the misallocation of scarce resources' (Hansard [1971]). He suggested the introduction of a two-tier tax system with the higher rate being applied to undistributed profits and hence the discrimination against distributed profits would be removed. A White Paper entitled *Reform of Corporation Tax* (Cmnd 4630 [1972] was published in March 1972 and the changes were introduced in the 1973 budget.

The final fiscal reform proposed in March 1971 was the replacement of purchase tax and selective employment tax by value added tax (VAT). VAT is a more broadly based and less discriminatory tax which is collected at each stage of production. The March 1972 budget saw the publication of a White Paper *Value Added Tax* (Cmnd 4929 [1972]) which explained the new tax. This system of indirect taxation brought the British system of taxation into line with the other member countries of the EEC. The tax was introduced in April 1973 along with the personal unified tax structure and corporation tax. VAT was introduced at a single rate of 10% although many goods (e.g. children's clothes and shoes) were zero rated. A refinement to the system was introduced by the Labour government in 1975 with luxury items incurring a new higher rate of 25%, later to be halved to $12\frac{1}{2}$%. The Thatcher government returned in 1979 to the original system with a single 15% rate tax.

1972–4: Further proposals for fiscal reform: tax credits and an inheritance tax
The 1972 budget has become known as the most reflationary of the decade, but before examining its effects on the economy we shall consider one of its alternative aims. The Conservative government intended to make further progress towards fiscal reform and in addition to the publication of the White Papers cited above the Government announced the publication of two forthcoming Green Papers.

The existing system of estate duties as a tax on wealth at death could be easily avoided by putting wealth into trusts or by giving it away prior to death. The Green Paper entitled *Taxation of Capital on Death: A possible Inheritance Tax in place of Estate Duty* (Cmnd 4930 [1972]) was introduced as a consultative document. The main aim of the tax was to transfer the liability for tax from the donor to the recipient of wealth. This new tax could also be avoided if the total wealth were distributed to several recipients because it is their lifetime acquisition of wealth that is the relevant criterion for taxation and an initial amount of receipts would be tax-exempt. This proposal was not put into effect, and the Labour government that followed in fact replaced estate duty by another donor-based tax, Capital Transfer Tax, in 1975.

The second major reform was in the form of Proposals for a Tax Credit Scheme (Cmnd 5116 [1972] which aimed to bring together the systems of personal taxation and social security benefits. As the Chancellor stated in his budget speech on 21 March 'In Britain we

have two systems existing side by side – a taxation system which
embodies a set of reliefs and allowances based on one set of principles
and a social security system which embodies a different set of
benefits and allowances based on a different set of principles.'
(Hansard [1972]). The scheme embodied a form of negative income
tax and attempted to bring together personal taxation and social
security benefits into one fiscal structure. Such a scheme has many
attractions for it would deal with the problem of the 'poverty trap'
and remove the need for many tax-payers to make claims for means-
tested benefits. This particular proposal received severe criticism from
Lord Kaldor (1973), a Labour Party adviser, and consideration of
introduction was abandoned when the Labour Party formed a government in 1974. Many of Kaldor's criticisms were arguably ill-founded
being based solely on the particular numerical example given in the
Green Paper. It seemed strange that a Labour Party would reject
what appeared to be a universal scheme. Kaldor argued for selectivity
on the grounds that it was the only way to help the poor, whilst the
Conservative Party was rejecting selectivity in favour of universality.

Thus these two later reforms did not come into being. Their demise
partly resulted from the election of a Labour government but also
from the unexpected death of Iain Macleod who was to have been the
Chancellor of the Exchequer during this period of Conservative government. It was he who had been the major driving force behind the
many proposals for fiscal reform proffered by the Conservative
government.

1972–4: Demand management: the Barber boom
During 1971 the level of unemployment approached one million unemployed. This was combined with a slowing in the rate of growth
and a worsening of the balance of payments. The budget introduced
on 21 March 1972 combined the aim of further progress towards
fiscal reform as discussed above with further aims of encouraging
British industry to expand and modernise to meet the challenge of
Europe and to get the economy growing at a sustained and faster
rate. The largest discretionary fiscal change of the period was achieved
mainly through income tax changes. It was thus to be a consumer
led boom. Even after an allowance for fiscal drag the effect of the
£960m charge in tax revenue through tax allowance changes was
expected to be substantial. Purchase tax was reduced to give a further
£135m reduction in tax revenue.

The general feeling at the time was that the high levels of unemployment and slow growth would mean that these reflationary measures would have little effect on the rate of inflation. At this time there was still an implicit belief in the Phillips curve and so it was generally believed that unemployment and demand pressures on inflation could not coexist. The balance of payments deteriorated and moved into deficit. It is debatable whether British industry was prepared or capable of satisfying a consumer boom at that particular time or of that particular magnitude. Thus the decision to float the pound was taken on 23 June 1972 to restore the balance of payments deficit.

Precisely by how much these measures aggravated the levels of inflation or crises on the balance of payments is open to considerable debate. In retrospect there are those who believe that the economy would not have recovered without a lever of the sort that was employed. At the time the Government was not prepared to see unemployment exceed one million nor a dramatic decrease in the rate of growth of the economy. Others believed that a large discretionary intervention of the type utilised was a sure recipe for disaster because of the reason already offered that the economy was not prepared for a particularly large consumer led boom.

As Blackaby [1978] has pointed out, the arguments have become essentially about the objectives which the Government chose and given a target of 500 000 unemployed combined with a 5% rate of growth the large stimulus was inevitable. In reality the target of 500 000 unemployed was reached by the end of 1973 and the 5% growth target by mid 1973.

Priority in the objectives of government policy began to shift after the 1972 budget as there was increasing concern with the accelerating rate of inflation and the wage explosion. Both the public expenditure plans announced on 19 December 1972 and the budget of 6 March 1973 were neutral (the latter seeing the introduction of the fiscal reform package). The Chancellor, however, announced restrictions in the growth of public expenditure through major cuts in road building and other local expenditures on 21 May 1973. Investment in nationalised industries was also cut. The rationale advanced for these restrictions was that public expenditure had been deliberately expanded at the end of 1971 to reduce unemployment and with unemployment falling and a growth rate of 5% there was no need to continue with a high growth programme. As Price [1978] has explained these cuts were also a reaction to criticism that the December 1972 plans would be potentially destabilising, particularly in late 1973/4 and during 1974/5. In any case the economy was now growing quickly.

In early November 1973 the Arab oil-producing nations announced a 25% minimum cut in oil supplies to the West – a decision which followed a 66% rise in the price of oil on 16 October and a 5% cumulative cut-back in oil production on 17 October. Oil prices were then doubled with effect from 1 January and the cut-back in production was to be eased. In the event it is uncertain how much of the deterioration in the balance of payments that followed was a result of the excessive growth in home demand and how much resulted from the unprecedented rise in oil prices. In response the Government on 17 December announced cuts in public expenditure totalling £1200m for 1974/5, although this did not prevent a substantial rise in public expenditure for 1974/5 in real terms. According to Blackaby ([1978], p. 73) the change in the terms of trade effected by a devaluation of approximately 9% between 1972 quarter 4 and 1973 quarter 4 accounted for virtually all the adverse change in the balance of payments which he suggests does not imply an excessive strain on domestic resources.

The Conservative government's period of office ended in March 1974 when the National Union of Mineworkers challenged the Government's pay policy. As a result a Labour government was elected and the new Chancellor, Mr Healey, presented his first budget on 26 March 1974.

1974–9: The Labour administration

1974–5: The first twelve months: increased budgetary activity
The Labour government took office at a time when the rate of inflation was beginning to rise rapidly and the balance of payments was in deficit. The output of the economy as a whole had been declining because of the three-day working week and the miners' strike. The main aims of Mr Healey's first budget were to make fullest use of the resources available, to improve the balance of payments and to arrest the momentum of inflation whilst at the same time recreating a sense of social unity by means of a fairer distribution of the tax burden. A major objective of the budget was the reduction of the PSBR which in 1973/4 had been in excess of £4000m. The budget proposals were expected to reduce PSBR to about £2700m.

The major changes were an increase in tax allowances which was expected to reduce tax revenue by £650m accompanied by an increase in the tax rate which would increase tax revenue by £940m. Further increases in tax revenue were to come from an extension of VAT to include more goods (£290m) and an increase in excise duties on, for example, alcohol and tobacco (£360m). The total increase in tax revenue was expected to be almost £1400m. This was used to give a substantial increase to expenditure on government transfers in the form of retirement pensions, and sickness, supplementary and unemployment benefits which amounted to £1240m. These were accompanied by food subsidies which amounted to £500m. This latter measure was introduced to reduce the prices of essential foods such as bread, butter and milk and thus were expected to reduce the general index of retail prices by about $1\frac{1}{2}$%.

The Chancellor, however, found it necessary to introduce a 'July package' on 22 July to slow down the rate of inflation, which was approaching 16%, by acting directly on prices without putting any strain on the economy as a whole and without upsetting the economy as a whole. VAT was therefore reduced from 10 to 8% and there was an increase in food subsidies of a further £50m. The PSBR was expected to rise by £340m and as such the measures were slightly reflationary. The Chancellor expected inflation to be cut by an initial $1\frac{1}{2}$% and by $2\frac{1}{2}$% by fourth quarter 1975. The rate of inflation, however, was to continue to rise until after mid 1975. As with most macroeconomic measures it is difficult to ascertain whether these measures reduced the rate of inflation to a level below that which would have occurred had the measures not been introduced. The measures should have been expected to increase demand pressure.

The Chancellor's third budget in less than eight months was presented on 12 November 1974, following an October election in which the Labour Party was re-elected with a small majority. The budget was again slightly reflationary to prevent the dangers of mass unemployment which was beginning to rise from the 500 000 base. The major change was in the determination of tax relief for stock appreciation in the calculation of corporation tax and the reduction in revenue for 1974/5 resulting from this change was expected to be £750m. This budget was also used to introduce three items of fiscal reform.

1974: Fiscal reform: capital transfer tax, wealth tax, development land tax and petroleum revenue tax

The first set of proposals for fiscal reform were announced by the Labour government in their first budget. A White Paper gave details for the proposed introduction of *Capital Transfer Tax* (Cmnd 5705 [1974]). This was published with a Green Paper on *Wealth Tax* (Cmnd 5704 [1974] on 8 August 1974. The new capital transfer tax would close several loopholes, which had made estates duty a largely voluntary tax, by taxing all transfers whether at death or during one's lifetime. An initial level of transfer of capital is taxed at a zero rate. This was to be combined with an annual wealth tax which taxed the ownership of wealth rather than its transfer on an annual basis. It was to apply to high levels of wealth holding and a minimum level of £100 000 was suggested. The Labour government was unable to introduce this latter measure before it was defeated in May 1979.

Two further methods of taxation were introduced by the Labour government in 1974. Petroleum revenue tax was to apply from 13 November 1974 and was chargeable on the profits from extracting (rather than refining) oil and gas under licence in the UK and its continental shelf. A development land tax had been proposed in a White Paper entitled *Land* (Cmnd 5730 [1974]). It was a tax to be paid on the development of land, to be generally payable when the development value was realised on disposal of land.

1975–7: Deflationary budgets and fiscal carrots

The public expenditure plans announced on 30 January 1975 showed a large increase in the public expenditure programme in order to stimulate the growth of the economy. Unemployment was approaching 800 000. As inflation began to approach 20% and with a large deficit on the balance of payments it was not surprising that the Government completely reversed the trend in reflationary budgets and began to deflate the economy in April 1975. Public expenditure plans were cut by £1100m for 1976/7 (£900m at 1974 prices) and tax revenue increased by £1251m). The major expenditure cuts were in its subsidies to nationalised industries (£480m), on food (£150m) and on housing (£65m). National industry investment was cut by £100m and defence expenditure by £110m (all figures at 1974 prices). The main increase in tax revenue came from an increase in income tax rates by 2p for all but the highest bracket, the introduction of a luxury rate for VAT and increased revenue duties, for example on cigarettes and alcohol. Vehicle excise duties were also increased.

Further cuts in public expenditure resulted from the public expenditure plans announced in February 1976. The public expenditure growth was limited to a $2\frac{3}{4}\%$ per annum rise but as the base from which these projections were calculated was cut in the previous budget the result was a reduction in the level of public expenditure.

The Government considered that its pay policy was successfully lowering the rate of inflation, and the budget presented on 6 April 1976 was aimed at continuing the attack on inflation as the key to a return to full employment, the regeneration of British industry and the achievement of a sound balance of payments. The Chancellor offered a broadly neutral budget which consisted of both unconditional and conditional measures. In his budget speech the Chancellor emphasised the value of real wage rather than money wage settlements and the benefits to society of a lower rate of inflation. A number of changes in personal taxation announced in the budget were conditional upon a further extension and reinforcement of the Government's counter-inflation policy. The unconditional measures would cost the Government £370m and the conditional measures a further £930m. The measures were conditional on the continual support by the TUC for a twelve-month negotiating period between wage settlements and an observation of a 3% incomes policy guideline. Larger pay increases meant that the conditional reliefs would be reduced accordingly.

Agreement on pay was reached in May and so the full tax concessions were allowed. This, however, did not prevent the introduction of a deflationary July package on 22 July 1976. The aim of the supplementary budget was to reduce the public sector's claims on resources, i.e. to prevent the public sector pre-empting private savings which productive industry would need to finance stockbuilding and investment to take full advantages of the export opportunities now open to us. The rate of inflation was declining and the Chancellor considered recovery to be imminent. Unemployment was approximately 1.3m and showing no sign of decline and the balance of payments was still in deficit. This is the reason why the budget speech was couched in terms of export-led growth. There were fears that the excessive PSBR would lead to an excessive growth in the money supply and thereby final inflation. Hence it was intended that PSBR should be reduced to a target of less than £9000m for 1977/8, and this proved to be a target which was easily achieved. The total cuts in public expenditure for 1977/8 were to total £1000m (at 1976 prices) and were announced not as panic measures but rather as an early announcement of the 1977/8 expenditure plans. In addition the employers' national insurance contributions were increased by 2%.

Further cuts of £1000m were announced on 15 December 1976 together with the sale of £500m of BP shares and an increase in duties on tobacco and alcoholic drink. This was to reduce further PSBR and to curtail growth in domestic credit expansion (DCE), the new monetary target set by the IMF as part of conditions for a standby loan to support the Government's policies to strengthen the balance of payments.

The balance of payments was restored to surplus in 1977 and with inflation on the decline Mr Healey felt that there was scope for a fiscal stimulus of £1500m mainly through a reduction in personal taxation which would amount to £2250m in a full year. The December measures were thus seen to have restored financial stability and confidence. Indirect taxes were raised to aid energy saving, the environment and transport and health policies. Once again a carrot was offered to the TUC for successful agreement on pay policy. The tax concessions promised in the budget were introduced on 15 July 1977 although the rate of tax was reduced by 1p rather than 2p with allowances being increased by larger amounts to compensate.

1977–9: The final years of the Labour government and fiscal reflation

Unemployment was soon to exceed 1½m for the first time since the war, so a quick acting stimulus to the economy was introduced on 26 October 1977. This supplementary budget was designed to have maximum effect on employment. Personal allowances that were due to be increased in April 1978 were backdated to April 1977, and pensioners were given a £10 Christmas bonus. The cost to the economy was expected to be £1000m for 1977/8 and £2000m for 1978/9 as increases in public expenditure amounting to £1000m were also announced. The PSBR was expected to rise to £7000m for 1978/9 a figure well within the Government's target of £9000m. The main increases in public expenditure were confirmed in January 1978 and included increases in child benefits, the number of free school meals and manpower training. These accounted for half of the proposed increase although some had been previously announced in July.

Further reflationary measures were announced in the April 1978 budget with the aim to increase net family incomes and to encourage incentives to industry. The stimulus to the economy amounted to £2500m and resulted almost entirely from cuts in personal taxation. Expenditure increases in pensions, child benefits and government services were paid for out of the Government's contingency reserves which had been introduced in January 1978. Unemployment was remaining at a persistently high level and the sole aim of the budget was to cure the unemployment problem.

Failure to reach agreement with unions on a continuation of pay policy helped to contribute to a weakened minority Labour government's defeat on a confidence motion and a general election was called for in May 1979. It was replaced, after a caretaker budget introduced to allow for the collection of tax revenues, by a Conservative government which was committed to monetary control, the restoration of incentives and to the limitation of public expenditure to that compatible with poor short-term prospects for economic growth. Much of the election campaign was fought around the alternative tax concessions proposed by the major parties.

1974–9: Fiscal reform: changes in personal allowances and Meade Committee proposals

During the latter period of the Labour government there were several changes in the method of calculating the personal allowance which is deductable from gross income in order to arrive at taxable income. Allowances for children and family allowances were phased out during the late 1970s and were replaced by a system of child benefits. This transition was completed in April 1979. Thus, rather than have an allowance against income which had a large marginal benefit for high tax-payers and a zero benefit for those who paid no tax, all parents were to receive a benefit of a fixed amount per child. This amounted to £4 per child in April 1979 and slightly more for single parent families. Insurance premiums were also to be paid net of tax relief deducted at the standard rate as the previous system of allowances were also biased against zero tax-payers and in favour of high income earners. The allowance for tax relief on mortgages was to remain at a maximum £25 000.

Personal allowances were also index linked to the retail prices index in the *1977 Finance Act* and thus changes to take account of inflation were automatically conceded. Thus the apparent generosity of a Chancellor when he restored the real value of personal allowances was removed but along with it an element of automatic stabilisation in the British economy was also removed.

The final fiscal reform introduced by the Labour government was the introduction of a lower rate tax band for personal income taxation in April 1978. The basic rate was at 34% but the first £750 of taxable income would be charged at the new lower rate of 25%. Whether this had any effect on reducing the extent of the 'poverty trap', whereby income earners who pay small amounts of direct tax face an effective rate of tax in excess of 100% due to lost social security benefits, is debatable. This problem was highlighted by the report of the Meade Committee [1978] although they were unable to offer a satisfactory method of overcoming it.

The report of the Meade Committee has been summarised by Peacock [1978], Brown, Bird and King [1978] and Bird [1979] and criticised by Prest [1979]. The proposals of the Meade Committee stimulated considerable discussion on publication in 1978 but although the 1979 election debate was mainly about fiscal reform the debate itself attracted little attention. The main proposal by the Meade Committee was for the introduction of an expenditure tax. This does not refer to indirect taxation but to a system of tax on income after an allowance has been made for eligible forms of saving. Thus expenditure is simply income minus saving. The major reasons given for proposed reform were that inflation combined with *ad hoc* modifications of the existing tax structure meant that the whole system contained a number of anomalous complications and inconsistencies. As with Kaldor's original plans for the introduction of an expenditure tax in 1958 it now seems unlikely that the Meade Committee proposals will be introduced.

1979: The End of the Decade: Conservative government and tight Monetary Control

Mr Howe's first budget in June 1979 was broadly neutral and was to herald a 'new beginning' for the British economy. There was a radical switch from direct to indirect taxation accompanied by cuts in public spending. The Government was committed to bring inflation under control through a tight monetary policy. In many respects the statements made by the Chancellor were similar to those of his Conservative predecessor in 1970. The aims were to reduce the extent of government intervention, to improve the efficiency of the government machine and to reduce government borrowing. The reduction in taxes on income were aimed at offering better incentives although these were countered by a large increase in VAT to 15%.

Spending was planned at an amount compatible with the objectives given and the poor short-term prospects for output. The Government stressed the need to earn the resources for improvements in public services through higher output. The government expenditure plans for 1980/1 (Cmnd 7746 [1979]) stated that 'Higher public expenditure cannot be allowed to proceed and thus prevent the growth in the private sector needed to finance it.' This reflects the monetarist belief that any increased public expenditure will 'crowd-out' private expenditure.

The neutral budget in June in which increased VAT amounting to £4700m countered the reduction in direct taxation of £4275m in a full year was followed by a very deflationary public expenditure plan announced on 1 November 1979. In this £3500m was cut from the previous expenditure plans for 1980/1. The Government further intended to cut PSBR by the sale of government assets amounting to £1500m. The immediate effects of these measures was to increase the rate of inflation through the increase in VAT. This was expected to be a short-term once and for all phenomenon as prices adjust to the tax changes.

The decade ended as it began with rising rates of inflation, rising levels of unemployment and a slow rate of growth. The only major difference is the high PSBR and the Government has taken steps to reduce it. The Conservative government and to a large extent monetary policy will be judged on the ability to prevent a sustained return to high levels of inflation. It appears willing to sacrifice a low unemployment target as a stick to encourage unions to negotiate 'sensible' wage increases. It will be interesting to see if the whole-hearted commitment to monetary policy can be maintained as the economy enters a severe recession. The dramatic rise in minimum lending rate (MLR) and mortgage interest rates will further increase the general index of retail prices and the Government will need to be strongly committed to avoid resort to further budgetary or direct controls on the economy, through an incomes policy for example. It will also be interesting to see whether the Government are able to restrict public expenditure without firm control of local authority spending which does not seem likely in the near future. Industrial unrest seems inevitable if the recession is to be severe and the ability to avoid a U-turn in policy will be severely tested.

Demand Management: Theoretical Developments in the 1970s

Short-term fiscal policy has attracted considerable criticism over the last twenty years and this criticism has extended not only to the macroeconomic policies employed by governments but also to the inadequacies of the theoretical framework on which these policy decisions are based. (See Eltis [1976 and 1977], Kahn [1977] and Worswick [1977]). Thus Eltis has argued that 'the precise simplifications of Keynes's model of 1936 are now obsolete' (Eltis [1976], p. 18). On the other hand there have been many developments to the IS–LM presentation of the Keynesian model since 1936 and we will consider the more recent developments below. Thus supporters of basic Keynesian policies have argued that, firstly, the problem has been a shortage of instruments needed to achieve all of the targets set by government and, secondly, that Keynesian policies cannot be judged at a time when governments use sudden and large changes in fiscal demand management instruments to achieve first this policy objective and then a totally different policy objective.

Nonetheless, the traditional IS–LM framework of Keynesian analysis has borne the brunt of much of the criticism from both policy-makers and monetarists. During the 1970s the framework has been amended to overcome some of these inadequacies and these amendments can be divided into three broad categories. The most common departure is the addition of an external sector in order to consider the problems of simultaneously achieving internal and external balance. The London Business School macroeconometric model has incorporated these particular amendments amongst others which have led to the development of its model into what is now referred to as an international monetarist model. The second amendment is to introduce a government budget restraint which imposes a dynamic structure on the model. Finally there have been several attempts at incorporating inflationary expectations and other forms of uncertainty into an IS–LM framework with an employment sector. The majority of these changes have been made on a piecemeal basis with one amendment being made at a time although there is now a growing body of literature which utilises all of these amendments in what can be described as 'complete macroeconomic models'.

The IS–LM framework has also been extended to question the effectiveness of fiscal policy as a tool in controlling the macroeconomy. More recently it has once again become the vogue to question whether fiscal policy 'crowds-out' private expenditure. The theoretical reasons for making this statement have been summarised by Carlson and Spencer [1975]. The possible 'crowding-out' of fiscal policy has also been examined using 'complete macroeconomic model' and the results summarised in Turnovsky [1978]. The question of whether an increase in government spending causes a fall in private spending has been asked by many economists including Keynes himself who considered that crowding-out would be caused by a change in expectations. Increased government activity would cause expectations of the future to diminish thus causing both the IS and LM curves to shift left counteracting any reflationary fiscal policy. Investment declines to shift the IS curve to the left and there is an increase in the speculative demand for money causing a shift in the LM curve also leftwards.

The main amendments are contained in some of the more recent macroeconomic textbooks (for example Westaway and Weyman-Jones [1977]) and are briefly summarised below. The balance of payments can be taken to consist of both a current and a capital account. If the aggregate level of prices and the rate of exchange are both assumed fixed the combinations of the rate of interest, r, and the level of real income, Y, that will lead to external balance can be derived. In the case of the rate of exchange, that is considered to be an instrument of policy that is fixed by the government.

The locus of the combinations of r and Y that will result in the balance of payments being equal to zero (i.e. neither in surplus nor deficit) is given by curve EB in Figure 1.7. An increase in real income will cause imports to rise and with exports constant lead to a worsening of the balance of payments on the current account. This can be countered by a compensatory improvement in the capital account which will result from an increase in the rate of interest. If r rises, more capital will flow into the domestic economy. Hence the EB line slopes upwards and points above (below) the line to give combinations of r and Y which will result in a balance of payments surplus (deficit). Furthermore a devaluation (revaluation) of the exchange rate will shift the EB curve to the right (left). We are now in a position to analyse the policy mixes that will lead to both internal and external balance.

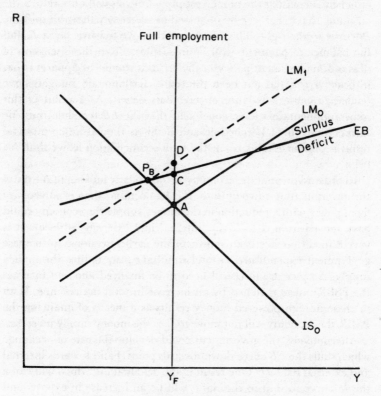

Figure 1.7   The IS–LM model with an external sector

As an example one case will be examined (alternative policy mixes are discussed in Westaway and Weyman-Jones [1977]). Let us assume that the economy is at full employment, but the balance of payments is in deficit as represented by point A in Figure 1.7. If the government takes no action there will be a drain on the economy's financial resources needed to finance the deficit thus causing a reduction in money supply. This will continue until the *LM* curve passes through point *B* (as given by LM_1). At *B* there is unemployment. The government can stimulate aggregage demand (to remove the unemployment) either by increasing the money supply – but this will only return the economy to point A – or by increased fiscal activity that will shift the *IS* curve to the right. The economy will move towards point D and the balance of payments will be in surplus. From the discussion of demand management policy in the 1970s it should be apparent that in practice this has not been the result. Reflationary budgets have tended to cause a balance of payments deficit. As a result of this some commentators have concluded that the *EB* schedule must be steeper than the *LM* schedule and if this is the case the empirical result is obtained. This is not the only reconciliation as we shall see below.

In order to prevent the economy automatically moving to B from A the government has two options. If it had combined an expansionary fiscal policy with a reduction in the money supply the economy could have moved from A to C (i.e. internal and external balance). It is very difficult, as has been shown in the earlier sections, to increase government expenditure, G, and simultaneously reduce the money supply. An increase in G will need to be financed and will increase the PSBR unless matched by an increase in total tax revenue. If an increase in high-powered money results as a means of financing the PSBR the economy will not move to C as the money supply increases.

Alternatively, the government could devalue the rate of exchange which shifts the *EB* curve down towards point A and towards internal and external balance. One result of the devaluation, which will cause the *IS* curve to shift to the right, will be an increase in exports and a reduction in imports. Provided the *LM* curve remains unchanged there will be excess aggregate demand in the economy. Thus a devaluation needs to be accompanied by internal deflation if internal and external balance is to be achieved. (The possibility of flexible exchange rates will not be considered here).

To return to the apparent conflict between the theoretical effect of reflationary fiscal policy causing a balance of payments surplus and the reality of an induced deficit, we note that this model has not considered the methods of financing a reflationary budget (the second major criticism of the traditional IS–LM approach). During the 1970s reflationary budgets led to large increases in the PSBR which can be financed either by issuing debt or by printing money. There is an obvious limit to the amount of debt that can be issued, and it has also to be remembered that interest must be paid on debt issued which may in turn lead to further increases in the PSBR thus making the situation worse. Alternatively the PSBR can be financed by printing money which causes an increase in the monetary base and a much larger increase in the money supply through the process of money creation. Thus the shift to the right of the *IS* curve is accompanied by a rightward shift in the *LM* curve. Obviously the final result will be dependent on the amount by which each curve shifts but it is possible that the combined shifts will lead to the intersection of the *IS* and *LM* curves at a point below the *EB* line (i.e. a point at which the balance of payments is in deficit).

Thus the consideration of the method of finance and the inclusion of a budget restraint which allows for interest payments on debt issued is of importance in determining the effectiveness of fiscal policy. These considerations are fully discussed by Turnovsky [1978], but some of the conclusions that have been derived using 'complete' macro-economic models will be summarised below.

Adding both interest payments to the budget restraint and wealth effects to a complete macroeconomic system indicates that if all bond finance is used it will be more expansionary than all monetary finance although stability of the system is brought into doubt. (The opposite result to that given by the standard IS–LM analysis). The system also implies that monetary authorities will have little ability to control either the money supply or the rate of interest through the open market sale of bonds. However, if all monetary finance is used to finance an increase in government expenditure, the system will not only be stable but the expenditure multiplier will equal the inverse of the marginal rate of tax. Blinder and Solow [1973] have obtained similar results using a continuous time model with a budget restraint that includes interest payments in order to attack the crowding-out hypothesis. They have shown that crowding-out can only occur if the system is unstable and this has not been the case.

Brunner and Meltzer [1972] also arrived at the same conclusion using a model that allowed the price level to be determined endo-genously and further adding a banking sector. Their model included markets for real assets, financial assets and current output. They further permitted wealth holders to choose amongst money, bonds, real capital and current expenditure. This gives a model with a different orientation to those based on the standard IS–LM approach. Including interest payments in the budget restraint once again gave the result that debt finance is more stimulative than money finance.

Turnovsky [1978] has shown that these results are sensitive to specification changes and as Carlson and Spencer [1975] have pointed out they do not accord with the empirical results attained for the USA which seem to indicate that debt finance is not very expansionary. In some cases the empirical investigation has shown negative values for government expenditure multipliers thus supporting the general crowding-out hypothesis. Keynesian macroeconomic models have thus been amended to allow for their inadequacies during the 1970s although the perverse combination of high rates of inflation and high levels of unemployment, which were evident in the 1970s and appear to be continuing into the 1980s, have yet to be explained. The Keynesian macroeconomic model with all its amendments has difficulty in both explaining and incorporating inflation and its effects and as such is still open for modification but then so are other models of the macroeconomy. Macroeconomics is still a relatively young discipline and we are still awaiting an Archimedes to spill the bath water although we need to ensure that the baby is not spilt with it. No matter how good we become at modelling the macroeconomy we will still need to allow for political and social targets when determining macroeconomic policy.

References

Bird, P. J. W. N. [1979], 'An Expenditure Tax for the UK?', *National Westminster Bank Review*, August 1979, pp. 32–9.

Blackaby, F. T. (ed.) [1978], *British Economic Policy 1960–74*. Cambridge University Press.

Blinder, A. S. and Solow, R. M. [1973], 'Does Fiscal Policy Matter?', *Journal of Public Economics*, Vol. 2, 1973, pp. 319–38.

Brown, C. V., Bird, P. and King, D. N. [1978], 'Tax Reform in the UK', *Economics Association Occasional Paper*.

Brunner, K. and Meltzer, A. H. [1972], 'Money, Debt and Economic Activity', *Journal of Political Economy*, September–October 1972, pp. 951–77.

Carlson, K. M. and Spencer, R. W. [1975], 'Crowding-out and Its Critics', *Federal Reserve Bank of St. Louis Quarterly Review*, December 1975, pp. 2–17.

Chrystal, K. A. [1979], *Controversies in British Macroeconomics*. Philip Allan.

Cmnd 4515 [1970], *New Policies for Public Spending*. London: HMSO.

Cmnd 4653 [1972], *Reform of Penal Direct Taxation*. London: HMSO.

Cmnd 4630 [1972], *Reform of Corporation Tax*. London: HMSO.

Cmnd 4929 [1972], *Value Added Tax*. London: HMSO.

Cmnd 4930 [1972], *Taxation of Capital on Death: A possible Inheritance Tax in place of Estate Duty*. London: HMSO.

Cmnd 5116 [1972], *Proposals for a Tax Credit Scheme*. London: HMSO.

Cmnd 5705 [1974], *Capital Transfer Tax*. London: HMSO.

Cmnd 5704 [1974], *Wealth Tax*. London: HMSO.

Cmnd 5730 [1974], *Land.* London: HMSO.

Cmnd 7746 [1979], *The Government's Expenditure Plans 1980/1.* London: HMSO.

Eltis, W. [1976], 'The Failure of Keynesian Conventional Wisdom', *Lloyds Bank Review*, October 1976, pp. 1–18.

Eltis, W. [1977], 'The Keynesian Conventional Wisdom', *Lloyds Bank Review*, July 1977, pp. 37–41.

Hansard, House of Commons Parliamentary Debates, 30 March 1971, Vol. 814, col. 1383.

Hansard, House of Commons Parliamentary Debates, 21 March 1972, Vol. 833, col. 1383.

Institute of Fiscal Studies [1978], *The Structure and Reform of Direct Taxes*, Report of a committee chaired by Professor J. E. Meade. George Allen and Unwin.

Kahn, Lord [1977], 'Mr Eltis and the Keynesians', *Lloyds Bank Review*, April 1977, pp. 1–13.

Kaldor, N. [1973], 'A critique of the Green Paper Proposals' in Select Committee on Tax Credit, Vol. 11, June 1973, pp. 211–32.

Kay, J. A. and King, M. A. [1978], *The British Tax System.* Oxford University Press.

Meade, J. E. [1978], see Institute of Fiscal Studies [1978].

Peacock, A. [1978], 'Do we need to reform direct taxes?', *Lloyds Bank Review*, July 1978, pp. 28–40.

Posner, M. (ed.) [1978], *Demand Management.* Heinemann Educational Books.

Prest, A. R. [1979], 'The Structure and Reform of Direct Taxation', *Economic Journal*, Vol. 89, no. 354, 1979, pp. 243–60.

Price, R. W. R. [1978], 'Public Expenditure' in Blackaby, F. T. (ed.) [1978].

Turnovsky, S. J. [1978], *Macroeconomic Analysis and Stabilisation Policy.* Cambridge University Press.

Westaway, A. J. and Weyman-Jones, T. J. [1977], *Macroeconomics: Theory Evidence and Policy.* Longmans.

Worswick, G. D. N. [1977], 'The End of Demand Management?', *Lloyds Bank Review*, January 1977, pp. 1–18.

2 Money Supply and its Control

by Geoffrey E. J. Dennis*

Introduction

The reputation of monetary policy has experienced a considerable revival in the Western world during the 1970s. This reappraisal of the role and influence of monetary policy has been as apparent in the UK as in other countries; as a result the instruments and *modus operandi* of monetary policy have been gradually transformed during the decade. In this chapter certain themes of UK monetary policy will be examined with reference where appropriate to actual events. Many controversies have existed in this area and this chapter will consider the issue of money supply control, the instruments of monetary policy, monetary targets and the tactics and instruments of debt management.

Theoretical Background

Academic and official opinion on the appropriate role for monetary policy has shifted significantly in the postwar period. A major influence on the debate over monetary policy was the Radcliffe Committee [1959]. The Radcliffe Report rejected money supply control because the volatility of the velocity of circulation made the relationship between money and nominal income very unpredictable. Instead the Committee argued that a broader concept of liquidity to include money 'people think they can get hold of' was the major influence on expenditure. The structure of interest rates which would be manipulated to control the stock of liquidity was the cornerstone of monetary policy. Expressed in this form, the Radcliffe Report did

*I would like to thank the members of the Loughborough and Nottingham Universities Banking Group, especially Max Hall, David Llewellyn and Brian Tew, for their comments and discussion of an earlier draft of this chapter.

not reject monetary policy although money itself was played down.

In the 1960s monetary policy was conducted in a way only partly sympathetic to the Radcliffe approach. The conflict of monetary policy was that while interest rate adjustments were needed to control liquidity, the requirements of debt management were for stable rates, at least in the short run. This was based on the belief that the demand for public sector debt would be maximised if the price of this debt and therefore the rate of interest on it were stable. This conflict between debt management and liquidity control was resolved in the 1960s through the imposition of direct controls on the growth of bank advances allowing interest rates to be consistent with the requirements of debt management. In this respect monetary policy did not follow the recommendations of the Radcliffe Committee which was aware that advances controls would create a 'fringe' of unsatisfied borrowers that would be diverted to the uncontrolled sector. The Committee therefore recommended the use of advances ceilings for brief, emergency periods only.

The expected growth in the uncontrolled financial institutions in response to ceilings on the lending of the controlled sector occurred on a large scale in the 1950s and 1960s. However in the second half of the 1960s, in response to this growth and the aggressive fund-raising policies of certain foreign banks, the non-clearing banks became subject to the same lending ceilings. Despite these, the growth of such institutions led to a reduction in the total volume of deposits and credit in the clearing bank sector and so to a diminution in the influence of the monetary authorities.

The attempt to control as many sources of credit as possible was, however, neither very systematic nor particularly effective. Within this policy, money supply control was not totally eschewed. In November 1967 in a Letter of Intent to the International Monetary Fund, the Chancellor of the Exchequer, Roy Jenkins, stated that the growth of the money supply in 1968 would be limited to its expected growth in 1967. This was followed by a second Letter of Intent in May 1969 in which a limit of £400m for domestic credit expansion was created for 1969/70. While these were the first examples of money supply targets used in the UK, the concern with the growth of the money supply that they represented was an isolated episode encouraged by the need to borrow from the IMF in the wake of the devaluation of sterling in November 1967.

Against this background, the changes in the operation and role of monetary policy in the 1970s have been gradual. Despite the existence of a series of major events or 'watersheds', the greater responsibility afforded to monetary policy in the 1970s has been the result of the evolution of a series of trends. Three main factors should be isolated. Firstly, there was general dissatisfaction with the monetary arrangements that had developed by the end of the 1960s. Secondly, the rise of the monetarist school significantly influenced the conduct of policy. In particular, emphasis was placed on the stability of the velocity of circulation (and therefore the demand for money) which ensured a considerable, although lagged, role for the money supply in the determination of nominal income. A key element of the doctrine is the rejection of the rate of interest as the focus of monetary policy in favour of the money supply. (See Friedman [1968] for a simple survey of the monetarist doctrine). Thirdly, inflation becoming the major economic problem in the 1970s contributed to the rise of monetary policy, which is conventionally viewed as having its greatest role to play in an inflationary environment.

The trends in the development of monetary policy that have symbolised the 1970s include a gradual change in the balance between fiscal and monetary policy to a situation in the late 1970s where the latter is considered to be as important or even more so than the former. Within monetary policy itself, there has been a significant move towards the control of monetary aggregates and away from interest rates as targets of policy. Finally, monetary policy is increasingly seen as influencing the economy in the long term with its short-term role being much more ambiguous.

Despite important events such as competition and credit control (CCC) in September 1971, the floating of sterling in June 1972, the introduction of the 'corset' in 1973 and monetary targets in December 1976 and the abolition of exchange control in October 1979, these trends in monetary policy evolved gradually; there were no dramatic policy shifts. Indeed, the instruments through which monetary policy is conducted have in fact changed little (except, in certain cases, in name) since 1970. Such an opinion is validated by the fact that retrospectively some of the major changes in monetary policy outlined in the previous paragraph were in part speedily amended. Thus, the new competitive environment introduced into the monetary system in September 1971 was soon followed by the restoration of discriminatory controls through the introduction of the 'corset'. Sterling floated freely for about twelve months only and for much of the rest of the decade its level was heavily influenced by the intervention policies of successive governments. At the time of writing (December 1979), it is not clear how 'permanent' the introduction of money supply targets and the abolition of exchange control may be.

A final point of major theoretical importance has been the changes in policy assignment in the 1970s. Throughout the 1960s and into the 1970s the UK utilised the familiar Keynesian assignment of policies. In simple terms fiscal policy was used to control demand, monetary policy to achieve balance of payments equilibrium (with assistance in 1976 from a change in the exchange rate) and prices and incomes policies to control the rate of inflation, the last being a less significant problem than in the 1970s. The floating of sterling in June 1972, did release monetary policy to a certain extent from the external objective to be replaced by exchange rate changes. However how real this change was in practice and how much one benefit of floating rates – namely the independence of monetary policy from the rest of the world (Laidler and Nobay [1975]) – was gained is very debatable. It is correct to argue that at the end of the 1970s the main objective of monetary policy is the control of inflation either in tandem with, or in the absence of, prices and incomes policies. In addition as monetarism gains support, there is greater acceptance that monetary policy may have little long-run influence on real income so that the level of unemployment is viewed primarily as a microeconomic problem related to the structure and flexibility of the labour market. (Laidler [1976]).

While the above assignment of policies to particular macroeconomic objectives is not uncontroversial, it does reflect the shift in academic and official opinion in the 1970s towards money supply policies.

Competition and Credit Control and the Reserve Base

With the introduction of CCC in 1971, the reserve ratio arrangements of banks were altered; as a consequence of some of the effects of this reform, a wide-ranging debate on the control of the money supply through the monetary base developed in the late 1970s. During the 1960s the clearing banks observed an 8% cash ratio and a 28% liquid assets or liquidity ratio. The banks could use cash (including balances at the Bank of England), money at call with the discount market and commercial and Treasury bills to satisfy the 28% ratio. The cash ratio, in particular, developed as a prudential control and although the banks in 1946 formally agreed to adhere to the ratio, no attempt was made by the monetary authorities to operate on the cash holdings of the banks to control the level of bank deposits. The simple bank credit multiplier mechanism was inappropriate, as the Bank of England provided without penalty all the cash needed to satisfy the ratio.

On the other hand, the liquidity ratio had a greater role to play in monetary policy. In 1955 the authorities imposed a 30% ratio on the clearing banks which in 1963 was reduced to 28%. The objective of this ratio was to limit the banks' ability to create credit (i.e. increase advances) through the manipulation of their holdings of defined liquid assets. (Given that the clearing banks alone were controlled by these ratios, their competitive position vis-à-vis other banks was weakened which contributed to the growth in the business of the latter). A debate developed concerning the relative merits of the alternative ratios. The 'old orthodoxy' view was that control of the money supply was possible through the cash ratio. However those who favoured the 'new orthodoxy' argued that this ratio was irrelevant as the authorities automatically supplied the cash demands of banks as they wished to stabilise short-term interest rates. Therefore control of the money supply through the liquidity ratio was both more feasible and desirable in these circumstances (see Cramp [1971] and Fletcher [1978] for a survey of this debate).

Although it was largely made a historical relic by the replacement of the two ratios in 1971, the discussion is important in the context of the monetary base debate of the 1970s as demonstrated below. Meanwhile in 1971, the new orthodoxists claimed a hollow victory by the introduction of the 12½% reserve asset ratio in place of the cash and liquidity ratios. The ratio, which was part of the CCC reform, stipulated that 12½% of the value of banks' eligible liabilities should be held in certain eligible reserve assets. Eligible liabilities included all non-bank domestic and overseas sterling deposits of less than two years' maturity. The relationship between the new reserve asset ratio and the old liquidity ratio is exemplified by the inclusion in the former of balances of banks at the Bank of England (but not special deposits), Treasury bills, local authority bills, money at call with the discount houses and listed brokers, commercial bills (up to 2% of eligible liabilities) and government securities with one year or less to maturity. (See Bank of England [1971c]). In addition, the clearing banks agreed to hold an average of 1½% of the value of eligible liabilities in the form of balances at the Bank of England. This may be likened to the former cash ratio, but multiplier control through the $1\frac{1}{2}\%$ ratio was clearly not envisaged.

In addition, under the CCC system, the clearing banks' interest rate cartel, whereby agreed rates were paid on deposits and an agreed scale levied on advances, was abandoned. This long-standing price-fixing agreement had symbolised the stagnant competitive atmosphere in clearing banking in the 1960s. The reserve asset ratio was to be supplemented by a special deposits scheme. Through this, the authorities could call for deposits which would be frozen at the Bank of England and not qualify as reserve assets. Having a similar effect as a variable reserve ratio, the object of special deposits was to drain excess liquidity from the system when circumstances warranted this action. The quantitative lending ceilings that destroyed the competitive nature of clearing banking in the 1960s were abolished although the authorities reserved the right to offer qualitative guidance on lending. Finally, greater fluctuations in interest rates on government debt than had occurred in the 1960s would be permitted through less active intervention by the authorities in the gilt-edged market. This reform, consistent with the desire to achieve greater control of the money supply, will be discussed later in the context of debt management policy.

The reasons for the introduction of CCC may be traced to the problems of the monetary system in the 1960s. The lack of competition among the clearing banks, symbolised by the interest rate cartel and ceiling controls, was widely disliked. To encourage equity all banks were subject to the new reforms. Other less compelling reasons for the changes were the desire to control the money supply more closely, even at the cost of interest rate fluctuations, and the wish of the new Heath government to foster competition and so match the demand for and supply of funds through the market.

In the immediate aftermath of the new system's appearance, most comment concerned the definition of reserve assets and the possibility of money supply control under the new arrangements. The reserve asset ratio, involving a considerable number of short-term assets, is very complicated. The supply of some of these is largely beyond the control of the authorities, e.g. money at call with the discount market and commercial bills, while the existence of non-bank holdings of certain assets provides the banks with the opportunity to purchase these at times of reserve asset pressure. A particular problem is the inclusion of Treasury bills as a reserve asset. The fact that residual financing of the public sector borrowing requirement (PSBR) is provided by sales of Treasury bills to the banking system has prevented the authorities from controlling the volume of reserve assets, as they have been unwilling to see interest rates fluctuate so much that at all times the appropriate amount of long-term debt is sold to the non-bank public. In this respect, fiscal and monetary policy are closely linked.

Therefore, close control of the money supply has not been facilitated by the $12\frac{1}{2}\%$ ratio. However this need not be a criticism of CCC as the authorities stated that they would not seek 'to achieve some precise multiple contraction or expansion of bank deposits' (Bank of England [1971a]) through the use of the reserve asset ratio and special deposits. The novelty of CCC lay in its attempt to control the money supply through the operation of free competition in the market for funds. With the abandonment of lending ceilings 'the allocation of credit is primarily determined by its cost' (Bank of England [1971b]). Through interest rate movements, the desired growth of the money supply would be achieved. This experiment in the operation of free market forces was not, however, immediately tested. In September 1971 the new Government was still concerned to reflate the economy in the attempt to achieve a 5% annual rate of growth of output. The budget in March 1972 was very expansionary with the Chancellor actually seeking a monetary growth rate that was 'high by the standards of past years'. However the experiment was not long-delayed. With the collapse of confidence in sterling culminating in the abandonment of fixed parities and the speedy withdrawal from the EEC 'snake in the tunnel' exchange rate arrangement in June 1972, the rapid erosion of the balance of payments surplus, and the increasing awareness that higher inflation would be a consequence of the expansionary policies, economic restraint was gradually imposed. Interest rates began to rise in June 1972. Minimum lending rate (MLR), which had replaced bank rate in October 1972 and was based on a formula related to Treasury bill rate, rose to 9% by the end of the year and, after a slight moderation in early 1973, to 13% in November 1973.

Much more seriously for the monetary authorities, the growth of the money supply exploded upwards. M3 (the broad definition of the money supply) rose by 60% in the two years from December 1971. This was clearly unacceptable to a Government seeking 'only' 5% growth, which explains the readiness to see short-term interest rates increase. However, the demand for credit appeared not to respond. The fear had been expressed that the demand for credit was sufficiently inelastic with respect to interest rates that only very high rates would clear the market for credit. The possibility that the free-market experiment would fail if such interest rates were 'unacceptably' high carried with it the logical consequence that direct controls on the banking system may be indispensable to monetary control.

Such a view was encouraged by the series of interventions in the market for credit that began in August 1972. On that occasion, the Bank of England requested the banks to

> make credit less readily available to property companies and for financial transactions not associated with the maintenance and expansion of industry.
>
> (Bank of England [1972a], p. 329)

This first use under CCC of qualitative guidance was followed by eleven further 'requests' during the 1970s. Meanwhile, attempts were made to hold down rates of interest and simultaneously to reduce the rate of monetary growth. To this end, the supplementary special deposit scheme ('the corset') was introduced in December 1973. This sought to limit the growth of banks' interest-bearing eligible liabilities (IBELS) by forcing them to deposit a proportion of any excess growth over a stipulated figure at the Bank of England. Although not a return to the mandatory ceilings of the 1960s, the corset effectively discouraged the banks from raising interest rates to attract new funds for the expansion of credit. It also effectively stifled competition among the banks.

The misfortune of this difficult period for monetary policy was compounded by the effects of CCC and the subsequent interventions on relative interest rates. When under reserve asset pressure, banks will be more willing to increase deposit rates (to attract new funds) than lending rates. It may then become profitable for prime bank customers to arbitrage from bank advances to certificates of deposits (CDs) or other wholesale bank deposits. Such 'round-tripping' led to an artificial or cosmetic increase in the money supply during 1973 and the elimination of this phenomenon was one of the main objectives of the 'corset'.

It may be argued that the experiment in competitive banking effectively ended with the introduction of the 'corset' in December 1973. Certainly the gradual erosion of the free market principles of

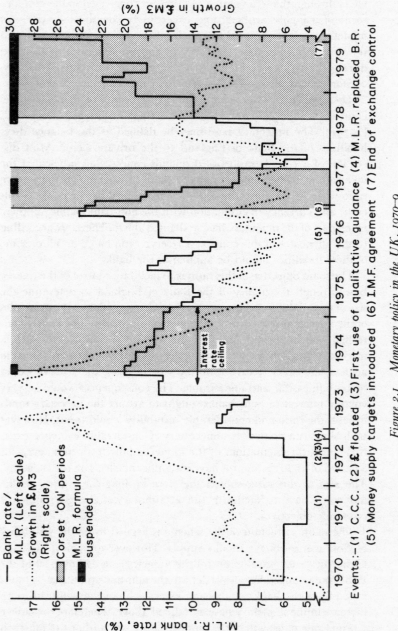

Figure 2.1   Monetary policy in the UK, 1970–9

Events:– (1) C.C.C. (2) £ floated (3) First use of qualitative guidance (4) M.L.R. replaced B.R.
(5) Money supply targets introduced (6) I.M.F. agreement (7) End of exchange control

—— Bank rate/
       M.L.R. (Left scale)
······· Growth in £M3
       (Right scale)
▓ Corset 'ON' periods
■ M.L.R. formula
   suspended

Growth in £M3 (%)

M.L.R., bank rate, (%)

Interest
rate
ceiling

CCC through the series of interventions in 1972–3 led to the development of a highly artificial and exceedingly complicated system of monetary management. When such observations are combined with the wide swings in monetary growth and interest rates as occurred during the 1970s (see Figures 2.1 and 2.2), it was natural that discussion should turn to further reform of the monetary system.

Therefore in the later years of the 1970s, the idea of 'monetary base' control was widely discussed (see Bank of England [1979*b*]; Greenwell's [1979]). The monetary base may be defined as the balance sheet liabilities of the Bank of England to the private sector. Most discussion of a reserve ratio based on this concept has advocated the inclusion of banks' balances at the Bank of England in the reserve ratio with the possible addition of currency held by the banks (vault cash) and currency in circulation with the non-bank public, all these being part of the monetary base as defined above. Therefore according to the advocates of this control, a reserve ratio based on all or some of these liabilities should be applied to the banks.

The main objective of this ratio is to facilitate control of the reserve base through the ability of the Bank of England to determine the size of their liabilities. Through this and the operation of the principles of the fractional reserve ratio, the money supply could be closely controlled. An important point in this debate is how rigidly such a monetary base scheme would be operated. If the banks were forced to achieve the exact reserve ratio on a daily basis, the scheme would be both infeasible and undesirable. The consequences would be very volatile interest rates as banks sought to attract the necessary funds to fulfil the ratio and considerable instability would result. However such short-run control is unnecessary. Considerable evidence exists that short-run fluctuations of the money supply from trend even for a period of up to six months have insignificant effects on the economy. The aim of this ratio should therefore be long-run control of the monetary base to facilitate the attainment of the government's economic objectives.

The main attraction of the scheme is argued to be the possibility of close control of the money supply. However to achieve this, the authorities must *actually* control the monetary base. Any part of the PSBR not financed by sales of debt to the non-bank public or by funds raised from the banks or through external financing will lead to an increase in the monetary base as defined above. Therefore to achieve a target rate of growth of the money supply, the authorities must sell the appropriate amount of debt to attain the target level of the monetary base (see the section on debt management policy). The cost may be high and volatile rates of interest may ensue. Money supply control is feasible but the problems of inconsistent fiscal and monetary policies would remain.

It is not certain that the 'corset' would be abandoned in the wake of a monetary base scheme. The costs of the scheme in terms of high interest rates could be mitigated by the continuation of the corset. However the abandonment of the corset could be used as a bargaining counter for the introduction of a monetary base scheme. A key benefit of the scheme would be that residual financing of the PSBR through Treasury bill sales to the banks would not inflate the monetary base. As a result, short-term debt instruments would carry more of the burden of government financing.

Despite some persuasive arguments in favour of a monetary base approach, a weight of professional opinion is ranged behind the status quo. Bankers have long been concerned over the consequences of close control of the money supply through a monetary base ratio. The infeasibility of the extreme version of the ratio is used to demonstrate the impracticality of the whole approach.

A major worry concerns the consequences of such a scheme for the discount houses. With money at call no longer a reserve asset, the subsidy received by the market from these assets would be lost. However the position of the houses as the buffer between the Bank of England and the banks (and therefore the lender of last resort function of the former) would be unimpaired. Any loss of income resulting from the ending of the subsidy could be balanced by the abolition of the 'undefined assets multiple' control imposed on the discount houses in 1973 (Bank of England [1973]). With such changes, the outlook for the discount houses, would be uncertain but not necessarily disastrous.

The Instruments of Monetary Policy, 1973–9

Events in the testing period for monetary policy in the second half of 1973 set the pattern for the remainder of the 1970s to the extent that 'the corset' and the suspension of the MLR formula (both of which were introduced in autumn 1973) have been central to the conduct of monetary policy subsequently.

The first new instrument of monetary policy in this period, a ceiling on the interest rate payable on certain bank deposits, was introduced in September 1973. This control has been frequently used in the USA in the postwar period – being known there as Regulation Q – but this was its first use in the UK. All banks were required to observe a ceiling rate of 9½% on deposits of £10 000 or less. The measure was justified in the following way:

> The increases in short-term interest rates which took place in the first half of the year under review curtailed the flow of funds into the building societies, which were constrained in raising their own rates because of the effect on the cost of mortgages.
>
> (Bank of England [1974], p. 7)

By this measure it was hoped to channel a greater volume of funds to the building societies, thereby forestalling a politically unpopular increase in the mortgage rate.

The success of the ceiling was however limited. Despite it, the mortgage rate was increased to 11% in the same month whilst inflows into the building societies did not improve significantly until the first quarter of 1975 when money market interest rates had begun to ease. Indeed, in April 1974 the first of five successive monthly loans of £100m was made to the societies to increase their stock of available liquidity. (The loans were repaid by 1976). The ceiling was abandoned in February 1975 by which time it was redundant anyway as the rate on seven-day deposit accounts had fallen to 9%. Further intervention occurred from April 1978 when the Joint Advisory Committee on Mortgage Finance imposed a ceiling on the monthly rate of new mortgages granted by building societies.

Despite the introduction of the formula to determine MLR in October 1972, the authorities retained the power to introduce

> a change in the lending rate independent of these arrangements ... if, for example, it was required to signify a shift in monetary policy.
>
> (Bank of England [1972b], p. 443)

This waiver was first used in November 1973 when MLR was raised to 13% as an indication of the authorities' intentions at a time of increasing inflation and monetary expansion and when sterling was weak. The formula was reinstated in January 1974. A second use of this discretionary power occurred on 7 October 1976 when MLR was raised to 15%; however Treasury bill rates moved into line so that the formula was restored on the following day. When rates began to fall from their peak levels in early 1977, the authorities wished to slow the pace at which these reductions were occurring. Therefore between February and May 1977 the formula was abandoned to keep MLR above the level dictated by the market. Finally, in May 1978, MLR was (in all but name) replaced by bank rate when the indefinite suspension of the formula was announced. The latest move, above all, reflected the concern of the authorities with the competitive experiment in monetary policy in the 1970s. The fluctuations in interest rates that followed the introduction of CCC have at times simply been too great to allow MLR to be determined by the market.

The third innovation in monetary policy in late 1973 was the most important. In December, the supplementary special deposits scheme, commonly known as the 'corset' was introduced. Since then it has, arguably, become the most important instrument of monetary policy. The scheme placed a limit on the growth of interest-bearing eligible liabilities over a particular six-month period. Should this rate be exceeded, special deposits are called on a sliding scale determined by the degree of excess growth. Initially the scheme set a growth rate of 8% of the average value of IBELs in April, May and June 1974 from the base which was defined as the average level of IBELs in October, November and December 1973. The special deposits call rate was 5% (of the excess) for an excess growth of up to 1%, 25% for an excess growth of between 1 and 3% and 50% above that. At the end of this initial six-month period, a growth rate of $1\frac{1}{2}$% per month was permitted over and above the initial 8% limit. This represented a relaxation of the limits on IBELs' growth. In addition, in November 1974, the call rates were effectively lowered with the 5% rate applying to an excess growth of up to 3% and the punitive 50% rate only coming into effect when the growth rate was exceeded by 5% or more. The scheme was discontinued in February 1975 as the banking system in general was well inside the 'corset' limits at a time of weak demand for credit.

The 'corset' was reactivated in November 1976 with a 3% growth of IBELs permitted before penalty over a six-month period from the base of August–October 1976 to the average IBELs level in February, March and April 1977. Although the same call rates were used as before, the low growth limit and the retrospective base-setting forced the banks to restrict the growth of IBELs very considerably to avoid penalty. On this occasion the $\frac{1}{2}$% monthly growth rate was in operation until the scheme was again abandoned in August 1977.

Finally, the scheme was again reactivated in June 1978 and continued in operation until the end of the decade. The maximum six-month growth rate of IBELs, on this occasion, was 4%, the retrospective base being the average of six monthly observations from November 1977 to April 1978 and the limit being applied to the average of the August, September and October 1978 IBELs levels. After this initial six-month period, the growth rate of IBELs allowable without penalty was raised to 1% per month. Call rates were unchanged.

The main aim of the 'corset' is to limit the growth of IBELs and thereby restrain the rate of monetary expansion while keeping interest rates down. This would be achieved by banks refraining from active bidding for new deposits which may lead to their incurring a 'corset' penalty. An immediate objective in late 1973 was to reduce the number of arbitrage transactions or 'round-tripping' caused by the particular structure of interest rates in existence then. In addition, with bank interest rates kept artificially low, the demand for public sector debt should increase which, in turn, would assist in controlling the growth of the money supply.

The corset has been very successful in reducing the rate of growth of both IBELs and the money supply (see Figure 2.1) – certainly more so than the long-standing ordinary special deposits scheme which is still in operation although now of considerably reduced importance. However the scheme has had a number of undesirable side-effects (see Greenwells [1978]). Firstly, cosmetic reductions in IBELs have been achieved by banks without affecting sterling M3. Examples of transactions that achieve such reductions include the switching by the public of funds from deposit accounts (included in IBELs) to current accounts (excluded from IBELs) and the transfer by banks of call loans in the discount market into market loans, the latter being negative IBELs to offset the growth in IBELs elsewhere in the banks' balance-sheet. Such liability management has become a crucial element of banking in the 1970s. Secondly, sterling M3 itself has been subject to distortions as a result of the operation of the corset. The limits on the growth of IBELs have encouraged disintermediation, i.e. direct lending from surplus sectors to deficit sectors with 'bank acceptances' becoming the main vehicle of this practice. These are bills of exchange accepted by a bank and then rediscounted (i.e. sold) in the banking sector with the non-bank public or with overseas residents. To the extent that these are purchased in the non-bank private sector, both IBELs and sterling M3 are unaffected. The only role played by the bank is the acceptance of the bill; although it does not act as a financial intermediary, a flow of credit is created. Net acceptances of the banking system rose from virtually zero in June 1978 to nearly £1000m one year later. Correcting the IBELs and sterling M3 series for these acceptances, the 'excess' growth rates in June 1979 were estimated at 5.77% of the total for IBELs and 2.03% for sterling M3 (Coghlan [1979]). Therefore the effects of the corset may have been to reduce the rate of growth of the IBELs and sterling M3 series, but the costs in terms of reduced inter-bank competition, increased disintermediation and considerable distortion to published figures have been great. The net effect of such distortions is to reduce the reliability of money supply data thereby casting some doubt on the accuracy of the monetary targets programme based on such figures.

Money Supply Targets

Within a decade of the first use of a money supply target in 1967, such targets had become the central element of the monetary policy of successive governments. The progress towards this situation was, however, gradual. The introduction of CCC in 1971 and the floating of sterling in June 1972 were seen as milestones on the path towards greater control of monetary aggregates.

However the unambiguous origin of money supply targets was in 1976. In the April budget, the Chancellor of the Exchequer, Denis Healey, suggested that the growth of the money supply (the broader M3 definition) should be in line with the growth in nominal Gross Domestic Product (GDP). In July, this was quantified as a M3 growth target of 12% for the financial year 1976/7. The practice of announcing targets for monetary growth and the PSBR was formally established in December 1976 under the aegis of the IMF. Given the fragile position of sterling and the low level of foreign exchange reserves, the UK authorities were virtually forced to adopt the monetary strictures required by the IMF in return for a stand-by credit of $3.9bn (see Chapter 9).

Details of the monetary targets adopted in December 1976 and after are set out in Table 2.1 with the actual out-turn included in parentheses. A number of points should be noted from Table 2.1. Firstly, for a medium-sized open economy such as the UK the IMF prefers the monetary target to be defined in terms of domestic credit expansion (DCE). Therefore the announced money supply target in

December 1976 was a residual which was to be consistent with the more important DCE target. In practice, however, since April 1977 the DCE target has become less significant. Secondly, Table 2.1 also specifies target levels for the PSBR which were included in the Letter of Intent to the IMF for the two-year period from April 1977. Thirdly, the replacement of the M3 target by one based on sterling M3 was undertaken in December 1976 in the belief that the non-sterling components of M3 are relatively unimportant for the domestic economic situation, while the sterling value of such non-sterling deposits will fluctuate as the external value of sterling changes.

Table 2.1   UK monetary targets and performance

		PSBR(£bn)	DCE(£bn)	%Δ£M3
1976/7 (April)	Target		9.0	9–13[a]
	Out-turn		(4.9)	(7.2)
1977/8 (April)	Target	8.7	7.7	9–13
	Out-turn	(5.6)	(3.8)	(14.4)
1978/9 (April)	Target	8.6	6.0	8–12
	Out-turn	(9.2)	(7.3)	(11.6)
1978/9 (October)	Target			8–12
	Out-turn			(13.4)
1979/ (June)–	Target	8.25		7–11[b]
80 (April)				
1979/ (June)–				7–11[b]
80 (October)				

[a] M3. (Sterling M3 was introduced in late 1976).
[b] Annualised rates.

The choice of the monetary aggregate to be used as a target has a long history which pre-dates the advent of money supply targets. The object must be to identify an aggregate which is representative of monetary conditions, includes all the unambiguous components of the money supply and is relatively free from distortion; this is, in fact, an almost impossible task. While the M1 definition of money including currency held by the non-bank public and sterling 'sight' deposits is too narrow, a broader definition such as sterling M3, which includes time deposits and public sector deposits, suffers from the drawback that it is less stably related to the level of nominal income than is M1, while in recent years it has been distorted through the effects of the corset. Sterling M3 does however have the compensating and possibly decisive advantage that it may be linked easily with official statistics on the PSBR, DCE and bank lending. Finally, the call has been regularly heard in the late 1970s for an even broader series that includes deposits at other financial institutions, in particular, building societies. Series for such alternative definitions are available (e.g. Bank of England [1979*c*]; Greenwells Monetary Bulletins). The temptation to use multiple targets to avoid the choice problem is considerable. However the main danger of this solution is that the alternative target variables may yield different signals. For example in 1977/8, DCE at £3.8bn fell short of the target of £7.7bn, while sterling M3 grew at 14.4% which exceeded the target range of 9–13%. When multiple targets are used, great care is needed to ensure that they are consistent with each other to prevent the confusion such as occurred in 1977/8.

Figure 2.2 which shows the growth of sterling M3 since the 1960s also includes the target ranges. Although sterling M3 exceeded the target in the early part of the 1976/7 period, the revival of sterling and the gilt-edged market in early 1977 following the IMF agreements led to little growth in the aggregate in the six months to April 1977. The sterling M3 target for 1976/7 was accordingly undershot. Experience in 1977/8 was almost exactly opposite to this. Steady growth in sterling M3 to December 1977 left the series within the target range. However as interest rates, which had fallen throughout 1977 (with MLR reaching 5% in October), began to rise and the inflation and balance of payments outlooks worsened, sales of government debt virtually ceased. As a result, sterling M3 grew at an alarming rate and ended well above the target range with the actual growth being 14.4%.

The introduction of rolling targets in April 1978 was partly in response to the large increases in sterling M3 in the latter part of 1977/8. From that date, a new target was to be specified every six months so that the target period was continually rolled forward (e.g. in October 1978 a new target running for the year to October 1979 would replace the existing target). Although the danger of excessive elasticity in the operation of money supply targets is created by this move, this was felt to be outweighed by the advantages of the scheme. The main one was to reduce the seriousness of money supply figures which moved the series away from the target, towards the end of the target period, as happened in April 1978. Fixed-period targets allow no time to correct such excessive growth within the

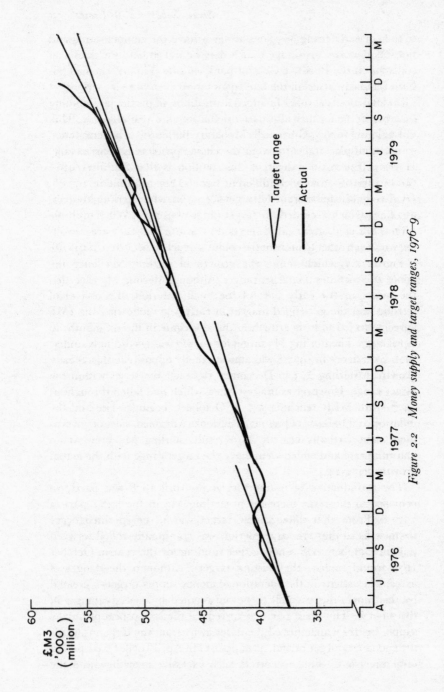

Figure 2.2 Money supply and target ranges, 1976—9

current period. Therefore a smoother pattern of monetary growth should follow the introduction of rolling targets when the objective would be to return the money supply to the target path by the end of the succeeding six-month period.

The 8–12% target for 1978/9 was attained although with the growth rate being at the top of the range, the new target for the year beginning in October 1978 was exceeded in the first six months of its course and indeed the authorities failed to reduce monetary growth sufficiently for that target to be attained by October 1979. The introduction of the annualised 7–11% target by the new Conservative government from June 1979 represented a slight tightening of policy.

The shift to money supply targets in the UK has not occurred in isolation from other countries (see Pringle [1977]; McClam [1978]). The primary reason for the new approach to policy has been the failure of demand management or 'fine-tuning' policies to solve the economic problems of the 1970s. In particular, the serious world-wide inflation encouraged the adoption of a different approach to economic policy. Monetary targets have been made more feasible in the floating exchange rate era of the 1970s. However despite this, certain strong currency countries, notably Germany and Switzerland, have regularly failed to attain these targets due to the large flows of funds into and out of these countries (Foote [1979]). Such countries have now reverted to exchange rate targets. Therefore it is not obvious that a highly open economy can attain the independence of monetary policy from floating exchange rates which the theory postulates. The attractions of the monetarist doctrine have contributed to the introduction of monetary targets, while for the UK the pragmatic response to the IMF negotiations was a point of major importance in the development of money supply targets.

In the UK the long-run feasibility of money supply targets has however been questioned. Apart from the openness of the UK economy, the debate over the stability in the demand for money in the 1970s (e.g. Artis and Lewis [1976]) has cast some doubt on this policy. Most importantly, the authorities must have the ability to control the money supply itself. The large proportion of the national debt held in long-term government securities places a considerable burden on the capacities of primary and secondary debt markets. Slight changes in sentiment in the gilt-edged market may therefore have dire effects on the controllability of the money supply. The whole area of debt management is crucial for monetary policy and is considered in the next section.

Debt Management Policy

The relationship between the objectives of managing the national debt and monetary control was brought much more sharply into focus in the 1970s than it had been earlier in the postwar period. This was mainly due to the combination of considerably increased levels of the PSBR and higher rates of inflation in the 1970s. In 1968/9 the PSBR was £0.46bn and in 1969/70 it was actually negative (−£0.54bn). However in the nine financial years since then (to 1978/9) it has averaged £5.63bn, peaking at £10.6bn in 1975/6 which accounted for $10\frac{1}{4}\%$ of GDP. The reliance on the gilt-edged market to raise sufficient funds to finance these deficits without substantial monetary financing was therefore enormous. At a time of higher inflation when fixed-interest gilt-edged securities are less attractive, the need for careful nurturing of debt markets is obvious. In addition with the greater concern over monetary control and the eventual introduction of money supply targets, the appetite of gilt-edged investors continuously had to be encouraged.

The link between fiscal and monetary policy originates from the fact that a positive PSBR will lead to a rise in the money supply automatically and unless compensatory financing is arranged. Therefore the authorities will seek to sell both marketable and nonmarketable debt to the non-bank public which, by reducing the money supply, effectively returns the money supply to its previous level. (Assistance may also be gained from the external financing of the public sector). Any residual PSBR may be financed by sales of non reserve-asset debt (e.g. government bonds) to the banks or by bank lending to the public sector. Such transactions lead to a rearrangement of bank assets but no change in their level and so the once-for-all increase in the money supply resulting from the positive PSBR remains. Finally, the remainder of the PSBR is covered by sales of reserve asset debt (e.g. Treasury bills) to the banks or by an increase in notes and coin; in both cases high powered money rises and there may be a multiple increase in the money supply.

If the authorities wish to constrain the growth of the money supply, they will seek to maximise the sales of government debt to the non-bank public. In this way monetary financing of fiscal policy will be avoided. The importance of debt-management policy to the achievement of money supply targets is therefore obvious.

However from 1960 to 1968, the clear objective was the maximisation of the attractiveness of long-term government debt, with the control of the money supply being a minor element in the authorities' policy (Bank of England [1966]). The need to raise large amounts of finance in the gilt-edged market to meet government expenditure plans and to replace maturing debt was as true in that period as in the 1970s. However it was felt that this would be more successfully achieved through the establishment of an appropriate structure of interest rates, with little concern in the consequences for the money supply. Policy sought to keep gilt-edged prices broadly stable. This involved 'leaning into the wind' – buying and selling to iron out price fluctuations – and refraining from selling on a falling market (Tew [1978]). (In fact before 1960, price falls were allowed if the market was weak – there was no 'leaning into the wind' on the buying side). This was based on the assumption that market demand for gilts would be maximised when prices were stable. It was believed that the market was dominated by sceptics, with extrapolative expectations, such that when prices fell, investors, expecting further falls, either sold debt or stayed out of the market, forcing prices down again, so that the expectation was self-fulfilling. Any expansion of bank lending that followed this policy was controlled through the imposition of direct lending limits.

Although a slight modification in these gilt-edged market 'support' policies occurred in 1968 to allow greater price fluctuations, the formalisation of a new set of tactics did not occur until the CCC system was established in 1971. Through this document, debt management policy was modified in the following ways:

(a) The Bank will no longer be prepared to respond to requests to buy stock outright, except in the case of stocks with one year or less to run to maturity.

(b) They reserve the right to make outright purchases of stock with more than a year to run solely at their discretion and initiative.

(c) They will be prepared to undertake, at prices of their own choosing, exchanges of stock with the market except those which unduly shorten the life of the debt.

(d) And will be prepared to respond to bids for the sale by them of 'tap' stocks and of such other stocks held by them as they may wish to sell.   (Bank of England [1971a])

The clear objective of the new policy was to improve the control of the money supply even at the cost of both higher and more volatile interest rates.

The results of the new tactics were not particularly dramatic although undesirable consequences have followed particularly at times of great uncertainty in the markets, while the Bank of England has in general withdrawn support when there was a combination of falling prices and a high PSBR. But the authorities have always resisted actually *selling* gilts on a falling market, for fear of causing massive market disruption as prices fell because it would be a breach of faith to investors who had purchased stock as prices were falling. They continued to do this, effectively limiting the possibility of debt sales to periods when the market was rising. The 'selling' tactics adopted by the authorities have therefore remained largely unchanged since the 1950s with the significant developments being restricted to 'buying' policies.

At times since 1972, the authorities have actually bought stock on a falling market. Support phases of this type occurred most notably in the second quarter of 1972 (which included the period in June when sterling was floated after a brief but intense currency crisis and a shortage of bank liquidity caused the authorities to establish a two-week sale and re-purchase agreement with the banks), and also in the final quarter of 1974. Yields on gilt-edged securities have fluctuated more in the 1970s in pursuit of the more flexible debt management tactics and money supply control. While the average monthly yield fluctuation on twenty-year stock was 0.15% between 1967 and 1969, (Morgan [1973]), this rose to a peak of 0.85% in the bull market in the first nine months of 1977. Despite such fluctuations the market's capacity has not been impaired. Morgan noted that while average monthly transactions in debt of over five years' maturity totalled £717m in 1967–9, this had risen to £1736m in 1970–2 and more recently to £4456m in the first nine months of 1977.

The major concern with debt management policy in the 1970s has been the effect of the new 'control' policy on the market in a period of great uncertainty. When investors are expecting interest rates to rise, they will in general stay out of the market until they believe an interest rate peak has been reached. The existence of 'buyer strikes' of this type causes an increase in the monetary financing of government expenditure ensuring that eventually a substantial upward movement in interest rates is necessary to encourage gilt sales and to reduce the demand for bank credit. Such periods of famine have led to the phenomenon known as the 'Duke of York' effect whereby an interest rate hike occurs to what is hoped will represent a peak so that gilts sales are resumed with rates gradually falling, generating capital gains for the investor. This effect was exploited successfully in 1975 and most spectacularly in 1976–7 when MLR fell rapidly from a peak of 15% in October 1976. Sales of gilts amounted to £3180m in the final quarter of 1976 and as much as £5218m in the first three quarters of 1977. It is likely that if interest rates have reached their peak in late 1979, new opportunities will exist to sell debt on a rising market when rates eventually turn down.

The 'Duke of York' tactic has been very successfully utilised in the 1970s. However at least two sources of concern result from its operation. Firstly, while gilt-edged securities are successfully sold the cost in terms of higher interest costs for the life of this debt is considerable. Secondly, the combination of highly volatile interest rates on government debt and the relatively sticky interest rate structure of the building societies, in particular, disrupts the flow of funds into those institutions. The sensitivity and political importance of building societies' mortgage lending rates makes such disruption very undesirable to the authorities.

Much discussion in the late 1970s has concentrated on possible methods of increasing the demand for government debt to resolve the conflict between high government spending and monetary control with generally lower and less volatile interest rates, and also to ensure that the 'correct' amount of debt is sold to attain a particular money supply target. To facilitate these objectives, three new types of stock have been introduced in the 1970s (Bank of England [1979a]). In March 1973, a convertible stock, which enables the investor to convert the short-term stock into a long-term security at a particular date and at predetermined terms, was issued. Whether such a stock is an attractive investment depends on the investor's expectations of future interest rate movements. Secondly, a partly-paid stock was introduced for the first time in 1977. Issues of this type spread the cost of purchase and enable the authorities to permit closer matching of expenditures with receipts. Thirdly, floating-rate issues were also made for the first time in 1977. These should be more attractive than fixed rate debt at a time of rising interest rates as they compensate an investor in terms of greater interest payments when stock prices are falling.

Such new types of debt instrument have had only limited success, however. Other ideas have been suggested to assist the smooth operation of debt management policy. At present, gilt-edged securities are issued through a 'tap' system. Under this system, new issues of stock are made at regular intervals, with the date of issue usually being determined by the state of the market. If the demand for a new issue is insufficient at the issue price, the unsold securities are taken up by the Bank of England, to be sold later. Although some price variation has occurred in this system in the 1970s, the amount of stock sold remains essentially at the whim of the investor. It has been argued that a 'tender' system whereby the whole issue is sold on a particular day, with the price finding its own level in the market, should replace the 'tap' system. The key advantage of the 'tender' method (which is used both in the USA bond market and for Treasury bill sales at home) is that money supply control is facilitated. However official concern is that the interest rate fluctuations which would accompany the tender system would harm the long-term stability of the gilt-edged market, while it is not even clear that long-term demand for debt would rise at all; it may even fall. In addition, the maturity structure of the debt would shorten.

Notwithstanding these arguments, a partial shift towards the tender system occurred in March 1979. An issue of £800m of $12\frac{1}{4}$% Exchequer stock, 1999 was made with a minimum price quoted. Bids were requested and the stock allocated to the highest bidders. Although the issue was undersubscribed, insufficient stock remained for it to be retained as a tap. Therefore, a minimum price of £97.50 (below that originally stipulated) was accepted as the whole issue was sold by tender.

Summary

The 1970s has been a decade of considerable discussion and evolution in monetary policy. The role that monetary policy has been asked to play in an overall economic strategy has changed, particularly since the advent of monetary targets and the floating of sterling. The institutional environment in which policy is conducted has also experienced certain changes. The controlled banking system of the 1960s was replaced by a more competitive framework in 1971 only for the unacceptable side-effects of competition (namely high and fluctuating interest rates and rapid monetary growth) to force further change. With the imposition of the corset, the introduction of discretionary determination of MLR and the regular use of qualitative guidance, it may be argued that a new era of control over the activities of banks has merely replaced the previous system. The future for monetary policy in the next decade is uncertain, particularly so following the abolition of exchange controls in October 1979 (see Chapter 9). This development has important implications for monetary policy chiefly because of the possibility that domestic control measures such as the 'corset' may now be circumvented by the drawing of funds away from domestic banks and into the euro-sterling market. The consequences of this new environment for monetary policy were not totally clear at the end of 1979, but significant reform of the monetary system in the early 1980s to cope with the new situation is very likely.

References

Artis, M. J. and Lewis, M. K. [1976], 'The demand for money in the U.K., 1963–73', *Manchester School of Economic and Social Studies*, June 1976, pp. 147–81.

Bank of England Quarterly Bulletin [1966], 'Official Transactions in the gilt-edged market', June 1966, pp. 141–8.

Bank of England Quarterly Bulletin [1971a], 'Competition and Credit Control', June 1971, pp. 189–93.

Bank of England Quarterly Bulletin [1971b], 'Key Issues in Monetary and Credit Policy', June 1971, pp. 195–8.

Bank of England Quarterly Bulletin [1971c], 'Reserve ratios: further definitions', December 1971, pp. 482–9.

Bank of England Quarterly Bulletin [1972a], 'Bank Lending', September 1972, p. 327.

Bank of England Quarterly Bulletin [1972b], 'Commentary', December 1972, pp. 435–51.

Bank of England Quarterly Bulletin [1973], 'Competition and Credit: modified arrangements for the discount market', September 1973, pp. 306–7.

Bank of England Quarterly Bulletin [1979a], 'The gilt-edged market', June 1979, pp. 137–48.

Bank of England Quarterly Bulletin [1979b], 'Monetary Base Control', June 1979, pp. 149–59.

Bank of England Quarterly Bulletin [1979c], 'Components of Private Sector Liquidity', September 1979, pp. 278–82.

Bank of England [1974], *Reports and Accounts for the year ended 29 February 1974.*

Coghlan, R. T. [1979], 'Squeezing into the corset', *The Banker*, September 1979, pp. 35–9.

Cramp, A. B. [1971], *Monetary Management*. London: Allen and Unwin.

Fletcher, G. A. [1978], 'Cash Base Control of Bank Deposits and the British Banking System', *Société Universitaire Européene de Recherches Financiéres* (S.U.E.R.F.).

Foote, M. D. K. W. [1979], 'Monetary Targets: their nature and record in the major economies'. Paper presented to the City University Conference on Monetary Targets, May 1979.

Friedman, M. [1968], 'The role of monetary policy', *American Economic Review*, March 1968, pp. 1–17.

Greenwells Monetary Bulletin [1978], 'The corset and transactions within the Banking Sector', July–August 1978, pp. 1–19.

Greenwells Special Monetary Bulletin [1979], 'Proposed Changes to the Present Monetary System', March 1979, pp. 1–8.

Laidler, D. E. W. [1976], 'Mayer on Monetarism: Comments from a British point of view', *Kredit und Kapital*, pp. 56–67.

Laidler, D. E. W. and Nobay, A. R. [1975], 'Some current issues concerning the international aspects of inflation' in D. Laidler, *Essays on Money and Inflation*. Manchester: Manchester University Press, pp. 166–82.

McClam, W. D. [1978], 'Targets & techniques of monetary policy in Western Europe', *Banca Nazionale del Lavoro Quarterly Review*, March 1978, pp. 3–27.

Morgan, E. V. [1973], 'The gilt-edged market under the new monetary policy', *The Banker*, January 1973, pp. 19–24.

Pringle, R. [1977], 'New approaches to monetary policy', *The Banker*, November 1977, pp. 45–50.

Radcliffe Committee [1959], *Report on the Working of the Monetary System*, Cmnd 827. London: HMSO.

Tew, J. H. B. [1978], 'Monetary Policy', Part 1 in F. T. Blackaby (ed.) *British Economic Policy 1960–74: Demand Management*. Cambridge: Cambridge University Press, pp. 218–57.

3   Incomes Policy

by Peter J. Dawkins

Introduction

After the general election of June 1970 the incoming Heath government was determined not to use a prices and incomes policy. Similarly,
the general election of March 1979 brought in a government committed against the use of such a policy. That is how the 1970s began and
ended. However in the intervening years prices and incomes policies
were in fact operated most of the time. Indeed during the 1970s there
was a continuation of the growing willingness of postwar governments
to place constraints on the growth of incomes in the fight against
inflation. However despite such policy developments there has still
not emerged a widespread acceptance of the need for an incomes policy.
Even the Labour government elected in 1974 disputed the virtue of
an incomes policy except of a very voluntary nature, when coming
into office. The new Conservative government in 1979 have shown a
more fundamental opposition to incomes policy than any in the postwar period. The current scepticism of incomes policy arises for a
number of reasons. First, incomes policies tend to become unpopular
with the electorate and face vehement opposition from sections of the
workforce after a time, and have had much to do with the fall of
governments. Second, the great problem of inflation has continued
despite the use of incomes policies. Third, monetarist thought which
tends to argue that incomes policies are not only useless but positively
harmful, has been growing considerably. These observations are particularly pertinent to the 1970s. The main aim of this chapter is to
consider the experience of the 1970s in the light of such observations.
If incomes policies are to continue into the 1980s it is hoped that
previous experience will provide useful guidance for the policy-
makers.

The Meaning and Theory of 'Incomes Policy'

It could be argued that the government always has some kind of incomes policy. In that the government has become an increasingly important part of the economy, its behaviour must be a very important influence on incomes. In a broad sense then, it might be said that the government always has an incomes policy, which may be more, or less, interventionist. However this chapter adopts a narrower definition. An incomes policy here is regarded as a systematic attempt by government to influence the level or structure of incomes at source. The most significant form of incomes policy is the 'prices and incomes policy' which aims to control the growth of incomes and at the same time prices, as a form of macroeconomic policy against inflation. Indeed the terms 'incomes policy' and 'prices and incomes policy' tend to be used interchangeably. That is largely true of this chapter also. However there are cases of incomes policies with quite different objectives from that of prices and incomes policies. Minimum wages legislation which is widespread in the United States is an example of this. In the UK in the 1970s equal pay legislation for women is the outstanding example. The effect of the *1970 Equal Pay Act*, and its effect on prices and incomes policy is considered below. However, it is prices and incomes policies *per se* which form the focus of attention of this chapter.

Prices and incomes policies have been used as a weapon against inflation. A cost-push theory of inflation provides the usual rationale. In particular if trade unions can exert upward pressure on wage costs, independent of the level of demand in the labour market, they can promote inflation. This can be regarded as giving an upward bias to the Phillips curve relation between the rate of change of money wage rates and the level of unemployment which, following Lipsey [1960], was generally regarded as confirming a demand-pull theory of inflation, with unemployment a proxy for excess demand. The aim of incomes policy in the light of this cost-push theory is to negate the inflationary effect of trade union pushfulness, by placing constraints on increases in wages and forcing the Phillips curve down. Thus incomes policy represents an attempt to reduce the level of inflation without affecting the level of employment. During the 1960s and particularly the 1970s, observations relating wage inflation and unemployment moved very much away from the traditional Phillips relation. Table 3.1 shows the predicted and actual levels of wage inflation with respect to the prevailing levels of unemployment in the period 1960–79. The discrepancy from the Phillips relation reported in column 3 gives one key to the reason why incomes policies were

used in the 1970s. It was feared that acting upon demand to return
to lower levels of inflation would require very high levels of unemployment. Even if it were necessary to some extent to act upon demand
it was hoped that an incomes policy would help to soften the blow.

Table 3.1   Inflation in the UK: annual data 1960–79

	(1) Change in retail prices (%)	(2) Change in wage rates (%)	(3) Displacement of Phillips curve (%)	(4) Unemploy- ment (%)
1960	1.0	4.1	0.0	1.5
1961	3.4	3.4	−1.2	1.3
1962	2.6	4.4	+1.6	1.8
1963	2.1	4.3	+2.5	2.2
1964	3.3	3.8	−0.3	1.6
1965	4.8	4.6	−0.6	1.3
1966	3.9	3.3	−1.3	1.4
1967	2.5	5.9	+4.0	2.2
1968	4.7	7.1	+5.2	2.3
1969	5.4	5.7	+3.8	2.3
1970	6.4	13.5	+11.9	2.5
1971	9.4	12.1	+11.4	3.3
1972	7.1	11.0	+10.4	3.6
1973	9.2	12.2	+10.7	2.6
1974	16.1	29.4	+28.9	2.5
1975	24.2	25.4	+25.4	3.9
1976	16.5	11.8	+11.8	5.2
1977	15.8	5.8	+6.0	5.7
1978	8.3	18.1[a]	+18.2	5.7
1979	13.4	15.6	+15.6	5.4

Sources: Figures for 1960–77 from Prest and Coppock [1978], p. 43. Later Data from
Department of Employment Gazette. For an account of the derivation of
this measure of displacement see A. R. Prest and D. J. Coppock [1978]
pp. 42–3.

[a] This figure is greatly influenced by nationally negotiated rates of wages of engineering
workers remaining unchanged between February 1976 and April 1978.

For a more extensive exposition of the relevant macroeconomic
theories including the monetarist objectives see Trevithick and
Mulvey [1975], Chapters 4–7.

Prices and Incomes Policies in the 1970s: A Summary of Policy Developments

Incomes policies had been used at various times in the postwar period (see Blackaby (ed.) [1978], Chapter 8) with the latest attempt by the Labour government involving a certain amount of statutory intervention, as administered by the National Board for Prices and Incomes (NBPI). However in the latter part of the policy the wage limits had ceased to be effective and in 1970 the new Conservative government, reflecting its non-interventionist philosophy soon abolished the National Board for Prices and Incomes (NBPI). Employers in the private sector were advised of their responsibility to resist irresponsible wage demands and were warned that they would not be rescued by government if they got into trouble. The same principle applied in the public sector in theory, but the Government itself showed a special interest in settlements adopting the $n - 1$ strategy such that each successive wage settlement should be 1% less than the last. The policy had some success with the postmen, but was broken by the miners, who created a state of emergency as a result of industrial action, and finally secured an increase in average earnings in the region of 17–20% on the recommendation of the Wilberforce Court of Inquiry. With inflation increasing the Government sought a voluntary agreement on wages and prices with the TUC and the CBI, but failed, and in November 1972 it introduced a statutory freeze on wages and prices. The second stage of the Conservatives' policy, commencing in April 1973, marked the beginning of a new style and elaborate statutory policy which was to last until the downfall of the Government in February 1974. On the wages side the policy was universal and much more comprehensively monitored than ever before by the newly created Pay Board though large firms faced greater notification requirements than small ones, on the basis that if big settlements were restrained, smaller ones would tend to follow suit. Another new development was that wage limits were to be on the average amount paid per head by the firm, rather than on wage rates agreed at the national level, in an attempt to avoid any wage drift that might occur because of increases at the plant level and to allow for flexibility within firms. With regard to prices, a separate body, the Price Commission was established and a price code introduced. In manufacturing, price controls were based on the principles of 'allowable costs' (with firms having to demonstrate that they had gained no advantage in profits from an above average increase in productivity) and a reference level for profit margins based on the best two trading years in the last five. In distribution, prices were not controlled on the basis of 'allowable costs', but on the basis of reference levels for gross and net profit margins.

Stage Two of the pay policy (that which followed the freeze) commenced in November 1972, and involved a £1 per week + 4% maximum increase, subject to a maximum of £250 per annum per person. Such wage increases could only take place once in a twelve month period. The economy was in a period of very rapid expansion now with unemployment falling quickly, and earnings increased by rather more than the guidelines would have suggested. However part of this was a result of the payment of settlements deferred by the wage freeze, and increases resulting from equal pay legislation (see section on wage guidelines and special cases). However the policy did not face major opposition or outstanding clashes which might lead to its breakdown. But it had been known that the second stage was to be replaced in November 1973 by the third stage. The Conservatives, worried about possible problems of opposition from the trade unions, introduced some flexibility into Stage Three, and the possibility that threshold agreements could be made whereby employees would be compensated for increases in prices in excess of 7%. The basic pay guidelines were for a maximum increase of 7% or £2.25 whichever was the greater (plus threshold agreements), subject to a maximum of £350 per person per annum. Exceptions could be argued on the basis of low pay and unsocial hours, the latter designed specifically to provide a loophole for the National Union of Mineworkers to use. (The NUM's annual conference in July had reached unanimous approval for a claim for increases ranging from 22% for face workers to 46% for underground workers on minimum weekly rates). The new pay code came into operation on 7 November 1973. By 12 November the miners had rejected an offer from the Coal Board, who had attempted to make full use of any flexibility in the new code. Unfortunately, the policy had no additional built-in flexibility, though while the miners' dispute continued, the Pay Board published a report on relativities, (Pay Board [1974]), and the Government turned the Pay Board into a Relativities Board. However before the Relativities Board had reported on the miners' case, a power crisis and a three-day week had been encountered, and the Prime Minister had called an election in an attempt to achieve electoral support for the Conservatives' policies, an election that they lost in February 1974. Thus the statutory incomes policy ended, though the Pay Board continued to administer the pay code for some months after the change of government, and a lot of people enjoyed a number of intermittent pay increases on the basis of threshold agreements because inflation was beginning to increase markedly.

Central to the new Labour government's policy package was the 'social contract', which had emerged from joint discussions between the Labour Party and the TUC and was outlined in a joint publication (TUC–Labour Party Liaison Committee [1973]). The Labour government undertook to implement certain policies favoured by the TUC including repeal of the *1971 Industrial Relations Act* and the implementation of price and rent control. In return the TUC agreed that wage increases should not exceed the level necessary to compensate for price increases between main settlements. It was also understood that there should be twelve months between pay agreements. However this guideline experienced widespread evasion, and there was a wages and prices explosion. A run on the pound in summer 1975 provoked the introduction of social contract 'mark 2'. The new policy which was agreed with the TUC, involved a £6 per week maximum on wage increases and a freeze on incomes over £8000. The Government was to ensure observance in the public sector. In the private sector, if an employer broke the pay limit, the whole pay increase would be disallowed as a cost justifying price increases. The Government did not seek legal compulsion *per se* for the wage limits but prepared legislation which it would ask Parliament to support if the pay limit were endangered. This policy period was certainly accompanied by a significant reduction in the rate of inflation though wage rates increased by as much as 17.5% at an annual rate. However TUC support was maintained and social contract mark two moved into Phase Two in August 1976. This phase was to tighten up on wage increases. There was to be a 5% guideline, but subject to a minimum increase of £2.50 and a maximum of £4 per week. The Government promised income tax concessions if the TUC accepted the policy which it duly did. Phase Two was a period in which wage rate increases were reduced to something less than 5% per annum. However, price inflation actually increased and the trade unions became strongly opposed to the continuance of such a policy. Phase Three was introduced in August 1977, relaxing its pay limit to 10% and allowing for special cases on the basis of restoring differentials or self-financing productivity deals, but it did not receive TUC support. To reinforce the existing arrangements whereby price increases based on excessive wage claims were disallowed, a sanctions policy was introduced, such that pay settlements inconsistent with the pay guidelines would be taken into account in public purchasing policy and in the placing of contracts. During Phase Three wage rates increased by more than 15%, but price inflation was reduced to single figures. Although the TUC's policy of no support continued, the Government was encouraged by the single figure inflation result, and attempted to sustain this improvement in Phase Four with a limit of 5% on wage increases, while allowing for exceptional cases established on the basis of independent recommendations. It was in this period that the policy finally broke down. Growing hostility to the sanctions policy in industry was reflected in Parliament where the Government was defeated on this issue. Thus sanctions ended. The low limit of 5% also faced great hostility from certain groups, and there followed a 'winter of discontent' with a number of industrial disputes affecting the public, particularly that involving manual workers in local government. In March 1979 the Government, attempting to keep its incomes policy intact, announced that the Standing Commission on Pay Comparability (the Clegg Commission) was to be set up. However in May 1979 the Labour government was defeated in a general election.

It should be added that throughout the period of the Labour government's incomes policy the Price Commission had been kept intact. Indeed the existence of a statutory prices policy had been a necessary condition for the initial agreement with the TUC in the context of the social contract, and the *Prices Act 1974* extended the prices policy by providing the Secretary of State for Prices and Consumer Protection with the power to subsidise certain foods. However the price code had to be amended in 1976, and replaced by a new code in 1977, because company profits had been squeezed. The 'allowable costs' provision of the original price code was subject to a 50% productivity deduction, which was later reduced to 20% and then abolished in 1976. The new code inaugurated by the *Price Commission Act 1977*, described the duty of the Price Commission to be to restrain the prices of goods and services 'so far as to be consistent with the making of adequate profits by efficient suppliers'. The new code involved less rigorous price controls and selectivity in investigations, (see Smith and Swann [1979]).

The new Conservative government, which took office in May 1979, had fought an election campaign based on free market principles.

Prices and incomes policy was regarded as an alien notion and abandoned. Thus the Price Commission was abolished. It is interesting to note, however, that the Government has not found it appropriate to abolish the Clegg Commission as it enters the 1980s. In this sense at least it might be regarded that its abandonment of incomes policy is less than absolute. However the essential anti-inflation strategy of the Conservative government is based on monetarist thought and on a tight money policy. In the public sector this is reinforced by the provision of expenditure ceilings such that increases in wages above a certain level would seem to imply redundancies. The Government has urged public sector employers and employees to take heed of this fact in their wage bargains and as such could be regarded as pursuing an incomes policy, loosely defined, in the public sector. Time will tell whether this becomes more formal intervention so as to accord more clearly with our definition of incomes policy. In the private sector, it is hoped that the unemployment consequences of excessive wage settlements with a tight monetary policy in action, will restrain wage settlements to allow the anti-inflation policy to succeed without unemployment consequences that are too drastic.

Recurring Features, Themes and Problems of Incomes Policy
Even by a strict definition of incomes policy then, such a policy was in action for most of the 1970s. As previous experience suggested there are certain themes and problems in the implementation of such policies that are typically encountered. Experience of the 1970s allows a broader examination of these factors.

Introduction, stages and breakdown of incomes policies
Examination of incomes policies in the 1970s confirms the previous experience of 1958, 1961 and 1966 that such policies are typically introduced in a crisis. In 1972 mounting inflation was accompanied by a deteriorating balance of payments and rate of exchange, so that in November 1972 a freeze was introduced. The Labour government responded similarly to the crisis it faced in 1975, when the wages and prices explosion under social contract mark one had precipitated a sterling crisis. In this case a £6 maximum rather than a freeze was introduced. However bearing in mind the new heights inflation had reached in 1974–5, the implications of this limit for the slow-down of wage increases was comparable to the freezes imposed in previous crises. Policies since the early 1960s had also moved into a second

stage in which the limits to wage increases were relaxed somewhat. The Conservatives' policy in 1973 followed this principle with the introduction of £1 + 4% after six months of a wages freeze. In contrast the Labour government's policy was actually tightened in Phase Two, introduced in August 1976. However this might be explained by the fact that the Government was trying to reduce inflation from such a high level and thus had two stages in which wages were allowed to increase by less and less, rather than 'slamming the brakes on' in one go. However, in Phase Three, the Labour government did relax the rules by allowing for increases of up to 10%. But then the Labour government tried something distinctly new by reducing the wage limit to 5% in Phase Four. In so doing it appears to have been suggesting that it regarded incomes policy as a more permanent feature of economic policy than did previous governments who tended to relax incomes policy constraints with the avowed aim of returning to 'free collective bargaining'.

However, while the stages of the Conservatives incomes policy may have differed significantly from those of the Labour government that followed it, both policies came to similar ends. Certain trade unions, in particular the miners in 1974 and local government manual workers in 1979, challenged the policies in their final stages with industrial action which had a considerable effect on the general public. In the general elections which followed close upon these disputes, the governments which had tried to stand firm were defeated. In the 1960s the Conservative government's policy (1961–4) and the Labour government's statutory policy (1966–70) had also ended in electoral defeat. The experience of the 1970s then does not seem to provide any greater hope than previously existed about the possibility of successful incomes policy on a permanent basis, though this may have something to do with the fact that incomes policies have typically been introduced in a crisis. As long as it is thought that an economic policy can be successful without an incomes policy, this is likely to be a recurring phenomenon. Perhaps the policy of the new Conservative government will be seen as a severe test of this hypothesis. If they turn to incomes policy it may become regarded as a more necessary feature of economic policy on an ongoing basis.

Voluntary v. statutory policies
One of the major debates concerning the operation of incomes policy is whether such policies should be voluntary or statutory in their

application (see, for example, Blackaby [1972], pp. 16–17). Clearly there must exist a certain level of consensus in the acceptance of an incomes policy, and in that sense a statutory policy without sufficiently widespread support cannot be expected to succeed. However there is quite a strong argument that to ensure that a basic consensus is actually converted into wage restraint, a certain amount of compulsion may be appropriate. The Labour government in the 1960s attempted voluntary agreements on incomes policy between December 1964 and July 1966, but the crisis that followed led them to obtain statutory support for their freeze and a certain amount of statutory back-up to the following stages of its policy. The experience of the 1970s confirms similar tendencies. The Conservative government attempted to obtain voluntary consent for an incomes policy in 1972, but without sufficient agreement and faced with a crisis in November 1972, it introduced a statutory freeze. The following Stages (Two and Three) involved the most complicated statutory intervention in wage and price determination ever attempted.

The incomes policy under the Labour government (1974–9) embodied similar traits, but made the distinction between a voluntary and a statutory policy less clear. Indeed it is probably more appropriate to talk of compulsory rather than statutory incomes policy, as the Labour government used certain devices, which did not require legislation *per se*, in an attempt to impose its policy. Initially in social contract mark one, its approach was very much one of a voluntary agreement with the TUC. However during this period there was widespread evasion of the wage guidelines, and a wage and price explosion, tending to confirm the need for a certain amount of compulsion in the application of an incomes policy. The consequent sterling crisis in 1975 led to the introduction of social contract mark two. As we have seen, this was still regarded as an essentially voluntary policy involving TUC consent, but nonetheless it was supported with the threat of legal intervention. The Government actually prepared legislation which it would have asked Parliament to support if the pay limit were endangered. An additional device, which was introduced in Stage Two of this policy, was that of conditional tax reliefs. If the wages policy was accepted, these reliefs would be enacted. Thus a 'carrot' was dangled (see Chapter 1) to induce agreement on wages policy. Such agreement could be regarded as 'voluntary', but the Government was clearly using a certain amount of its power of statute to achieve such agreement. In Stage Three of the policy another innovation was introduced – that of sanctions. This involved the use of a 'stick' against those employers who contravened the wage guidelines. This policy of sanctions was such that pay settlements inconsistent with the pay guidelines, would be taken into account in public purchasing and the placing of contracts. The Government was clearly not using statutory intervention here to enforce its pay policy. However it was seeking to compel employers to comply with the policy on the basis of its importance in the economy as a purchaser. The policy was thrown out towards the end of the Labour government, partly because its application had been somewhat secret and inconsistent, thus causing great uncertainty and even hostility in certain areas of British industry. Even before sanctions, the Government had been using its statutory powers with regards to prices in applying its incomes policy. The Government would not allow firms which made excessive pay settlements to reflect these settlements in higher prices to the consumer. So while the policy was still ostensibly voluntary, the Government was using its power of statute and its importance as an economic agent in the economy to attempt to compel employers to abide by the wage guidelines in their wage settlements.

One of the arguments that might be lodged against the kind of complicated statutory intervention that the Conservative government undertook between 1972 and 1974 is that it gives rise to inflexibility. It is difficult for the Government to use its discretion as a policy proceeds. Indeed the Conservatives found themselves in something of a tight corner when the Coal Board stretched the Stage Three guidelines to their limits in attempting to give the miners an increase in pay very much above the average, but nonetheless failed to achieve a settlement on this basis. In the end, the Government responded by asking the Pay Board to act as a Relativitities Board which could facilitate exceptional treatment for special cases. The Labour government's policy was somewhat more flexible in that it could use its powers of intervention in a more discretionary way. However such discretion, particularly with regards to the use of sanctions, was used in a somewhat inconsistent and secret way. The uncertainty and hostility that this engendered in British industry, helped to lead to the policy's downfall. Indeed the Labour government also established a body towards the end of its policy, to provide for a more formal consideration of special cases, namely the Clegg Commission. This, taken along with the Conservatives' experience with Stage Three, suggests the need for the establishment of an institution to provide a

certain degree of flexibility in the implementation of an incomes policy
– hopefully applied in a way that is sufficiently consistent to give the
policy credibility and consent.

Finally, on this issue of the role of statutory intervention, experience
of the 1970s suggests that the Conservatives are more likely to resort
to statutory controls if they adopt an incomes policy than is a Labour
government. Although the latter may resort to a certain amount of
statutory intervention, it is more likely to use its special relationship
with the trade unions to achieve voluntary consent and to attempt
to persuade and cajole the trade unions rather than to emphasise
statutory controls in its incomes policy. When the Conservative
government sought voluntary agreement in 1972, it failed. In contrast
the ideologies of the trade unions and the Labour party are more likely
to give rise to a joint approach to government involving a certain
amount of wage restraint on behalf of the trade unions. That was the
basis of the social contract. However it would seem that when this
special relationship is increasingly tested by dire circumstances and a
Labour government's inability to produce the goods desired by the
unions, the government is likely to turn towards compulsion in its
application of an incomes policy.

Wage guidelines and special cases
One problem that was confronted by incomes policies before the 1970s
was that wage norms tended to become minima. The response of
governments then had been to set maxima on the basis that at worse
they might become norms. This would seem to be a sensible approach.
However major problems remain. At what level should such a
maximum be established? Is there a problem of wage drift? Should
a wage limit be expressed in absolute or in percentage terms? Should
exceptions be allowed, and if so for what reasons?

There is an argument that wage guidelines should allow workers
wage increases which at least compensate them for rises in prices, so
that their real wages are not eroded. However there are problems
with this. If inflation is running at a high level, then to allow wage
settlements to be based on the current rate of inflation, as measured
by changes in prices over the previous twelve months, entails high
wage increases which hardly help to restrain inflation. Social contract
mark one embodied this very problem as it followed this principle of
compensation for price increases between settlements twelve months
apart. So even if wage increases had not exceeded this guideline they

would still have been high because of the high rate of inflation that prevailed. However the problem of applying the compensation principle may be less severe if based on a twelve-month rule than if based on threshold agreements. The threshold agreements resulting from Stage Three of the Conservatives' policy in 1973–4 meant that every time the price index went up another full percentage point in addition to the basic 7% allowable, workers were compensated. Every such increase may be expected to fuel the inflationary process further. The principle of threshold agreements may be reasonable if based on a pure wage-push theory of inflation such that prices will only go up if wages go up. However, if there are some demand-pull forces at work as well or if inflation results from increasing import prices, the consequent threshold agreements can set up a cost-price spiral. In fairness to social contract mark one, this was one of the problems it had to face, as a legacy of the previous government's policy.

Typically then, incomes policies have attempted to restrain wage increases below the existing level of inflation in the hope that inflation will follow suit. Prices policies accompany the wages policies in an attempt to ensure that prices do follow suit. In extreme cases such attempts to restrain inflation involve freezes. However, as a freeze must follow more closely upon some groups' wage increases than upon others, such drastic action is regarded by certain groups as having hit them hardest. This stores up problems for the post-freeze period of attempting to sort out such anomolies. When inflation is running at a particularly high level a freeze may be too drastic in this respect. Putting the brakes on steadily may be the sensible policy in this situation, as followed by the Labour government in their Stages One and Two of social contract mark two. Indeed although freezes have generally been quite effective for their duration – and the Freeze of 1972–3 basically falls within this category – if incomes policy is regarded as a useful policy tool, it may be more likely to succeed, and store up less problems if used in a more gradualist way.

A concept that has frequently been discussed in relation to incomes policy is that of 'wage drift'. There are various definitions of wage drift (see Office of Manpower Economics [1973]), but there are basically two aspects of concern to incomes policy. First, if nationally negotiated wage rates are constrained, the shortfall at the national level may be replaced by increases in earnings at the local level. This could be for one of two reasons. First, it may be because of pure drift as defined by Phelps Brown [1962] whereby labour costs are increased by arrangements 'outside the control of the recognised procedures for scheduling rates' (p. 340). Such a phenomenon bodes ill for incomes policy which can only really act upon recognised procedures. The other way in which earnings increases at the local level may be of great importance is as far as formal procedures at the local level supplant national agreements. Evidence presented by Brown and Terry [1978] suggests that this has been an increasingly important feature of British industry. This gives rise to greater optimism about the role of incomes policy as long as it acts upon agreements at the plant level. Such has been the approach of incomes policy since Stage One of the Conservatives' policy in 1972. The other aspect of wage drift more loosely defined is the increase in earnings in excess of wages rates as the result of payments on top of basic pay resulting, for example, from premia for overtime or shift-work. As these are percentage mark-ups which tend not to change, their importance depends upon the number of hours worked, which will depend upon demand factors. It will also depend upon the number of hours that make up normal hours of work. In fact in the 1970s positive wage drift of this type has only been very significant in 1977. In some years, such as 1978, it was quite significantly negative.

If wage maxima are established in absolute terms and as a result workers generally receive similar absolute increases regardless of their existing levels of income, then wage differentials measured in percentage terms can be expected to narrow. Such a narrowing is reinforced by inflation which erodes the value of a given level of income. On the other hand, the trade unions have shown a certain aversion to limits based on percentage increases which in the 1970s has typically led to limits being based either on absolute increases, such as the £6 in phase one of social contract mark two, or a limit which includes at least a certain absolute element, such as the £1 + 4% with a £250 maximum in Stage Two of the Conservatives' policy in 1973, or the 5% with a minimum of £2.50 and a maximum of £4 in Phase Two of social contract mark two. While such a tendency to favour the relatively low paid compared with the relatively high paid may help to gain a policy's acceptance in the first instance, the danger of antagonising higher paid groups and of affecting the inflow of labour into the higher paid occupations is a real problem. It was in the light of these factors that the social contract mark two in the end had to turn to simple percentage limits. We return later to the complicated question of the effect of incomes policy on wage differentials.

Most groups of workers usually think that they deserve special treatment within an incomes policy. In some cases the argument for special treatment may be very strong. A number of criteria have been used for judging special cases in various incomes policies. In particular, productivity deals, low pay and the maintenance or restoration of established differentials have cropped up from time to time. There are however problems with allowing for special cases. Most groups of workers can probably find some apparently sound basis for special treatment. If special cases become numerous the concept becomes meaningless and the basic wage guidelines become irrelevant. The Conservative government (1970–4) therefore allowed for no special cases until Stage Three when unsocial hours or low pay could be used as the basis for special treatment. However this led to a lack of flexibility in the Conservatives' policy in dealing with anomolies and special problems as they emerged. In the end they set up the Relativities Board to deal with this very problem. Unfortunately it was too late. However, if on the other hand special treatment of certain groups is allowed for, quite apart from ensuring that this special treatment has only limited applicability, there is the danger that criteria for special treatment may become contradictory. For example special treatment for low pay or productivity deals may upset established differentials. The problems here are acute, and the nature and the relative importance of the criteria depends on how important relative wages are in the allocation of labour on the one hand, and on workers' attitudes and militancy on the other. What is clear is that incomes policy in the future has to confront this problem more rigorously. The establishment of the Relativities Board in 1974 and the Clegg Commission in 1979 were both after-thoughts. Such institutions should be established earlier in the life of an incomes policy.

Finally with regard to special cases, there were two pieces of legislation in the 1970s that gave rise to certain groups being imposed upon incomes policies as special cases by independent statute. These were the *1970 Equal Pay Act* and schedule 11 of the *1975 Employment Protection Act*. The Equal Pay Act sought to force employers to pay men and women equally for doing the same, or broadly similar, work. It was due to have effect from 29 December 1975, the lag of five and a half years designed to give firms and organisations sufficient time to introduce equal pay without being too disruptive. Table 3.2 does suggest a significant narrowing of the sex wage differential as a result of this legislation. It has been shown that the effect of the Act on female wages was spread out over the 1970s (Department of Employment Gazette [1975] and Bosworth and Dawkins [1979]), but, as Table 3.2 suggests, its greatest effect would appear to have been in the period 1974–6. As far as prices and incomes policies were concerned then, the effect of the Equal Pay Act was probably at its greatest in the early stages of the social contract, but it also gave rise to exceptional increases during the preceding Conservative government's incomes policy and to some extent in later phases of the social contract. Schedule 11 of the Employment Protection Act, especially concerned with low paid workers, became a method for some unions to circumvent the Labour government's incomes policy. This was by no means confined to low paid workers. Those in professional occupations, represented for example by ASTMS, were important users of this provision. A detailed discussion of schedule 11 can be found in Bercusson [1976] and Wood [1978], but basically it allowed for the possibility of legally binding settlements in cases where an employer was observing less favourable terms and conditions of employment than the 'recognised' terms and conditions, which had been settled by an agreement or award between substantially representative employers' associations in comparable employment in the same trade, industry or section. The Central Arbitration Committee explicitly stated that its decisions were not related to the current pay policy (Wood [1978], p. 83).

Table 3.2   The female–male earnings ratio, 1970–8

	Average gross weekly earnings (excluding overtime pay) all industries and services					
Year	Manual males (1)	Manual females (2)	(2)/(1) (3)	Non-manual males (4)	Non-manual females (5)	(5)/(4) (6)
1970	26.8	13.4	0.50	35.8	17.8	0.50
1973	31.9	18.9	0.59	46.7	24.4	0.52
1974	36.6	22.7	0.62	52.7	28.3	0.54
1975	47.8	31.2	0.65	66.3	39.2	0.59
1976	61.7	42.4	0.69	87.3	53.5	0.61
1978	69.1	47.7	0.69	96.3	58.5	0.61

Source: *New Earnings Survey.*

As we move into the 1980s, the effect of the Equal Pay Act on negotiated wage rates is virtually complete, and schedule 11 faces repeal. Similar problems may however emerge in the future if equal pay legislation is strengthened or if the government were for example to adopt minimum wages legislation.

Price controls

It is fairly clear that to obtain the acceptance of a wages policy a government must at the same time institute a prices policy. Consequently the incomes policies of the 1970s have gone hand in hand with a prices policy – hence the title 'prices and incomes policy'. Indeed the price controls instituted by the Conservative government in 1972 involved the most elaborate intervention in this field ever attempted. Some of the details were discussed in section 2, and a more detailed discussion can be found in Smith and Swann [1979]. Furthermore a statutory prices policy, administered by the Price Commission, was maintained by the Labour government after 1974 even though the statutory wages policy was abolished.

Experience of prices policy in the 1970s would appear to suggest certain lessons. First, stringent price controls can be expected to cause a profits squeeze which may become intolerable. Second, if profits-push inflation exists, there may be some scope for a prices policy independent of a wages policy. However the scope here would seem to be limited and to lie rather in the realms of competition policy (see Chapter 6). Otherwise prices policy against inflation must be related to a wages policy. If the wages policy is not statutory nor monitored by some kind of wages board, the body implementing a prices policy can therefore be expected to become involved in assessing wage increases. It would seem sensible to ensure that if there is a prices and incomes policy in operation, the establishment involved in its implementation should be designed to consider wages as well as prices. Furthermore the Chairman of the Prices Commission from 1973 to 1977 has argued that just as it is unreasonable to have a statutory wages policy without a statutory prices policy, it is unreasonable to have a statutory prices policy without a statutory wages policy (Sir Arthur Cockfield [1978]).

The establishment of institutions

During the 1950s and 1960s various bodies set up in relation to prices and incomes policies, came and went, as various governments came and went. There was the Council on Prices, Productivity and Incomes, the National Incomes Commission and then the National Board for

Prices and Incomes. This saga continued into the 1970s. The Price Commission and the Pay Board were both set up by the Conservative government in 1972. The Conservatives proceeded to turn their Pay Board into a Relativities Board, which was later abolished by the succeeding Labour government. However the Labour government did find it appropriate to establish the Standing Commission on Pay Comparability (The Clegg Commission) in 1979 for reasons similar to those that had led to the establishment of the Relativities Board under the previous Conservative government. Although they abolished the Pay Board the Labour government did keep the Price Commission in existence. It was the next Conservative government, in 1979, which abolished that.

This experience of the establishment and abolition of similar institutions to monitor developments in prices and incomes and to administer prices and incomes policies would seem to suggest the virtue of some kind of more permanent institution. Considering the great problems that emerge and re-emerge in relation to price and pay codes, discussed in preceding sections, it would seem that the body of experience and knowledge that a more permanent institution would build up could be expected to improve the chances of a successful incomes policy being operated. It may be that the tradition of non-intervention in wage bargaining in the UK and the nature of a two-party system will prohibit this. However it is at least an idea that should be discussed. The increasing involvement of ACAS in industrial relations (see Chapter 5) may be interpreted as a growing acceptance of the role of government in wage bargaining and makes the establishment of a more permanent body to monitor prices and incomes a more likely possibility.

The need for a policy mix

The 1970s has witnessed a great debate about the cause(s) of inflation. That the debate continues suggests that empirical verification for one or other theory has not been sufficiently powerful to close the debate. Indeed the quest for a cause of inflation may be a pointless exercise. For example to establish that there is a strong causal link as well as a correlation between the rate of growth of the money supply and the rate of inflation need not lead to the simple conclusion that to control inflation monetary policy is alone sufficient. Put another way the use of bargaining power by trade unions to push up wages may not lead to inflation unless accompanied by money supply growth. However such a push on wages creates pressure on government to accommodate the wage increases to maintain the level of employment. The new Conservative government in 1979 however has taken the view that monetary policy should be sufficient. The threat of unemployment in the private sector should be sufficient to restrain wage demands. There is an argument, however, that labour does not bargain in aggregate, and bargainers at the micro level believe that the costs of excessive wage increases can be passed on to others (Llewellyn [1980]). Thus, at least in the short-run, a tight monetary policy, may not be sufficient to restrain wage increases in line with the fall in money supply growth. The consequences for unemployment may be so severe as to render monetary policy alone unacceptable in the fight against inflation. It may prove necessary to constrain wage changes as well by some form of incomes policy.

Thus even if one accepts a great deal of monetarist thought, incomes policy need not be redundant. Any evidence that supports alternative socio-political or cost-push theories reinforces the argument. What is clear, however, is that if an incomes policy is adopted, it should be accompanied by an appropriate fiscal and monetary policy. It is not sufficient to restrain wage increases, while pursuing an expansionary monetary and fiscal policy. Ending wage controls can then be expected to release pent-up demand. In the 1970s it is the Conservatives' incomes policy (1972–4) that illustrates most clearly the problems of an inappropriate policy mix. Restraint on incomes was not accompanied by restraint in monetary and fiscal policy. The 'Barber boom', engineered in the budget of 1972, ran counter to the incomes policy established in the same year. A study by Stevenson and Trevithick [1977] of monetary policy and prices and incomes policy has shown that the velocity of circulation tends to decline during periods of incomes policies and returns to its 'normal level' upon their removal. This has been because monetary policy has not been sufficiently restrictive during periods of incomes policy, and the latter constrains spending in an artificial way by reducing the velocity of circulation. On the removal of incomes policies this pent-up liquidity is released, allowing for the acceleration of inflation. The Conservative policy (1972–4) was an outstanding example of this. It was a period of rapid growth in the money supply, accompanied by a very significant reduction in the velocity of circulation. When the policy was removed the velocity of circulation increased markedly, and there followed a period of rapid inflation. Thus incomes policy does constrain the growth in spending by constraining wage increases, but it will not have a lasting effect unless accompanied by a sufficiently restrictive monetary policy. Stevenson and Trevithick [1977] concluded that 'Both prices and incomes policies and restrictive monetary–fiscal policies are necessary to reduce the rate of inflation. Neither policy can work satisfactorily if implemented independently of the other.' (p. 31).

It should be added, however, that the domestic economy cannot isolate itself from the international economy, and inflation is an international phenomenon. In fairness to their policy the Conservatives (1972–4), as well as failing to find an appropriate policy mix, faced the very considerable problem of a rapid inflation of world commodity prices.

The Macro and Micro Effects of Incomes Policies

In this section an attempt is made to evaluate the effects of incomes policies in the 1970s at the macro and at the micro level.

Table 3.1 showed that despite the use of incomes policies, wage and price inflation was a major problem throughout the 1970s. Having said that, there were two 'wages explosions': the first occurring at the beginning of the decade, the second in 1974–5. Both of these were effectively 'policy off' periods, even though in the latter case the social contract mark one was supposed to be restraining wage increases. In fact during social contract mark one basic hourly wage rates increased at a rate equivalent to 32% per annum, while price inflation was running at 24.4%. In contrast during the freeze in 1972–3 there was an increase of 1.2% in the index of hourly wage rates and 2.3% in the price index (annual rates of 3.6 and 6.9% respectively as far as it is legitimate to express these increases over a four-month period at an annual rate). Also the Labour government's incomes policy, introduced in the latter half of 1975, was accompanied by a moderation of price inflation in its first two phases. However there are problems associated with interpreting this evidence as implying the success of incomes policy in attacking inflation. In particular 'policy-on' and 'policy-off' periods should not be regarded as independent. In other words periods of wage and price restraint may be artificially constraining inflation, and when removed result in the release of pent-up forces and result in a wage and price explosion. Indeed the critics of incomes policy would argue that the 1970s were characterised by unsuccessful attempts to restrain inflation by incomes policies, which inevitably broke down, releasing pent-up demand. The high average level of inflation suggests that an alternative approach to inflation should be adopted. In particular the monetarists point to the growth of the money supply (see Chapter 2) and the need for a strict monetary policy. Against this, however, there is the strong argument that a successful anti-inflation policy requires the appropriate policy mix incorporating constraints on money supply growth and on the growth of wages.

Monetarist macroeconomics has cast considerable doubt on the efficacy of incomes policy. Furthermore at the micro level monetarists argue that incomes policies disrupt the operation of the wage mechanism in allocating labour, constraining the behaviour of wage differentials. (See Brittan and Lilley [1977] and Owen Smith and Dawkins [1978]). Here we consider some of the evidence on wage differentials.

First Brown [1976] undertook a study of forty engineering factories employing 80 000 people in the West Midlands in the period between August 1972 and summer 1975, a period which included all three stages of the Conservatives' statutory policy between 1972 and 1974 as well as the social contract mark one. As far as the application of the incomes policies was concerned, he found that the Conservatives' policy from 1972 to 1974 was broadly speaking adhered to, but that the social contract mark one was widely evaded. Brown presented very interesting evidence about the inter-factory differentials of machinists, electricians, storekeepers, labourers, machinists and assemblers and canteen workers. While there was no evidence that incomes policy alters the extent to which the ranking of firms in terms of wage payments changed over time, clear evidence was put forward that differentials among similar workers in different factories narrowed markedly during the Conservatives' incomes policy from 1972 to 1974, then widened during the social contract mark one. However Brown also considered skill differentials, for example the difference between the average wage paid to a machinist and that paid to an electrician and so on. While it was clear that these skill differentials became more compressed during the period under investigation, it was not possible to attribute this to incomes policies. First this compression was most marked during social contract mark one. Second this compression was the continuation of a phenomenon which had been ongoing throughout the twentieth century. Third, the actual compression of skill differentials during the statutory incomes policy was actually less than that which would have been predicted on the basis of adherence to the wage guidelines.

Another study of vertical wage differentials has been reported by Fallick [1979]. This study was based on a consideration of salary changes for non-manual workers in the public sector and shows, for example, a very substantial narrowing of salaries between clerical workers and managerial staff since the 1950s. This narrowing was concentrated in the 1970s. Also junior staff within managerial, administrative and technical groups have enjoyed significantly larger increases than senior staff since the 1950s with the narrowing process again concentrated in the period after 1969. Fallick argues that because incomes policies in the 1970s have tended to involve at least in part a wage limit which is expressed in absolute terms, much of this narrowing of occupational wage differentials can be attributed to these policies. However, because the narrowing process does not seem to have especially related to 'policy-on' periods (1969–72 was a policy-off period), there may be an alternative explanation. One such is that rapid price inflation gives rise to a narrowing of occupational differentials. This was the explanation that Brown preferred in explaining the narrowing of the skill differentials in his study, which was particularly pronounced during the wage and price explosion during social contract mark one. This theory is in keeping with that of Routh [1965] and Turner [1952] who argued that such compression during times of inflation is explained by the widespread preference for flat rate rather than percentage pay increases. Brown reinforces this argument by referring to attitude surveys which suggest a willingness to give exceptional treatment to the low-paid during times of rapid inflation. An alternative or complimentary explanation might rely on the effect of money illusion; thus if the narrowing of occupational (vertical) differentials is leading to skill shortages (see Chapter 4), putting the blame on incomes policy may be misplaced.

A study by Metcalf [1977] of the effect of incomes policy on the industrial wage structure, going back to 1948 but incorporating data up to 1975, showed fairly convincingly, using multiple regression analysis, that the wage structure has widened prior to incomes policies and narrowed following their introduction. This, taken along with the evidence from Brown's study of inter-factory differentials, suggests, in contrast to the evidence on occupational differentials, that incomes policy does have a significant narrowing effect on horizontal differentials. Following the competitive market model this could be interpreted as incomes policy causing a misallocation of labour among plants and among industries. Metcalf's own interpretation based on sound empirical results is that the narrowing of the industrial wage structure results from an incomes policy's resistance to cost-push inflation which has the effect of widening the industrial wage structure; that is to say, unionised industries have higher earnings than non-unionised industries and when there is cost-push inflation this disparity becomes greater. This causes the wage structure to widen in the years prior to incomes policies, and to narrow as incomes policies take effect.

Conclusions

Inflation has not been brought under control in the 1970s despite the use of incomes policies for most of the decade. These policies have all eventually broken down, the last ending with the Labour government's defeat in May 1979. However there are certain things that can be said in defence of incomes policy as a policy weapon, using the 1970s as an example. First such policies tend to be introduced in a crisis by governments who have not planned them and administered by new institutions. Bearing in mind that the government must to some extent be involved in the process of wage determination, particularly in the public sector, and given that most governments in recent history have turned to incomes policy in a crisis, there is a strong argument that planned and systematic intervention with an ongoing incomes policy, applied in a more gradualist way rather than 'slammed on' in crises, would be more likely to produce successful results. Second, the adverse experience of the Conservative government in the early 1970s stresses the importance of an appropriate policy mix. Fiscal and monetary policy should be complementary to incomes policy.

It should be added that the argument that an incomes policy is bound to be harmful because of its effect on the allocation of labour may be based on a model of the labour market that is more competitive than accords with the real world. Also the narrowing of occupational differentials which has occurred in the 1970s may well not be the result of incomes policy but rather of inflation itself. It may be however that incomes policy narrows inter-plant and inter-industry differentials, but this might be because of its resistance to the effect of unionisation on differentials rather than to a resistance to the market mechanism. However, while changes in supply and demand may not imply adjustment in wages and employment according to the normal competitive market mechanism, substantial changes in supply and demand can be expected to require wage adjustment after a certain lag. Thus the implementation of incomes policy should take care to allow for flexibility where there is a strong case for changes in relative wages to improve labour mobility. Indeed it is perhaps the careful provision for flexibility which policy-makers must confront more rigorously in the future. The destruction and creation of various institutions in relation to incomes policy, which has continued in the 1970s, has not improved the chance of any future incomes policies to deal with this problem successfully.

References

Bercusson, B. [1976], 'The New Fair Wages Policy: Schedule 11 to the Employment Protection Act', *Industrial Law Journal*, Vol. 5, no. 3, September 1976, pp. 129–47.

Blackaby, F. (ed.) [1972], *An Incomes Policy for Britain*. Proceedings of a Conference Organised by the NIESR and the SSRC. Heinemann.

Blackaby, F. (ed.) [1978], *British Economic Policy 1960–74*. Cambridge: Cambridge University Press.

Brittan, S. and Lilley, P. [1977], *The Delusion of Incomes Policy*. London: Temple Smith.

Bosworth, D. and Dawkins, P. J. [1979], *Female Patterns of Work and Associated Renumeration Facilities and Opportunities*. Report to the EOC–SSRC Joint Panel.

Brown, W. [1976], 'Income Policy and Pay Differentials', *Oxford Bulletin of Economics and Statistics*, Vol. 58, no. 1, pp. 27–49.

Brown, W. and Terry, M. [1978] 'The Changing Nature of National Wage Agreements', *Scottish Journal of Political Economy*, Vol. 25, no. 2, June 1978, pp. 119–33.

Cockfield, A. [1978] 'The Price Commission and the Price Control', *Three Banks Review*, no. 117, March 1978, pp. 3–25.

Department of Employment [1975], 'Further Progress Towards Equal Pay', *Department of Employment Gazette*, August 1975, pp. 747–53.

Fallick, J. L. [1979], 'Pay Policy and Labour Supply: Some Neglected Considerations', *National Westminster Bank Review*, February 1979, pp. 7–18.

Lipsey, R. G. [1960], 'The Relation Between Unemployment and the Rate of Change of Money Wage Rates in the United Kingdom 1862–1957: A Further Analysis', *Economica*, Vol. 27, February 1960, pp. 1–31.

Llewellyn, D. T. [1980], 'Can Monetary Targets Influence Wage Bargaining?', *The Banker*, Vol. 130, no. 647, January 1980, pp. 49–55.

Metcalf, D. [1977], 'Unions, Incomes Policy and Relative Wages in Britain', *British Journal of Industrial Relations*, Vol. XV, no. 2, pp. 157–75.

Office of Manpower Economics [1973], *Wage Drift*. London: HMSO.

Owen Smith, E. and Dawkins, P. J. [1978], *Incomes Policy: The Macro and Micro Implications*. Loughborough Papers on Recent Developments in Economic Policy and Thought no. 10, Department of Economics, Loughborough University.

Pay Board [1974], *Problems of Pay Relativities*, Cmnd 5535. London: HMSO.

Phelps Brown, E. H. [1962], Wage Drift, *Economica*, Vol. 29, no, 116, pp. 339–56.

Prest, A. R. and Coppock, D. J. [1978], *The UK Economy: A Manual of Applied Economics*. London: Weidenfeld and Nicolson.

Routh, G. [1965], *Occupation and Pay in Great Britain 1906–1960*. Cambridge: Cambridge University Press.

Smith, P. and Swann, D. [1979], *Protecting the Consumer*. Oxford: Martin Robertson.

Stevenson, A. A. and Trevithick, J. A. [1977], 'The Complementarity of Monetary Policy and Prices and Incomes Policy: An Examination of Recent British Experience', *Scottish Journal of Political Economy*, Vol. 24, no. 1, February 1977, pp. 19–31.

Trevithick, J. A. and Mulvey, C. [1975], *The Economics of Inflation*. Glasgow Social and Economic Research Studies 3. London: Martin Robertson.

Turner, H. A. [1952], 'Trade Union Differentials and the Levelling of Wages', *Manchester School of Economics and Social Studies*, Vol. 20, no. 3, pp. 227–82.

TUC–Labour Party Liaison Committee [1973], *Economic Policy and the Cost of Living*. London: The Labour Party.

Wood, P. [1978], 'The Central Arbitration Committee's Approach to Schedule 11 to the *Employment Protection Act 1975* and the *Fair Wages Resolution 1946*', *Industrial Law Journal*, Vol. 7, no. 2, June 1978, pp. 65–83.

4 The Labour Market

by Derek L. Bosworth and Robert A. Wilson

Introduction

Any survey of the effects of government economic policies in the labour market is immediately faced with the problem that almost all economic policy impinges in one way or another on the labour market. One option is to concentrate purely upon those policies explicitly directed at employment such as those concerned with measures to subsidise labour, job training or employment protection. However this would gloss over the very important effects on the labour market that result from demand management, the government's own role as an employer, and policies directed at the structure, conduct and performance of individual industries and firms in both private and public sectors. This chapter attempts to provide a broad survey of all the major effects on employment of government policy since the mid 1960s. Discussion is concentrated on those policies which in our view had significant effects on the labour market as well as those directed purely towards employment.

Immediately following this introduction we include an overview of the main trends in employment in the UK economy since 1950. This provides a back-cloth to the discussion of policy and also serves to put the experience of the 1970s into historical perspective. The next section on aggregate demand and the demand for labour concentrates on the effect of budgetary policy and other policies concerned with demand management on the labour market and discusses the success of governments in achieving the full employment objective. Then we move on to consider the effect of the increase in the size of the public sector in the labour market. Policies concerned with the structure of the economy, industrial policy and regional policies are next briefly discussed. We then consider the measures introduced to improve the mobility of labour. Our next section covers policies on training and education.

The various special measures concerned with providing temporary assistance to disadvantaged groups are at this point discussed, followed by examination of the effects of the reorganisation of the government employment services. The next part of the chapter contains a review of the various measures introduced in the 1970s that have affected the legal background to the employment contract. In the final part, we provide a brief examination of the likely trends in the 1980s, including an examination of the probable effects of technological change and the prospects for work-sharing.

Background: Employment in the UK Economy since 1950

In the 1950s and early 1960s total employment in the UK economy grew rapidly from just over 22.5m in 1950 to almost 25.5m by 1966. Furthermore, this increase of almost three million occurred at the same time as a substantial running down of Her Majesty's armed forces, a group which had to be absorbed into other employment. This growth in employment was shared by both males and females, although employment in the case of the latter grew at a much faster rate (1.1% per annum compared with 0.5% for males). The main trends are clearly illustrated in Table 4.1. The overall growth in employment between 1956 and 1965 was primarily a result of expansion in the service sector, but it also reflected growth within manufacturing and in government. During the period up to 1966 unemployment remained very low, rarely if ever exceeding 500 000, or a rate of 2.0%. The economic cycle during the period can only really be observed in terms of relatively faster or slower rates of growth rather than boom or slump as such.

It is clear from Table 4.1, however, that the year 1966 was a watershed. After this year the employment picture altered very dramatically. This is reflected in the rapid decline in employees in employment, the employed labour force and the working population until 1972. During this period the population of working age grew very slightly and so this decline cannot be attributed to demographic factors. There has been no shortage of hypotheses about the cause of this break in trend. The introduction of Selective Employment Tax (SET), the Redundancy Payments Act and earnings related unemployment benefits have all been cited at various times as being the main causal factor. Other explanations have been in terms of a 'shake-

Table 4.1   The principal postwar trends in employment and hours of work

	Employees in employment 000s			Self employment 000s	HM forces 000s	Employed labour force[c] 000s	Unemployed 000s	Working population[d] 000s	Normal weekly hours of manual workers[e]		
	Males	Females	Total						Men	Women	All
1950	13722	7036	20758	1802	697	23257	298	23555	44.4	44.5	44.4
1951	13767	7203	20970	1798	835	23603	207	23810	44.4	44.5	44.4
1952	13772	7144	20916	1794	880	23590	336	23926	44.4	44.5	44.4
1953	13796	7245	21041	1791	870	23702	311	24013	44.3	44.5	44.4
1954	13954	7450	21404	1789	845	24038	254	24292	44.3	44.4	44.4
1955	14086	7616	21702	1787	809	24298	210	24508	44.3	44.4	44.4
1956	14244	7721	21965	1782	767	24514	215	24729	44.3	44.4	44.3
1957	14294	7764	22058	1778	708	24544	276	24820	44.2	44.4	44.3
1958	14220	7664	21884	1774	620	24278	406	24684	44.2	44.3	44.3
1959[a]	14262	7747	22008	1770	569	24347	420	24767	44.2	44.3	44.2
1959[b]	14102	7315	21417			23756	420	24176			
1960	14314	7579	21894	1766	518	24178	326	24504	43.0	43.4	43.1
1961	14482	7745	22228	1750	474	24452	287	24739	42.3	42.3	42.3
1962	14590	7858	22447	1738	442	24627	406	25033	42.1	42.2	42.1
1963	14613	7892	22505	1725	427	24657	496	25153	42.0	42.1	42.0
1964	14746	8066	22812	1710	424	24946	349	25295	41.9	42.1	42.0
1965	14856	8223	23080	1696	423	25199	299	25498	41.0	41.2	41.0
1966	14853	8410	23253	1681	417	25351	281	25632	40.3	40.5	40.3
1967	14504	8303	22808	1762	417	24987	503	25490	40.2	40.4	40.2
1968	14306	8344	22650	1786	400	24836	542	25378	40.1	40.2	40.1
1969	14184	8436	22619	1853	380	24852	518	25370	40.1[e]	40.1[e]	40.1[e]
1970	14002	8470	22471	1902	372	24745	555	25300	40.1	40.0	40.1
1971	13714	8408	22122	1909	368	24399	724	25123	40.0	40.0	40.0
1972	13608	8512	22120	1899	371	24390	804	25194	40.0	40.0	40.0
1973	13771	8891	22662	1947	361	24970	575	25545	40.0	40.0	40.0
1974	13659	9131	22790	1925	345	25060	542	25602	40.0	40.0	40.0
1975	13536	9174	22710	1886	336	24932	866	25798	40.0	40.0	40.0
1976	13392	9152	22544	1886	336	24766	1332	26098	40.0	40.0	40.0
1977	13376	9285	22661	1886	327	24874	1450	26324	(40.0)	(40.0)	(40.0)
1978	13354	9356	22710	1886	318	24914	1446	26360	(40.0)	(40.0)	(40.0)
1979	n.a.	n.a.	n.a.	n.a.	n.a.	n.a.	n.a.	n.a.	(40.0)	(40.0)	(40.0)

Sources: Data on employment, hours of work and stoppages from *DE Gazette; British Labour Statistics Yearbook, 1976; British Labour Statistics, Historical Abstract 1886–1968.* Data on days' holiday from DE, *Time Rates of Wages and Hours of Work.*

Notes: [a]Statistics up to 1959[a] are on a national insurance card count basis.
   [b]Statistics from 1959[b] are on a census of employment basis.
   [c]Employed labour force = employees in employment and self employed plus HM forces.
   [d]Working population = employed labour force + unemployment;
   [e]Previous years – average of April and October, this and later years – October only.
   [f]Affected by power crisis, February 1972.
   [g]Includes public holidays, weights applied in aggregating are relative employment in SIC orders.
   [h]Days for certified incapacity for sickness and invalidity.
   [i]Industries and services covered by regular earnings enquiries.
   ( ) Denotes estimate.

Actual weekly hours of manual workers[f]			Working Overtime		Working Short-time		Days' holiday per year[g] (manu-facturing)	Sick days per annum[h]	
Men	Women	All	Percentage of all operatives (%)	Average hrs/week per operative on overtime	Percentage of all operatives (%)	Average hrs/opera-tive on short-time		Male	Female
47.3	41.7	45.9	n.a.	7.3	n.a.	14.8	n.a.	n.a.	n.a.
47.9	41.6	46.3	n.a.	7.5	n.a.	13.0	14.5	n.a.	n.a.
47.5	41.2	45.9	20.9	7.7	3.8	15.0	14.9	n.a.	n.a.
47.9	41.8	46.3	24.0	7.8	1.0	11.1	15.2	n.a.	n.a.
48.4	41.8	46.7	26.5	8.0	0.7	11.4	15.6	12.79	16.38
48.9	41.7	47.6	27.5	8.0	0.8	13.3	16.0	12.79	16.28
48.6	41.3	46.8	25.7	7.9	1.5	10.9	16.3	12.29	15.78
48.4	41.2	46.6	26.1	7.8	1.1	10.5	16.4	12.49	15.68
47.9	41.0	46.2	23.1	7.6	2.8	14.0	16.4	12.69	16.08
48.3	41.4	46.6	26.4	7.6	1.3	11.9	16.5	12.89	16.28
40.7	48.0	46.2	30.5	7.9	1.0	10.5	16.5	12.49	15.88
47.7	39.8	45.7	29.1	7.9	1.2	12.4	16.6	12.69	16.18
47.2	39.5	45.3	28.1	7.8	1.7	10.4	16.9	14.06	16.16
47.8	39.7	45.8	29.3	7.9	1.3	10.9	17.3	13.83	16.28
47.8	39.7	45.8	33.0	8.2	0.4	10.3	17.6	14.43	17.01
47.3	38.9	45.3	34.6	8.5	0.5	12.4	18.0	15.40	17.35
46.2	38.3	44.3	33.9	8.5	1.2	9.8	18.3	15.30	16.61
46.2	38.2	44.3	32.4	8.4	1.6	10.8	18.8	16.49	18.35
46.3	38.4	44.5	35.1	8.5	0.5	11.2	19.3	16.05	17.55
46.5[e]	38.1[e]	44.6[e]	35.7	8.5	0.5	13.0	19.7	18.87	19.16
45.7	37.9	43.9	34.4	8.5	0.6	12.4	20.2	16.45	17.50
44.7	37.7	43.2	29.8	8.1	1.6	11.8	20.6	16.45	17.51
45.0	37.9	43.5	29.9	8.2	2.6[f]	12.2[f]	21.6	17.51	18.51
45.6	37.7	43.9	35.0	8.5	0.4	15.0	22.6	17.57	18.07
45.1	37.4	43.4	33.0	8.4	4.5	14.5	23.6	16.84	17.91
43.6	37.0	42.2	30.3	8.3	3.2	15.6	24.6	16.84	17.91
44.0	37.4	42.6	32.2	8.4	1.6	11.7	25.6	n.a.	n.a.
44.2	37.4	42.5	34.6	8.7	0.9	17.4	26.6		
44.2	37.4	42.5	34.8	8.6	0.7	15.1	26.7		
n.a.	n.a.	n.a.					27.3		

out' of hoarded labour. Much of the debate was conducted in terms of a shift in the relationship between vacancies and unemployment (Department of Employment [1976], pp. 1093–9). It is probably fair to say, however, that despite a great deal of intellectual effort the full explanation remains to be found.

Two observations are perhaps worth making. The first is that the upward shift in unemployment after 1966 was of the order of about 300 000. The fall in employment appears to be significantly greater than this, although part of the fall in employees in employment may be explained by an offsetting increase in self-employment. The much slower growth of services and the rapid decline in industrial employment was clearly sufficient to outweigh the very rapid growth of government employment. Since 1974, however, even this source of employment growth has almost disappeared (Bosworth and Wilson, [1980]). The second point is that the experience of males and females was very different. Female employment if anything rose slightly between 1966 and 1972, while male employment plummeted. In the period from 1973 this difference was exacerbated with males receiving only a minor boost to employment while female employment rose almost continuously. This difference is partly an illusion caused by considering the labour input only in terms of heads and not hours. The major growth area in employment has been for part-time workers. On average part-time workers tend to work only half as long as full-time workers. If we adjust employment to a full-time equivalent basis, the growth in employment for females between 1972 and 1978 is reduced from almost 600 000 to about 400 000 full-time equivalents. Nevertheless the growth in part-time working can only partially explain the different experience of men and women.

There have been important changes in economic activity rates over this period (Bosworth and Wilson, [1980]). For males participation rates have fallen, particularly since 1966. This fall has been very rapid for younger males and to a large extent reflects a rise in educational participation. It has also been significantly more rapid in the case of those above retirement age. This fall in economic activity rates may go some way towards explaining the apparent discrepancy between the rise in unemployment and the fall in employment noted above. The picture has again been very different for females, although it is important to take account of marital status. Activity rates for unmarried females appear to have changed in a similar way to those for males, but in the case of married females things have been quite different with economic activity rates rising for all age groups including the very young and the very old. This rise appears to have decelerated in the 1970s.

The second dimension of the employment of labour services concerns the length of working day, week or year (i.e. the number of hours that employees work). Negotiated normal hours have shown a secular decline over the postwar period, falling from just below forty-five hours per week in 1950 to around forty hours in the 1970s. Actual weekly hours have shown a parallel trend from around forty-six for all manual workers in 1950 to forty-three by 1979, although they have declined at a slightly slower rate than normal hours. Thus, the ratio of actual to normal weekly hours for all workers has increased secularly. The ratio of actual to normal weekly hours of less than unity for women seems to be caused by part-time working, while the equivalent ratio of over unity for men is associated with overtime working. The growth in part-time working, dominated by women, is a major feature of the postwar employment scene, although this trend may now be levelling off (IFF [1979]).

The increasing overall trend in actual to normal weekly hours is reflected directly in a higher percentage of operatives on overtime and a longer average length of overtime per week. The increased gap between actual and normal hours is accentuated in the overtime figures by the fact that overtime is concentrated amongst relatively few workers. While short-time working does seem to have hit something of a high point in the mid 1970s (both in terms of numbers and average hours for those on short-time), there is no clear secular trend. The trends in lower number of working hours per week have occurred together with an impressive growth in the length of holidays (i.e. a reduction in the length of working year). Days of holiday (including public holidays) have increased from approximately fifteen per annum during the 1950s to nearly thirty per annum in the 1970s, as shown in Table 4.1. This has occurred at the same time as a secular increase in the average number of days sickness per year, also shown in Table 4.1, rising from nearly thirteen for males in the 1950s to around seventeen in the 1970s and rising for women from just over sixteen in the 1950s to about eighteen in the 1970s. Unofficial absenteeism will further augment this loss of working days, although there are no precise figures to allow comparison over the postwar period. Employers also lose working days through strikes. Strikers as a percentage of the employed workforce in the UK increased from around

3% in the 1950s to 6% in the 1960s and 7% in the first half of the 1970s (Bosworth and Wilson [1980]).

The third dimension of labour hours concerns the time at which labour services are used in the production process. Recent evidence confirms the continuing secular increase in shiftworking (IFF [1978]). The incidence of shiftworking amongst manual workers in the manufacturing sector has been growing at about 1% per annum throughout the postwar period, rising from about 12% in 1954 to 20% by 1964 and 34% by 1978. The increases in both overtime and shift-working are, at least in part, a reflection of the attempt by firms to maintain levels of capital utilisation in the face of declining average hours of work per employee. While shiftworking has, overall, been growing steadily, if unspectacularly, the incidence has been growing more rapidly for women than for men, although women are still under-represented on shiftwork.

Aggregate Demand and the Demand for Labour

By and large it seems reasonable to argue that the government achieved its full employment objective up until the mid 1960s, although at the expense of balance of payments deficits or more rapid inflation which made it unsustainable in the long run. The extent to which this 'success' was the result of, rather than in spite of, the governments' attempts at fine tuning, however, is open to debate (Blackaby [1978]). However, this should not be taken as an argument against the use of fiscal or budgetary policy to achieve full employment in times of deeper recession when problems of imperfect information and lags in implementation are less important. Furthermore, this decision does not imply that fiscal policy did not increase employment. Some crude calculations indicate that employment was about 5% above what it might have been with a neutral budgetary stance (Bosworth and Wilson [1980]).

Since 1970, however, it has been clear that governments of both parties have failed to achieve this basic objective. The economy was already moving into a recession when Mr Heath took office in 1970 and unemployment reached almost one million during the winter of 1971–2. The consumer led boom of 1973–4 was brought short by the oil crisis; unemployment then rose again to over one million in 1975 and has remained at a very high level since then. No government since 1974 has felt able to make full employment the main priority of policy. Instead they have concentrated their attention – albeit with little success – on reducing the rate of inflation.

As a result of this and the general state of the world economy, the UK economy in the late 1970s was running well below capacity, with all the associated consequences for employment and unemployment. No reliable measures of full capacity levels of output exist for the UK economy, but Wharton school methods suggest that the economy has been operating at up to 10% below capacity since 1975. Most current short-term and medium-term forecasts suggest that this loss is 'permanent' and will not be recovered in the near future (Lindley [1978]). The size of the gap between actual output and full capacity output is much larger than the equivalent gap in employment terms because productivity growth has been drastically reduced by the severity of the recession. If output had grown along the full capacity trend, productivity improvements would, from past experience, have been substantially greater than those actually observed (Bosworth and Wilson [1980]). We consider the implications of these trends for the future later.

The Growth of the Public Sector

While it might be argued that short-term effects of demand management have not significantly altered the pattern of growth of employment in the UK, this would not be true of budgetary policy and changes in public expenditure over the medium term. Public expenditure as a proportion of GDP has grown steadily since the 1950s, and this growth accelerated in the 1970s. The reasons put forward to explain this expansion of the public sector and its consequences have been numerous. Some commentators regard the expansion of the public sector as the cause of the UK's structural malaise (Bacon and Eltis [1978]). Others argue that it is just a symptom of problems inherent in the structure of the UK's trade (Thirlwall [1978]). Whatever its cause it has had a profound effect on the structure of employment in the UK economy.

The questions of whether this rise was deliberate or not and the extent to which it was the cause rather than the effect of the UK's structural decline are however important ones. The Bacon and Eltis thesis suggests that the market sector has been squeezed by the non-market (predominantly public) sector and that this has been responsible for the UK's slow growth rate. The rise in the share of the public sector has perhaps been exaggerated, especially if one concentrates on the share of resources actually taken by the public authorities for their own direct expenditure rather than this share plus the share of resources transferred within the private sector as emphasised by Bacon and Eltis (on this see Blackaby [1978]).

The argument that it is the rising incidence of taxation on the private sector that has been the real cause of the relatively slow rate of UK growth also seems unconvincing, except possibly for the most recent period (namely that since the late 1960s). Furthermore, the case for the market sector being deprived of labour seems to be rather weak given the overall slack in the labour market since 1966 and in view of the fact that the occupational composition of employment in the public sector is very different from that in, for example, manufacturing industries – Whitley et al. [1980], p. 648). The growth in government employment has primarily favoured part-time, non-manual females rather than skilled manual trades. We therefore find the argument that the short-term benefits to employment of expanding direct government employment are outweighed by the lower growth in the medium term unconvincing.

As we have already noted above government employment was the main source of additional jobs in the economy during the late 1960s and early 1970s. Without these jobs the employment picture would have been gloomy indeed! The areas of most rapid expansion have been in education and health services rather than in administration or defence. Whether this change was the result of explicit decisions to expand the size of the public sector or of a failure to control public expenditure, a shift of this magnitude is clearly of great significance. The major part of the growth in the share of employment occurs between 1955 and 1975. There is a slight acceleration around 1966/7 reflecting the fact that government employment was not affected in the same way as aggregate employment, most categories of the former growing on a steadily rising trend over this period. Offsetting changes of structure of an equivalent magnitude were occurring in other sectors of course, as indicated earlier.

Government Policy and the Structure of the Workforce

At various times the government has employed a whole armoury of weapons aimed at altering the structure of the workforce. The principal goal has been to reduce the mismatch between the supply of and demand for particular skills and, relatedly, to ensure that workers are in jobs where they make the highest possible contribution to the output of the economy. Attempts to influence the occupational structure of the workforce by training and retraining programmes are dealt with later. In this section, we deal with governments' attempts to alter the industrial and regional structure of the workforce.

A major innovation during the latter half of the 1960s was the introduction and use of the Selective Employment Tax (SET). The idea can be traced to empirical results based on 'Verdoorn's Law' (Kaldor [1966]). It was introduced with great rapidity in 1966 (Musgrave and Musgrave [1968], p. 38). While it redressed the balance of taxation between services and industry and raised tax revenues, it was primarily conceived as a way of shifting labour out of the service sector (thereby stemming the secular increase in the size of the service sector) into manufacturing where productivity growth was apparently higher. This was achieved by a per employee tax on all firms, firms in certain sectors were reimbursed (e.g. agriculture) and firms in the manufacturing sector were actually paid back more than the original value of the tax. The theoretical basis of the tax was ill-conceived (i.e. the direction of causality between output growth and productivity growth was never properly established), and it proved difficult and costly to administer. Thus, with the exception of Development Areas, the subsidy element was withdrawn as early as November 1967, reducing its structural impact and emphasising its revenue raising effects. The tax was wholly withdrawn in 1973.

SET is by no means the only example of a tax or subsidy aimed at altering the industrial structure of the economy. Indeed, it is just the tip of the iceberg. While nobody knows the precise figures for British industry, Denton et al. [1975] estimated that industrial subsidies amounted to about 7% of the UK central government's budget in 1970/1. Even at the time, this may have been an underestimate. Government expenditure on promoting 'trade, industry and employment' has been one of the fastest growing elements in total public expenditure in the decade up to the election of the Thatcher administration, rising 44% in real terms over the period from 1970/1 to 1975/6 (Burton [1979], pp. 4–7). Again, on balance, this growth may be something of an understatement. It is, however, an international phenomenon, with the possible exceptions of the US and West Germany.

While the overall aims of industrial subsidies are poorly defined, one clear area was the maintenance of employment. In some sense all forms of industrial subsidy are intended to be job-maintaining or employment creating. Some are directly aimed at subsidising employment itself, as discussed below. While they would appear to be successful at first sight because they remove certain numbers of individuals from the unemployment register, it has been argued that the jobs created in subsidised industries are largely, if not wholly, at the expense of jobs in the non-subsidised firms, i.e. the 'displacement effect' (see Burton [1979]). The displacement effect is smaller the larger the export component of the subsidised firms, as part of the effect is transferred abroad, as long as foreign countries don't take retaliatory action (Layard and Nickell [1977]). Burton ([1979], pp. 47–58) paints a gloomy picture of the longer term effects of prolonged and widespread government subsidies with the growth of subsidy-maximising firms – a common feature among firms was the attempt to maximise their grants for training from the ITBs (Industry Training Boards) – lowering profitability and increasing the number of firms that fall within the subsidy net. The harder-line taken by the new Conservative administration may therefore result in considerable short-term hardships amongst firms as they are weened-off the subsidy bottle (Finger [1974]; Burton [1979], p. 50). A parallel movement will be in the return of parts of the nationalised industries to the private sector and increasing restrictions placed on the powers of the National Enterprise Board which oversees many of the more heavily subsidised companies.

Problem firms and problem industries are often more highly concentrated in certain regions than others. With structural change comes the problem of occupational mismatch, a problem which is intensified if the rate of decline in overall employment opportunities caused by contraction and closures in a particular region exceeds the rate of increase in job opportunities that arise with the expansion of other firms and the establishment of new companies. The Thatcher government has made some alterations to the regional boundaries of Assisted Areas. On balance, it has reduced the numbers of areas that will be eligible for assistance and reduced the extent of assistance for other areas (Department of Employment [1979]). The total saving of £233m expected by the year 1982/3 must surely result in adverse effects on the level of employment in the affected regions. The overall result will again clearly depend on the displacement effects of the original subsidies. The principal approach to regional employment

problems remains one of taking jobs to the workers (whether by investment incentives in the Assisted Areas, job creation programmes or
schemes to defer redundancies), but there is still a smaller element of
help in the form of taking the workers to the jobs, e.g. the Employment
Transfer Scheme (see Department of Employment [1979]). If the
economy goes deeper into recession, the regional disparities can be
expected to become even greater, and it is hard to envisage even the
Conservative administration refusing to reverse its stance on this
matter.

Policies to Improve Labour Mobility

The active role of the government in the labour market can be traced
to two reports published in the early 1960s – National Joint Advisory
Council [1962] and National Economic Development Council [1963]
– that emphasised the need for intervention to ease the problems
caused by labour shortages since the war. The reports recommended
that the government take a more active role in training (see below)
and in improving the mobility of labour. The then Conservative
government advocated a voluntary scheme by employers to solve the
problems caused by the financial hardship to workers made redundant
as a result of structural change in the economy. It was left to the
1964 Labour government to take the first active steps in the form of
the *Redundancy Payments Act 1965*. The main elements in the Act were
that firms were to be charged a levy in addition to national insurance
contributions. This was paid into a fund which firms forced to make
redundancies could then call upon. Charges and payments were fixed
by statute and firms were required to give notice to local employment
offices to allow them to find new jobs for the displaced workers.
Although the introduction of this Act has been cited as a possible
cause of the 1966 'shake out' (or 'walk out' if one prefers the supply
side explanation) the overall effect seems to have been limited. The
size of the employers' contribution to the central fund has never
exceeded 0.2% of total wage costs. This does not represent the total
cost to employers however because only a fraction of the total redundancy payment can be offset by a rebate from the fund. Originally
this fraction was set at about 66% but from 1969 onwards it was
reduced to 50%. The average payment amounted to about twelve
weeks' pay. Assuming half of this was obtained from the fund this left
firms facing a bill for up to six weeks' pay. However the flow of persons

entitled to such benefits remained very small. Even in the 1971 recession they amounted to less than 0.4% of the employed labour force in each quarter (about 12% of registered unemployment) so the total effect on the national wage bill probably amounted to not more than 0.4% per annum on average. Clearly, however, individual firms might have paid considerably more than this.

Because the payment to the individual was not taxable the beneficial effect as measured in terms of weeks of pay is probably greater than the average figure of twelve weeks. In net pay terms, for an average individual, the payment would represent something more like fifteen to sixteen weeks' pay. This is perhaps a better indication of the size of economic and social cushion provided for employees, and might have been expected to have substantially aided the individual's ability to undertake job search.

Although the Redundancy Payments Act clearly provided important assistance to a large number of workers, it was still true that there remained a number of workers not entitled to this aid, notably those below the age of 18 and those who fail to qualify because of not having been incumbent in their jobs for more than two years. As Fryer [1973] has noted, these qualifications introduced a built-in bias towards making new entrants (either young persons or those previously made redundant starting a new job) redundant again. However, there is some evidence that firms were enabled by the Act to move away from the 'first in, first out' principle (Parker et al. [1971]). On the other hand it has been suggested that the emphasis on age and length of service in deciding upon individual payments may have led to employers' singling out older people as less likely to resist redundancy and so placed an unfair burden on those who might have the greatest difficulty in securing re-employment (Mukherjee [1973]).

The evidence on the question as to whether the labour 'shaken-out' was reallocated to more productive uses is less favourable. A review of the various studies conducted in this area emphasises the built-in tendency of the Act to increase redundancy amongst older workers and the less skilled because firms choose to hoard more skilled workers who might be more easily redeployed (Elliot [1978]). Further, the emphasis on the length of service with one employer actively discourages voluntary mobility because the individual thereby forgoes his right to a substantial redundancy payment. Almost all the studies emphasise the difficulty of individuals securing a new job and the need for improved information to supplement the individual's imperfect appreciation of the market situation and for retraining.

The other main measure introduced during this period with the object of reducing the economic and social burden to the individual of job displacement was the earnings related unemployment benefit scheme (ERUB). A major object of this policy was to encourage workers to accept unemployment as a feature of a changing economy and to ease the financial burden of finding new work. This measure has also been cited as a possible cause of the increase in unemployment after 1966 (Gujerati [1972]). However, more careful consideration of its effect suggests that although it substantially aided those in receipt of the supplement, in practice its effect was slight because of the small proportion of persons entitled to the supplement. It has been estimated that ERUB increased unemployment by 10% at the most (Nickell [1979]). As with the Redundancy Payments Act a large proportion of people were not eligible for this additional aid towards finding another job, and again it tended to favour more skilled workers who were likely to experience least difficulty in securing re-employment.

A major feature of government policy was the emphasis on compensation to the individual for loss of the old job, rather than providing assistance in the form of training to ease the problems in obtaining a new one (Mukherjee [1973]; Elliot [1978]). This was in marked contrast to the policies of other European countries (Mukherjee [1973], p. 17). By the early 1970s it was gradually recognised that there was a disproportionate emphasis on compensation as opposed to retraining. Mukherjee estimated that, up to 1971, £381m was spent on compensation for redundancies, while only £100m was spent on adult retraining and other services to ease redeployment. The attempts to redress this balance in the 1970s provides one of the subjects for the next section.

Training and Education
Although the government had taken some responsibility for training during the war, its role became insignificant during the 1950s. The provision of training was largely left to market forces. With the experience of the very tight labour markets of the 1950s, however, there was a need for more training than was being undertaken by firms on a voluntary basis and a more active role to be played by the government (National Joint Advisory Council [1962] and National

Economic Development Council [1963]). Intervention was advocated for three main reasons: (i) to share the cost of training more evenly across firms and to reduce the problems caused by poaching; (ii) to improve the quality of the training provided; and (iii) to provide an adequate supply of the skills required for a changing economy in the face of technological change.

The *Industrial Training Act 1964* provided for the establishment of (eventually twenty-nine) Industry Training Boards responsible for the promotion of training. The boards were able to impose a levy on employers and then to provide grants to firms providing training to the required standard. A Central Training Council (CTC), which replaced the old Industrial Training Council, was set up to advise the Secretary of State. At the same time, it was planned to double the numbers passing through government training centres. A cursory glance at the Department of Employment estimates of numbers undergoing training suggests that the 1964 Act led to an increased quantity of training. However, a comparison based only on the numbers of trainees is fraught with difficulties. First, the emphasis of the boards on keeping records, may have led to previously unrecorded training being included in post-1964 estimates. Second, there are problems concerned with the definition of training used before and after the 1964 Act. The figures collected by individual boards are perhaps less ambiguous, but again may reflect the gradual increase in the boards' influence as much as increases in training *per se*. Another indicator is the number of group training schemes which increased dramatically from 65 in 1964 to 600 and covered a much broader range of skills (Pettman [1973]). By 1976 however the CTC estimated that there had been a substantial reduction of on-the-job-training within industry between 1970 and 1976 (i.e. as much as 30–40%), a change that was only partly offset by the rapid expansion of centrally provided training (Lindley [1978], p. 22).

While there had undoubtedly been an improvement in quality of training as a result of improved information, better organised training schemes, etc., there were other problems with the new scheme. The administrative burden on both firms and boards was very large. The levy–grant system was regarded by many as being a very crude tool for achieving the objectives of the Act. It was initially rather inequitable, with many small firms paying a large levy which they could ill afford and generally being unable to introduce a training scheme to the required standard to offset this by receipt of a grant. Many boards attempted to ease these difficulties by introducing differential levies and in many cases exempting very small firms altogether. Perhaps the main difficulty however was the broad question of meeting national economic needs. Many boards were faced with the problem of whether to relate grants to the individual firm's requirements for training or to the industries' requirements (some firms producing a joint product, one of which was trained manpower in excess of their individual needs). No board felt able to tackle the more general question of the nation's future requirements as they took the narrow view that their responsibility lay only to their own industry and not to the workers within that industry (Mukherjee [1970], p. 109). Thus the scheme, based on individual industries, failed to deal with the problems of retraining workers made redundant, particularly in declining industries. With its emphasis on those already employed by firms attached to a particular training board, rather than the unemployed, the boards had no means of crossing industrial boundaries and permitting the reallocation of labour to expanding sectors. Displaced workers were dealt with only by the centrally organised Government Training Centres.

Thus far we have discussed criticism of the Act on its own ground. However it was also severely criticised from a more general point of view based upon its apparent conflict with the ideas developed in the theory of investment in human capital (see McCormick and Manley [1967]; Lees and Chiplin [1970]; Oatey [1970]; Ziderman [1978]). According to Becker's [1964] restatement of the theory of human capital firms will only pay for specific training, the benefits of which, by definition, cannot be poached. If firms require their workforce to be in possession of general skills, useful in more than one firm, these will be acquired at the expense of the employee, who will be able to appropriate all the benefits from his training. (This is not to say that firms will not provide facilities for training in general skills, but that, in this case, the employee will bear the costs of their provision). This suggests that the appropriate response to a need for manpower trained in general skills is to subsidise individuals (as in student grants) rather than firms (or, more correctly, to provide them with loans).

Most authors have recognised, to a certain extent, the limitations of Becker's analysis in terms of its application to a less than perfect world and attempted to modify it. For example, specific and general training need to be redefined in terms of the mobility of labour (Oatey [1970]). Nevertheless, despite these modifications their central conclusion is that the 1964 Act was misconceived in its emphasis on firms rather than individuals. On the other hand, it has been argued that these criticisms may be unwarranted if one fully recognises the dynamic nature of the training problem and the difficulties of operating in an imperfect world with less than complete information and distortions from the perfectly competitive market structure assumed in Becker's model (Pettman [1973]).

The limitations of the 1964 Act were recognised by the Conservative government in 1972 when, after much debate, it was announced that a Manpower Services Commission was to be established. This body was to supervise the work of the public employment services (renamed the Employment Services Agency) and a Training Services Agency, as well as having limited powers of job creation. It was originally proposed that the levy–grant system be abolished. Having provided an essential shock treatment it was now regarded as having fulfilled its purpose. However this suggestion was opposed by the trade unions and other commentators who feared that without the levy–grant system the boards would be powerless. The Training Services Agency was to co-ordinate the activities of the boards and take responsibility for centrally provided training schemes including a fivefold expansion of the Vocational Training Scheme, to be retermed the Training Opportunities Scheme (TOPS). At the same time there were various reforms of the Employment Services which are discussed below. By the end of 1974 all three bodies were established under the *Employment and Training Act 1973*.

Since then, the MSC has gradually evolved into a body as much concerned with the macroeconomic issues (such as full employment) as with the detailed arrangements for training (Manpower Services Commission [1976]). With the much higher levels of unemployment, which were now being experienced in the 1970s, the stress on encouraging mobility and redundancy had changed to one of alleviating the problems of unemployment by retraining and job creation. The likely prospects for employment in the future (see below) suggest that this trend is likely to continue with the need for more emphasis being placed on training for the individual rather than to meet industrial needs (Lindley [1978], Chapter 8). The MSC appears to recognise this, stressing the need to cope with the problems of those most at risk in the labour market and the need to return to full employment as much as the need to facilitate the restructuring of the labour force as required by firms (Manpower Services Commission [1978a]).

With continuing high unemployment the objectives of manpower and educational policies overlap to an increasing extent, especially in relationship to young people. The main objectives of educational policy have not been directly concerned with the labour market (although some might argue that greater emphasis should have been placed on vocational education). Nevertheless, educational policy has directly affected the number of new entrants to the labour force. We have already noted the dramatic decline in economic activity rates for young people. This decline in economic activity has been mirrored by a rise in educational participation and, in fact, it might be argued that, to a large degree, the former has been caused by the latter. It appears reasonable to argue that up until the mid 1960s there was a demand for education which was to a large extent unsatisfied. The publication of the Robbins Report (in [1963]) led to a major change in policy in this respect; it argued that higher and further education should be expanded in order to provide places for all those who wanted a place and could meet the entry standards. This led to a very rapid expansion in the capacity of the educational sector, coupled with more generous student allowances plus higher real incomes. These factors probably explain the change in educational participation without having to argue that there has been a change in tastes, although this may also have been a factor. Whatever its cause, its effect on the labour market was as great as any training measures – at least as far as young people were concerned. A second measure with a more obvious effect on the labour market was the raising of the school-leaving age in 1973. It has been estimated that in 1973 the number of people leaving school available for employment fell by about 300 000, a considerable proportion of the total stock of people of less than 18 years of age (about 25%) (Institute of Manpower Studies [1973]). The evidence for more recent years suggests that this was only a temporary phenomenon and that the flow of new entrants returned to normal in 1974 and thereafter.

Special Government Programmes for Employment and Training

From 1973 onwards various special measures were introduced by the Government to supplement TOPS. In addition various programmes were also developed to preserve jobs and create new job opportunities for those who would otherwise have been unemployed. They may be grouped into measures concerned with training, measures concerned with increasing employment and measures concerned with reducing labour supply, although the boundaries between these groups are blurred, particularly in the case of young people. For example, full-time training schemes take people out of the labour force temporarily. But they may have very different implications for future labour supply than, say, work-sharing or policies promoting early retirement. Other schemes may involve a mix of training and job creation.

In addition to TOPS the TSA introduced various other training schemes including special TSA courses for young people. Further measures were also introduced to sustain levels of recruitment into craft and technician training within industries beyond what would have been achieved under the auspices of the ITBs. Many of these measures, which may collectively be termed 'training in industry' (TI), involved on-the-job training for young people. The work experience programme (WEP), introduced in 1976, was also aimed at assisting unemployed young people by providing them with a spell of employment. Finally 'community industry' concentrated the same kind of attention as WEP on disadvantaged young people. These last two measures involved a mixture of training and job creation. A closely related measure was the Job Creation Programme which attempted to create new jobs for a limited duration. These schemes were replaced by the Youth Opportunities Programme and Special Temporary Employment Programme in 1978. The latter aim at providing a more permanent programme of work experience and training for young people and adults.

The second set of measures included the temporary employment subsidy (TES), the small firm employment subsidy, the recruitment subsidy for school-leavers and the youth employment subsidy. All these measures were aimed at directly increasing employment in the short term by payment of subsidies to firms to persuade them to defer redundancies or to employ extra people, particularly new entrants to the workforce. This approach is clearly in direct contradiction to the encouragement of labour mobility in the tight labour markets of the early postwar era.

It is clear that the various measures have had a small but significant direct effect on employment. Of these, TES, which applied to both adults and young people, was by far the largest measure (about 25% of beneficiaries were young people) (Department of Employment [1978a]). The total effect on employment and unemployment is more difficult to judge because at least some of the jobs saved by TES, for example, must have been at the expense of jobs displaced in firms competing with TES recipients. On the other hand, the multiplier effects of maintaining employment meant that the overall effect is perhaps an underestimate. A survey undertaken by the DE suggests that the measures did have a real effect on employment in delaying and in many cases preventing redundancies that would have otherwise occurred; furthermore their results suggest that the displacement effects were not too significant whereas there was evidence of quite strong 'knock-on effects' on suppliers to the recipients of TES (Department of Employment [1977a]). The DE therefore concludes that such subsidies represent good value for money because much of the cost is recouped in the form of higher taxes and lower unemployment benefits although such calculations have been disputed on technical grounds (see Burton [1979]). Nevertheless, it can be argued that such subsidies offset the bias against employment (particularly of certain disadvantaged groups) caused by subsidies to capital. It should be remembered, however, that these arrangements tend to concentrate on the short-term gains and ignore the longer-term problem that may arise from the inefficient use of labour by relatively inefficient firms and the build-up of a non-market orientated sector of employment (Burton [1979]).

Finally the third group of measures is concerned with the voluntary reduction in labour supply. The only measure of this kind introduced to date is the Job Release Scheme (JRS) whereby persons near to retirement age are offered a tax-free inducement to withdraw from the labour market subject to their replacement by someone from the unemployment register. In principle, however, there are various other possible schemes that have been mooted such as work-sharing. The take-up for the job release scheme was small; only about 13 000 participated in 1977.

The overall effect of the various measures has been to provide some aid to particularly disadvantaged groups such as young people. However this did not prevent their unemployment rate rising to over 15% in 1978. Similarly the various employment subsidies have only made a relatively small dent in the total unemployment stock. While the evidence from the DE's surveys indicate that many firms felt that the subsidies had enabled them to survive during temporary difficulties and that they were now able to maintain employment, about one-third of firms were forced to make workers redundant after TES payments ended. Very little evidence is available on the longer-term effects of the subsidies on the allocation of resources, but a policy of subsidising those firms in difficulty seems more likely to lead to misallocation than does a policy aimed at increasing the overall level of demand and allowing market forces to operate more freely.

Reorganisation of the Government Employment Service

The principle of the Employment Service (ES) is to place individuals in the appropriate type of employment as quickly as possible (Department of Employment [1978c], p. 791). At the end of the 1960s, the (then) Department of Employment and Productivity reported that the ES was not sufficiently efficient in fulfilling its primary responsibility. Thus the ES was reorganised in an attempt to increase the use of the service by employers and job-seekers, as well as to increase its efficiency. The most tangible sign of this reorganisation has been the emergence of a network of Jobcentres (and, as a transitionary feature, the emergence of 'restructured' employment offices). This new departure is associated with an important underlying division of functions between the government machinery that handles unemployment benefit and the part of the ES designed to place individuals in jobs. The first Jobcentre was only opened in 1973 – and they are still being introduced – but the performance of the new Jobcentres in filling vacancies has already been compared with restructured offices and employment offices, as well as other forms of recruitment (i.e. advertising and private employment agencies).

The MSC have claimed success by Jobcentres in various ways. Firstly in increasing the number and the range of notified vacancies (in fact, increasing its share of vacancies at a time when unemployment was rising) and secondly shortening the period between notification of the vacancy and the date at which the new employee started work. It feels there is an improved opinion of the ES amongst employers and that an increased percentage of job-seekers have been making use of the job information facilities. The MSC also claim a higher level of placings amongst Jobcentres than employment offices and a more favourable attitude towards Jobcentres amongst job-seekers. Finally, despite the higher cost of running Jobcentres, the MSC claim a lower cost per placing (Department of Employment [1978c], pp. 792–4; Manpower Services Commission [1978b]; Cairncross [1979], p. 22). The MSC's own calculations indicate that the introduction of Jobcentres has reduced registered unemployment by about 12 000 and thereby decreased the PSBR by some £40m per annum. The modernisation programme did, however, add some £15m to operating costs between 1975/6 and 1978/9 (see Manpower Services Commission [1979]). This part of the calculation, however, appears contentious, as we argue below.

The MSC would not argue that the changes have been completely successful. The modernisation programme will not be complete until the mid 1980s, and the MSC feels that more information about the local labour market and the services available from the MSC should be provided. It argues that there should be a shift in resources towards those in need of most help and towards those most likely to benefit from it. The MSC feels an initiative is needed to find a more effective means of eradicating skill shortages. Indeed the operations of the ES must become more cost effective and more care must be taken to ensure a higher degree of matching of persons to vacancies. Nevertheless although the MSC seems to be reasonably satisfied with the effects of the reorganisation to date, other commentators are more critical. Layard, for example, while admitting that the MSC has done well by its own objectives, complains that the stated objectives are poorly conceived ([1979], p. 22). Further, he argues that the upward trend in unemployment since 1966 may have been accentuated by the reorganisation of the ES, on the grounds that it has reduced communication between those who pay out unemployment benefit and those who match people to jobs. He also argues that the reorganisation has reduced the propensity to decrease benefits for individuals refusing satisfactory offers of work and diverted jobs towards the newly unemployed and away from the longer-term unemployed. In the light of these factors, Layard suggests that job advice and unemployment benefit facilities should be housed together and greater emphasis should be given to the longer-term unemployed. He feels there should be a regular evaluation of the position of those who have received unemployment benefits for long periods. Finally he advocated retention of the weekly, rather than the fortnightly, which was then only at the proposal stage, signing on period.

Changes in the Legal Framework

There have been a number of particularly important changes in the law relating to employment in the last decade. In particular, the legal framework has been modified in an attempt to protect certain disadvantaged groups, to ensure greater clarity for both employees and employers in contracts of employment and to improve industrial relations (see Chapter 5). The strike record of the early 1970s is testament to the fact that poorly designed industrial relations legislation can adversely affect economic performance. Other changes may be envisaged in the area of industrial democracy, following activity by the EC and the publication of the Bullock Report [1977]. Wider ranging changes in the international legal framework have also been called for (Robinson and Wilkinson [1977]).

Legislation to protect disadvantaged groups

The *Equal Pay Act 1970* (EPA) was intended to ensure that employers pay men and women equally for doing the same or broadly similar work (Department of Employment [1974]). The provisions of the Act became effective on 29 December 1975, thus allowing five and a half years to ameliorate the potentially disruptive effects of a sudden transition to equal pay. It is probably fair to say that there had been a secular trend towards equality in 'basic' rates of pay before the provisions of the EPA became effective, but the ratio of women's to men's average weekly earnings declined and the ratio of female to male average hourly earnings remained roughly constant when comparing the beginning and end-of-period, i.e. 1950 and 1971 (see Hebden [1978]). While later evidence indicates that all but 5% of establishments had introduced equal rates of pay by early 1979, it is also clear that a significant proportion of establishments did not complete the process until well after 1975 (Bosworth and Dawkins [1979], pp. 163–4). Data from the NES on gross weekly earnings (excluding overtime pay) in all industries and services does suggest a significant narrowing of the sex wage differential during the 1970s, particularly during the period 1974–6, although similar data on average hourly earnings shows a slight reversal in trend in 1978 (Seear [1979], p. 863).

The *Sex Discrimination Act 1975* (SDA) extended and to some extent revised the EPA, covering not just pay but most dimensions of employment (Home Office [1975]). Discrimination against both men and women became unlawful in areas such as advertising, education, training and employment. It encompasses the principle of the abolition of both direct (i.e. where a woman is treated less favourably on the grounds of her sex) and indirect discrimination (i.e. which is equal in a formal sense as between the sexes, but discriminatory in its *effect* on one sex) (Home Office [1975], pp. 3–4), but not in equal pay where only direct discrimination is outlawed.

The EPA might have been expected to have resulted in adverse employment consequences, particularly for women. These do not appear to have materialised for three reasons: (i) the EPA (and the SDA) would seem to have had little effect on employers' attitudes and womens' conditions of employment (Seear [1979], p. 864), although specific, if limited, improvements can be seen (see Bosworth and Dawkins [1979], pp. 219–21); (ii) the EPA did not become effective until after 1975 and the SDA was also law by this time; and (iii) there have been underlying changes in the pattern of employment favouring part-time (and therefore women's) employment (Elias [1978], p. 5; Mallier and Rosser [1979]). Nevertheless, since 1975 there has been a rise in female unemployment which, in percentage terms, is a much greater increase than male unemployment, although it started from a considerably lower base (Mallier and Rosser [1979], p. 62). It seems likely that the rise in female unemployment rate can be mainly attributed to slackening demand and an increasing propensity of females to register as unemployed.

Despite progress towards equal pay, there would seem to be a general feeling of discontent with the effectiveness of the EPA and with the machinery established to oversee it. It is not surprising therefore that there have been a number of calls for legislative change. At the one extreme it has been suggested that there is no need for the EOC, but, at the other extreme, there have been advocates of a much stronger body with much sharper teeth (more along the lines of the USA system). A middle-of-the-road solution, with a more active use of existing mechanisms, seems the most likely outcome (Seear [1979], p. 865). Almost certainly some change will have to be undertaken to harmonise the UK definition of equal pay for 'like work' with the EEC definition of equal pay for 'work of equal value', and this will involve a much greater use of job evaluation schemes. Another change, which the EOC is proposing, is the removal of restrictions in order to allow women to work under the existing health and safety provisions covering men (Collins [1979]).

The *Race Relations Act 1976* (RRA) is in many ways similar to the legislation discussed above. The RRA was passed at a time of growing fears about racial tension in order to strengthen UK law against racial discrimination (Commission for Racial Equality [1977]). The principle aim of the RRA was to eliminate racial discrimination, thereby promoting equality of opportunity between racial groups. The law was intended to promote equal treatment in advertising, education, training, employment and pay. The Commission for Racial Equality was set up to oversee the operation of the Act. The Commission is empowered to investigate suspected cases of discrimination, it may issue 'non-discrimination notices' and may take legal action where discrimination persists. Individuals who feel that they have been unlawfully discriminated against may take their case before an industrial tribunal.

Contracts of employment

There has been considerable activity in modifying the law regarding contracts of employment during the 1970s. The *Contracts of Employment Act 1972* re-enacted, with some amendments, the *Contracts of Employment Act 1963*. Since it was passed, the Act has been further amended (Department of Employment [1978*b*]). The main aim is to give employees a minimum period of notice on termination of employment under common law, although the conditions set out in the Act do not apply where the individual's contract already gave the employee superior terms. In addition the Act gives the employee the right to a written statement of the main terms of his or her contract of employment. The *Employment Protection Act 1975* (EMPA) is perhaps the most far-reaching legislation of the 1970s relating to conditions of employment (Department of Employment [1975]). The Act made important modifications to the machinery of collective bargaining (see Chapter 5). It focuses in particular on the extension of employees' rights in their terms of contract and extends these rights to a larger proportion of part-time workers. In certain respects the Act can be seen as an extension of the existing protection of employees, e.g. redundancy and unfair dismissal provisions (see Elliot [1978]), but employees have additional rights with regard to guaranteed minimum payments during periods of short-time working, continued pay during authorised sick-leave, maternity rights for expectant mothers (but not paternity rights for new fathers) (Department of Employment [1977*b*]), ability to join the union of workers' choice, time-off for trade union and public duties and receipt of wages even where employer is insolvent. In a survey of employers it was suggested by the majority of employers that the EMPA had little or no effect on their behaviour (Bosworth and Dawkins [1979], p. 221). The most important effect appeared to be the need to provide maternity leave as firms discovered difficulty in covering jobs. Indeed smaller firms suggested that this induced them to avoid employing women in the normal 'mother' age category. There has been some talk by Conservative Ministers of abandoning this provision, at least in small firms, but this seems likely to be resisted by employee groups and, indeed, the EOC is suggesting additional maternity provisions (Collins [1979]).

Prospects for the 1980s

As indicated earlier productivity growth accelerated in the 1960s, slackening again since the 1973/4 boom. Sargent [1979] has argued that the more rapid growth experienced in the 1960s can be interpreted as a temporary phenomenon as the economy adjusted to a higher level growth path, but that productivity growth has now returned to its slower, long-term trend rate of increase. It will probably not be possible to ascertain the true picture until the current recession has passed. If this hypothesis is correct, however, the prospects for employment in the 1980s might seem less gloomy than if productivity had continued to grow at the same rate as the 1960s. A faster growth in productivity would imply a more rapid displacement of jobs which would make the return to full employment much more difficult. This, however, ignores the implications for competitiveness, which, given the forces at work to cause the exchange rate to rise (North Sea oil), will deteriorate even more rapidly in these circumstances (Whitley et al. [1980]). The prospects for industrial employment in the 1980s in the light of these considerations therefore do not seem very bright (Cripps, et al., [1978]; Barker et al., [1979]; Lindley [1978, 1980a]; London Business School [1979]). Projections of employment of this type have been criticised by Beenstock [1979] who argues for the primacy of automatic stabilising market pressures to restore full employment. It seems likely, however, that Beenstock has overstated both the degree of flexibility of UK labour markets and the extent to which this type of projection is invalidated by the failure to incorporate features in the model for which there is no firm econometric evidence (see Lindley [1980b]). The need for a return to the objective of full employment pursued by active fiscal policy seems to us to be crucial if there is not to be a massive waste of human resources in the 1980s on a par with that in the 1920s and 1930s.

The prospects for hours of work are clear in one respect: we can expect the number of hours worked per week (and per year) to decline over the 1980s. The steady reduction in normal hours which temporarily halted during the 1970s, would appear destined to restart and continue into the 1980s. The same is also almost certainly true of actual hours. If past experience is anything to go by, actual hours will also decline, following, with some lag, the trend in normal hours. Certain changes in the trends in hours, however, may be envisaged. The lagged adjustment of actual to normal hours has dragged a larger and larger proportion of operatives into the 'overtime net'. To date this has suited trade unions, for it has allowed their members' earnings to be raised during periods of incomes policies and to give the impression of improving the quality of working life. As individual workers have been willing to decrease their actual hours of work more slowly than normal hours, this has alleviated the worst effects for employers on the reduction in the degree of capital utilisation. In the future, however, we may well expect to see government action to reverse this perverse trend in overtime and thereby reduce actual hours towards their normal level and even introduce work-sharing in order to maintain or create new jobs. In doing this, the government may well have to study the effects of its employer and employee taxes to find tax structures that encourage this movement. It should be added that the effects will almost certainly spill over into higher shift-working as firms attempt to maintain their levels of capital utilisation. The governments of the 1980s are therefore likely to be faced by a dilemma between the number of jobs and unsocial hours of work.

The big unknown in the whole equation lies in the effect of the new micro technologies. The 'computer chip' will certainly affect process technologies in ways that may reduce the numbers of workers required per unit of output and the number of hours each worker is employed. The new technology may, through the full automation of certain processes that take place at abnormal hours, reduce the expected levels of shift-working. The big question is whether the computer chips will also produce a whole range of new products (and the income to buy them) which will create new jobs. Whenever process changes have threatened jobs in the past, the growth in demand for labour to produce new products has always more than compensated. It is difficult to judge whether this will be the case with the present 'revolution', but it seems almost certain that we are faced by a very difficult transitional phase in job (and even life-style) restructuring.

References

Bacon, R. and Eltis, W. [1978], *Britain's Economic Problem: Too Few Producers.* London: Macmillan.

Barker, T., Williamson, W. and Winters, A. [1979], 'The Cambridge Multisectoral Dynamic Model, Description and Analysis', *Department of Applied Economics, University of Cambridge.*

Becker, G. S. [1964], 'Investment in Human Capital: a Theoretical Analysis', *Human Capital.* New York: National Bureau of Economic Research.

Beenstock, M. [1979], 'Do U.K. Labour Markets Work?', *Economic Outlook,* June–July 1979, pp. 21–31.

Blackaby, F. T. [1978], 'General Appraisal', Chapter 14 in Blackaby, F. (ed.) *British Economic Policy, 1960–74.* London: NIESR, pp. 619–55.

Bosworth, D. and Dawkins, P. [1979], *Female Patterns of Work and Associated Remuneration, Facilities and Opportunities.* Research Report to the EOC–SSRC Joint Panel.

Bosworth, D. and Wilson, R. [1980], 'Government Policy and the Labour Market', *Manpower Research Group, Research Paper, Centre for Industrial, Economic and Business Research, University of Warwick, Coventry.*

Bullock Report [1977], *Report of the Committee of Inquiry on Industrial Democracy,* Chairman, Lord Bullock, Cmnd 6706. London: HMSO.

Burton, J. [1979], *The Job Support Machine: a Critique of the Subsidy Morass.* London: Centre for Policy Studies.

Cairncross, F. [1979], 'Modernisation has Benefited all Groups of Job-seekers', *Guardian,* 5 November 1979, p. 22.

Collins, R. [1979], *Health and Safety Legislation: Should We Distinguish Between Men and Women?,* Manchester: Equal Opportunities Commission.

Commission for Racial Equality [1977], *A Guide to the New Race Relations Act, 1976: Employment.*

Cripps, F., Fetherston, M. and Ward, T. [1978], Chapter 2 in *Economic Policy Review,* Department of Applied Economics, University of Cambridge, March 1978.

Denton, G., Ocleireacain, S. and Ash, S. [1975], *Trade Effects of Public Subsidies to Private Enterprises.* London: Macmillan.

Department of Employment [1975], *Employment Protection Act: An Outline,* DE, EP no. 1, London: HMSO.

Department of Employment [1976], 'The Changed Relationship Between Unemployment and Vacancies', *Department of Employment Gazette,* October 1976, pp. 1093–9.

Department of Employment [1977a], 'Surveys Carried Out into Special Employment Schemes', *Department of Employment Gazette,* July 1977, pp. 692–6.

Department of Employment [1977b], *Employment Protection Act 1975: Employment Rights for the Expectant Mother,* DE, EP no. 4. London: HMSO.

Department of Employment [1978a], 'By Far the Largest Measure', *Department of Employment Gazette,* May 1978, pp. 544–6.

Department of Employment [1978b], *Contracts of Employment Act 1972.* London: HMSO.

Department of Employment [1978c], 'How Well are Jobcentres Working?', *Department of Employment Gazette,* July 1978, pp. 791–4.

Department of Employment [1979], 'Regional Industrial Policy', *Department of Employment Gazette,* September 1979, pp. 883–9.

Elias, P. [1978], 'An Analysis of Trends in Female Employment', *Manpower Research Group, Research Paper 37, Centre for Industrial, Economic and Business Research, University of Warwick, Coventry*, 1978.

Elliot, R. [1978], 'Industrial Relations and Manpower Policy', Chapter 13 in Blackaby, F. (ed.) [1978], pp. 564–617.

Finger, N. [1974], *The Impact of Government Subsidies on Industrial Management: the Israeli Experience.* New York: Praeger.

Fryer, R. H. [1973], 'The Myths of the Redundancy Payments Act', *Industrial Law Journal*, Vol. 2, March 1973, pp. 1–16.

Gujerati, D. [1972], 'The Behaviour of Unemployment and Unfilled Vacancies: Great Britain, 1958–71', *Economic Journal*, no. 82, pp. 195–204.

Hebden, J. [1978], 'Men's and Women's Pay in Britain, 1968–1975', *Industrial Relations Journal*, Vol. 9, no. 2, pp. 56–70.

Home Office [1975], *Sex Discrimination: a Guide to the Sex Discrimination Act 1975.* Home Office and CSO. London: HMSO.

IFF Research Ltd [1978], *Shiftworking in Manufacturing Industry, Great Britain.* Research Report to the European Foundation for the Improvement of Living and Working Conditions, Dublin, 1978.

IFF Research Ltd [1979], *Women at Work.* Survey Carried Out for the EOC–SSRC Joint Panel, 1979.

Institute of Manpower Studies [1973], 'The Effects of the Raising of the School-leaving Age on Labour Supply', *IMS Monitor*, Vol. 2, July 1973, pp. 50–61.

Kaldor, N. [1966], *Causes of the Slow Rate of Economic Growth of the U.K., An Inaugural Lecture.* Cambridge: Cambridge University Press.

Layard, R. and Nickell, S. [1977], 'The Case for Subsidising Extra Jobs', *London School of Economics Discussion Paper no. 15, Centre for Labour Economics, LSE.*

Layard, R. [1979], 'Have the Jobcentres Increased Unemployment?', *Guardian*, 5 November 1979, p. 22.

Lees, D. and Chiplin, B. [1970], 'The Economics of Industrial Training', *Lloyds Bank Review*, April 1970, no. 96, pp. 29–41.

Lindley, R. M. (ed.) [1978], *Britain's Medium Term Employment Prospects.* University of Warwick: Manpower Research Group.

Lindley, R. M., (ed.) [1980a], *Economic Change and Employment Policy.* London: Macmillan.

Lindley, R. M. [1980b], 'Approaches to Assessing Employment Prospects', Chapter 2 in Lindley (ed.) [1980].

London Business School [1979], *Economic Outlook, 1979–1983*, Centre for Economic Forecasting, London Business School, Vol. 4, no. 2, November 1979.

McCormick, B. and Manley, P. [1967], 'The Industrial Training Act', *National Westminister Bank Review*, February 1967, pp. 45–56.

Mallier, T. and Rosser, M. [1979], 'The Changing Role of Women in the British Economy', *National Westminster Bank Review*, November 1979, pp. 54–65.

Manpower Services Commission [1976]. *Towards a Comprehensive Manpower Policy.* London: MSC.

Manpower Services Commission [1978a], *MSC Review and Plan, 1978.* London: HMSO.

Manpower Services Commission [1978b], *Jobcentres: an Evaluation.* London: Employment Service Division, ES Paper 49, MSC.

Manpower Services Commission [1979], *The Employment Service in the 1980s.* London: MSC.

Mukherjee, S. [1970], *Changing Manpower Needs: a Study of Industrial Training Boards.* London: Political and Economic Planning.

Mukherjee, S. [1973], *Through No Fault of Their Own: Systems of Handling Redundancies in Britain, France and Germany.* London: Macdonald.

Musgrave, R. and Musgrave, P. [1968], 'Fiscal Policy' in Caves, R. (ed.), *Britain's Economic Prospects.* Brookings Institute Study, George, Allen and Unwin.

National Joint Advisory Council [1962], 'Report of the Working Party on the Manpower Situation', *Ministry of Labour Gazette,* Vol. 70, February 1962.

National Economic Development Council [1963], *Conditions Favourable to Faster Growth.* London: HMSO.

Nickell, S. J. [1979], 'The Effect of Unemployment and Related Benefits on the Duration of Unemployment', *Economic Journal,* Vol. 89, pp. 34–49.

Oatey, M. [1970], 'The Economics of Training With Respect to the Firm', *British Journal of Industrial Relations,* Vol. VIII, March 1970, pp. 1–21.

Parker, F. R., et al. [1971], 'A Survey Carried Out in 1969 for the Department of Employment', *Department of Employment Gazette,* March 1971.

Pettman, B. O. [1973], *Training and Retraining: a Basis for the Future.* Transcripta Books.

Robbins Report [1963], *Report of the Committee Appointed by the Prime Minister Under the Chairmanship of Lord Robbins, 1961–63,* Cmnd 2154. London: HMSO.

Robinson, J. and Wilkinson, F. [1977], 'What Has Become of Employment Policy?', *Cambridge Journal of Economics,* Vol. 1, pp. 5–14.

Sargent, J. R. [1979], 'Productivity and Profits in U.K. Manufacturing', *Midland Bank Review,* Autumn 1979, pp. 7–13.

Seear, Baroness [1979], 'Where Do We Go From Here? Equal Pay and Equal Opportunity', *Department of Employment Gazette,* September 1979, pp. 863–6.

Thirlwall, A. P. [1978], 'The U.K.'s Economic Problem: a Balance of Payments Constraint?', *National Westminster Bank Review,* February 1978, pp. 24–32.

Whitley, J., Wilson, R. and Smith, D. [1980], 'Industrial and Occupational Change', Chapter 4 in Lindley (ed.) [1980].

Ziderman, A. [1978], *Manpower Training: Theory and Policy.* London: Macmillan Studies in Economics, Macmillan.

5 Collective Bargaining

by Eric Owen Smith

Introduction

Two changes in the structure of collective bargaining became increasingly manifest during the 1970s. The first change has been lucidly analysed by Professor Phelps Brown [1973]. The collective bargaining system was exacerbating the problems created by expectational, market and procedural developments, whereas for many years it had adapted to change. It was the behaviour of these three variables which resulted in the second change. Government intervention in all aspects of the labour market and collective bargaining came to be seen as an increasingly important policy priority – a phenomenon discernible, at the latest, during the late 1960s. The government became a larger employer in its own right; legislatively, too, intervention has increased. All these developments conflicted with the long-held theory that Britain had a 'voluntary' system of collective bargaining.

Attention in this chapter is concentrated on various aspects of procedural disequilibrium, including the policy instruments designed to restore equilibrium. The development of this disequilibrium is briefly explored in the first section. This leads to an examination of the resulting change in policy prescriptions. Secondly, the *Industrial Relations Act 1971* (IR Act) is analysed. A third section deals with the *Trade Union and Labour Relations Act 1974* (TULRA) as amended in 1976 and the *Employment Protection Act 1975* (EP Act). In the fourth section policy attitudes at the end of the decade are examined. A final section analyses the position of trade unions in terms of their growth, structure and policy.

Recent Developments in Collective Bargaining

Since the Second World War *procedures* that once adjusted costs to prices have been pushing costs and prices up together because institutions have changed comparatively little while the forces that operate on them have changed dramatically. Labour unit costs of output have risen fastest in the UK in recent years, but this stems more from low productivity than from high money wage increases. Structural rigidities on both sides of the labour market contributed to the slow rate of productivity growth (Robinson [1972], pp. 300–1). These rigidities resulted not least from trade union restrictions on productivity growth and poor managerial quality (Ulman [1968], pp. 332, 335). With the advent of full employment *expectations* became based on comparisons among different groups of workers. Relativities apart, there was an expectation of annual improvement in real wages. But the product *market environment* also gradually became harder: increases in money wages and unit costs could not be as easily passed on to the consumer.

Expectations and the market environment have, therefore, recently been on collision course, one result of which has been a significant downward trend in profitability. The external pressure of a falling exchange rate gave a further fillip to inflationary pressure which has to be added to other similar strains on the collective bargaining system. As inflation increased relatively low-paid workers entered into the taxable brackets for the first time; together with the inflationary impact of SET and VAT, and even the lagged response to the domestic rate of inflation itself, confused expectations have resulted in an increasing wages scramble (Jackson et al. [1975]; Robinson [1972], p. 317). Indeed Phelps Brown is surely correct in stating that collective bargaining today is not between labour and capital, or employees and management, but between different groups of employees and between them as a whole and the inactive population (Phelps Brown [1973]).

These trends have led to widespread government intervention on the assumption that market forces were alone inadequate to resolve the problems. A whole battery of Acts designed to ameliorate structural rigidities have been introduced in the 1960s and 1970s thus modifying the so-called 'voluntary' (liberal or free) philosophy of collective bargaining. These have represented the other policy school, the 'legal-intervention' (collectivist) philosophy.

McCarthy and Ellis, and for that matter Weekes et al. [1975], all trace the initial disenchantment with the voluntary system back to the mid 1950s. Such disenchantment had been caused by the increasing number of strikes, the alleged abuse of trade union power and an uneconomic use of manpower. A gradual hardening of attitudes was discernible in the Labour governments of the 1960s. Threats of legislative solutions to unofficial strikes, the expectation of a tough report from the Donovan Commission and, ultimately, the White Paper *In Place of Strife*, all testified to this perceived need for a change in policy. There was indeed a tough note of reservation on industrial disputes from one member of the Donovan Commission (Andrew Shonfield). Meanwhile, the Conservative Party was actively developing proposals for a detailed legislative programme with such evocative pamphlets as *A Giant's Strength, Trade Unions for Tomorrow* and *Fair Deal at Work*. By the end of the 1970s Labour's Secretary of State for Employment (Albert Booth) was able to tell the House of Commons that the argument had moved from one about the necessity for legal intervention to an argument about the appropriate role for the law in collective bargaining. He continued to say that despite being a lifelong unionist, he believed that some rights are 'better enshrined in law than fought for through collective bargaining' (Hansard, 8 March 1979, cols 1551 and 1563). A few months later his Conservative successor stated that it was 'as sensible to say "keep politics out of government" as to say "keep the law out of industrial relations"' (Prior [1979], p. 11). Also by 1979 the failure of the voluntary collective bargaining system to adjust to changed conditions had frustrated its most zealous legal adherent (McCarthy and Ellis [1973], pp. 8–9, 144–5; Kahn-Freund [1979]).

Donovan and In Place of Strife

When the Donovan Commission was appointed in 1965, the position of what collective bargaining law already existed had been put into a rare tangle of confusion by the *Rookes v. Barnard* case which the courts had settled to their apparent satisfaction earlier that year. The precise legal implications of the case are still unclear but trade union leaders were advised that it had virtually nullified the protection given to unions by the *Trade Disputes Act 1906* (Moran [1977], p. 35; Thomson and Engleman [1975], p. 16; Crouch [1979], p. 48). This situation was far from unique in Britain. As the Donovan Commission pointed out in their Introduction, they were the fifth Royal Commission to be concerned with collective bargaining. Each one had been appointed as a result of an unexpectedly perverse judicial interpretation of the existing statutes. This Gilbertian situation stems from the fact that trade unions are in basic conflict with ancient common law because they restrain trade if their leaders call strikes or order picketing. Each statute must therefore attempt to define the degree of *immunity* trade unions will enjoy from the common law, but that definition will be tested by the judiciary against a back-cloth of ancient common law.

Three sources of confusion were therefore fundamentally to affect collective bargaining during the 1970s. First, there was a procedural disequilibrium; second, there was the voluntarist or legal intervention debate; third, the position of the law itself had in any case to be clarified. All three strands can be discerned in the attempts made by the Donovan Commission to arrive at some viable policy pre-scriptions.

The central theme of the Donovan Report was that Britain had two systems of industrial relations. One was the formal system embodied in the official institutions. The other was the informal system created by managers and shop stewards at a local level. The main implication was that the 'national' (i.e. industry-wide) agreements tended to be circumvented and supplemented at the level of the 'local' (i.e. plant-level) labour market. This is how the phenomenon of wage drift emerged – that is actual earnings at the workplace tending to exceed nationally agreed wage rates. It also accounted for the increas-ing number of unofficial and unconstitutional strikes. Unwritten agreements based on custom and practice were pervasive. Therefore

> The central defect in British industrial relations is the disorder in factory and workshop relations and pay structures promoted by the conflict between the formal and the informal systems. To remedy this effective and orderly collective bargaining is required....
>
> (Donovan [1968], para 1019)

In other words, while earlier commentators suggested that the unions had grown too powerful, Donovan concentrated on the growth in the bargaining strength of *work groups* at a *local* level. The crucial recommendation was that institutional reform should be introduced. It was considered that the amount of statutory intervention should be minimised and that the amelioration of collective bargaining problems would be best achieved through a reformed structure of collective bargaining. Indeed, free collective bargaining was seen as a desirable objective in its own right. The type of Act on industrial relations envisaged by the Commission was therefore basically designed to encourage reform along these lines. Measures intended to reform the institutions, as well as those conducive to economic efficiency, were to be introduced autonomously by employers and unions.

Several minority notes of dissent were appended to the Report. A particularly powerful note of reservation, which in essence challenged the major premise of the main Report, was entered by Andrew Shonfield. He argued that the growing dependence of people on the reliable performance of services in modern urban communities raised new problems if such services were disrupted by collective action. He went on to assert that strike action would continue to be a necessary element in the bargaining power of wage and salary earners 'as far ahead as one can see'. However, certain minimum standards of behaviour could reasonably be expected, and very special grounds would be needed to justify there being no legal rules to restrain powerful organisations. Although trade unions commanded the voluntary assent of those they represented, they should 'bargain in good faith'. Both unions and employers should be encouraged to treat collective agreements as contractural obligations enforceable at law. Strikes which endangered life and health should be made illegal and the immunity granted by the 1906 Act should be taken away from workers who refused to drop restrictive practices.

Hence neither the voluntarist nor the legal interventionist wings of the Donovan Commission sought to deny that problems existed. The contrast lay in the diagnosis of their cause and in the derived policy prescriptions. A lack of unanimity tended to render the final Report into a piece of political compromise.

In Place of Strife (1969) was the then Labour government's White Paper based on the Donovan Report. It confirmed the efficacy of collective bargaining in reconciling differences between workers and management. The reform and extension of collective bargaining was therefore seen as a primary policy objective to encourage basic reform. A Commission on Industrial Relations (CIR) was formed to supplement the work of the National Board for Prices and Incomes (NBPI) and the Department of Employment and Productivity (as it was then known). At the micro level more information was to be given by employers to their employees. However, 'new safeguards' for the community and individuals were also seen as policy objectives. An individual could appeal to the Registrar of Friendly Societies if he felt that he had been unjustly expelled from membership of a trade union. Moreover, a conciliation pause of twenty-eight days could be ordered by the Secretary of State during which strikes and lock-outs would have to be called off. The Secretary of State would also have had the power to order a strike ballot. It should be noted that these powers were to be conferred on the Secretary of State and were therefore seen as being overtly *political* in nature. Under the IR Act the Secretary of State applied to the courts and the judiciary made a *legal* decision as to whether a conciliation pause or strike ballot should be ordered. These latter proposals in *In Place of Strife* became known as the 'penal clauses' and they caused quite a furore in the trade union movement. A strident campaign against the clauses was mounted. Eventually, the TUC agreed to introduce its own procedure for avoiding strikes and the Labour government withdrew its proposals. After *In Place of Strife* the Labour government introduced a Bill, shorn of the offending clauses; it did so without enthusiasm and the Bill was never debated because it was overtaken by the 1970 General Election.

The Industrial Relations Act 1971

The controversial nature of the Act

By the time Conservatives were returned to office in 1970, employers' organisations had become even more perturbed by the worsening strike and wage inflation position, although they wished to see a flexible system of control which would be headed by an experienced Registrar. The unions were affronted by the Government's refusal to enter seriously the now accepted processes of consultation. The Government perceived the IR Act as putting 'on record the judgement of the community about what conduct is fair and reasonable' (McCarthy and Ellis [1973], pp. 74–5).

The events leading up to the withdrawal of the *In Place of Strife* proved to be a mild skirmish when compared with the bitter resistance mounted against the IR Act. Inside Parliament, its Committee stage was taken on the floor of the Commons, and it occupied more parliamentary time than any other piece of non-financial legislation since 1945. Barbara Castle, who as Secretary of State had sponsored *In Place of Strife*, subjected the Bill to fiery denunciations. Eric Heffer, erstwhile opponent of *In Place of Strife*, joined Barbara Castle on the front bench to assist in leading the parliamentary opposition. Although the debates took up one-third of the Government's parliamentary time in the 1970/1 session, most of the Bill's 170 clauses could not even be debated because of the extent of the detailed opposition. Outside of Parliament the TUC mounted a massive campaign of agitation and propaganda; consultation with the Government was boycotted when it became plain that the Bill was not going to be modified. When the Act became law, official TUC policy was to boycott the institutions set up under the Act.

The contents of the Act

Whereas Donovan had explicitly rejected the principle of transplantation of collective bargaining arrangements as being 'useless or even harmful' if social conditions in the two countries differed, *Fair Deal at Work*, on which the IR Act was largely based, implicitly drew heavily on the North American system of collective bargaining – a system in which the law plays a prominent part. It was hoped that adoption of the American law would result in a metamorphosis of the unofficial and short British strike into a more structured, predictable (and more protracted?) affair. Shonfield's plea to 'bargain in good faith' was explicitly reflected in the IR Act by concepts borrowed directly from the USA: 'bargaining agents', 'unfair industrial practice', 'agency shop' and 'emergency procedures'. The Act was constructed on eight 'pillars'. An analogy with a building is appropriate in the sense that the Government announced that no pillar would be removable as a result of consultation. The IR Act's authors hoped that this legal framework would induce the voluntary reform in collective bargaining which the Donovan Commission had advocated.

The first pillar enacted the right to belong or not to belong to a trade union. In effect, the IR Act's embodiment of both rights led logically to further sections which proscribed the pre-entry closed shop and which rendered a post-entry shop inoperable where individuals opted not to join a union. A North American notion was substituted for the closed shop. This was the agency shop. Provided a trade union registered under the Act (see below), and if it secured two-thirds majority in a ballot conducted by the CIR (now a legally constituted body) it was an unfair industrial practice on the part of an employer not to recognise the trade union and all affected employees were required either to join the appropriate union or to subscribe an amount equivalent to a union contribution to a recognised charity. Finally, as a result of a concession made during the passage of the

Bill through Parliament, an 'approved closed shop' was made permissible under certain exceptional circumstances.

The second pillar of the IR Act concerned trade union recognition. A Code of Industrial Relations Practice was drawn up – a document which illustrated practices which would ideally prevent the need to invoke the Act. The Code did not explicitly state that trade unions *should* be recognised: it gave advice on how recognition *might* be accorded. But, as a last resort, machinery was established under the Act by which a registered union could attempt to obtain statutory recognition. The National Industrial Relations Court (NIRC), a specially created division of the High Court, could require the CIR to examine and report on recognition issues brought to its attention by the Secretary of State, employers or a registered trade union.

Under the third pillar of the Act lay the notion of registration. A Registrar of Trade Unions and Employers' Associations would subject the rules of all applicants for registration to strict tests. Basically these tests were designed to control arbitrary discrimination in membership and ensure intra-union democracy. In the event, all trade unions already registered with the Registrar of Friendly Societies were automatically transferred to the new Registrar's provisional register. It was the decision on the part of all the leading trade unions to de-register which rendered the Act unworkable. The analysis returns to this later in this section.

The fourth pillar of the Act made all collective agreements legally enforceable unless the contrary was specified.

As far as the fifth pillar of the Act was concerned, only appointed representatives of registered unions could call for industrial action, unless a group of employees gave due notice of strike action.

The North American cooling-off period, or conciliation pause as it was termed under *In Place of Strife* and the IR Act, was part of the sixth pillar. Provision for a sixty-day period (twenty-eight under *In Place of Strife*) was made. Also if the Secretary of State deemed a national emergency to exist, he could apply to the NIRC for a strike ballot.

Both the seventh and eighth pillars were designed to induce parties to collective agreements to observe procedural agreements. Inter-union disputes over the establishment of, and participation in, those procedures would be reduced by introducing the concept of a bargaining unit within which only registered and recognised trade unions had bargaining rights.

The repercussions of the Act

The NIRC granted one conciliation pause and one strike ballot under the Act, both of which affected the railways. In April 1972 the Secretary of State obtained the pause for fourteen days in order to prevent the series of unofficial strikes and work-to-rules which had accompanied the protracted wage negotiations. The Government later obtained a NIRC order for a compulsory strike ballot. The result was a six to one majority in favour of industrial action and consequently there was a resumption of such action. Hence the ballot was counter-productive and there is evidence that the union's bargaining stance changed from the usual willingness to compromise to one of obduracy.

However, it was the TGWU and the AUEW which mounted the most determined opposition to the Act. The former was fined £55 000 by the NIRC, the latter a total of £208 000 in fines and costs (Lewis [1974]). In the case of the TGWU this marked approximately a year (March 1972–March 1973) of traumatic episodes which consisted of an intra-union dispute, a questioning of the role of its shop stewards, the imprisonment of five of its members and the need to formulate and negotiate a national agreement with respect to employment in the docks. The AUEW became associated with a membership issue, a closed shop case and a recognition dispute. The TGWU initially refused to appear before NIRC, the AUEW consistently refused to do so. (For that matter the TGW was in frequent private communication with the CIR). The NIRC dealt uncontroversially with nearly 1096 different proceedings during its existence, mainly appeals from industrial tribunals, but it was these few cases involving the TGWU and the AUEW which questioned its viability. These episodes are now briefly examined.

Early in 1972 an unofficial committee of dockers attempted to protect their diminishing employment opportunities by 'blacking' (refusing to handle) vehicles belonging to road haulage firms which had declined to sign an agreement which acknowledged that certain work on their containers ('stuffing and stripping') should be carried out by registered dockers and the drivers of container vehicles should belong to a union. The NIRC granted an injunction against the 'blacking' to a number of affected firms led by Heatons of St. Helens. In its absence, the TGWU was fined £5000 when the blacking did not cease, followed by a further £50 000 for a similar contempt.

Members of the commercial section of the TGWU employed at a container depot in London (Cobham Farm) now successfully applied for a NIRC injunction against the docks section of their union. On this occasion the case was brought against three named individuals, but the intervention of an hitherto unknown public figure (the Official Solicitor) at the invitation of the Court of Appeal prevented a national dock strike in protest against the threatened imprisonment of the named three. However, when the blacking and picketing grew more widespread the Midland Cold Storage Ltd (London) brought a case which resulted in the NIRC imprisoning five dockers. There was an immediate nationwide dock strike.

In the meantime, following the £55 000 fines, the TUC modified its policy and permitted its affiliates to defend their interests in the courts. The Heatons case had gone from the NIRC to the Court of Appeal and then to the House of Lords. The TGWU argued that it had instructed its dockers to cease their blacking action and they were acting beyond the scope of their authority by persisting in that action. The NIRC insisted that they remained official agents of the union. The Court of Appeal accepted the union's claim, displaying a great deal of perspicacity into the dual (and unique) function of a British shop steward as a representative of *both* his work group and his union. The House of Lords reversed this decision and this enabled the NIRC to release five dockers imprisoned as a result of the Midland Cold Storage case. This was done on the grounds that the Lords had shown the primary means of enforcing the law should be against the funds of organisations *and* not against individuals.

There were thus two main consequences of the TGWU case. First, it was unlikely that the IR Act could be enforced by using penal sanctions against individuals. Secondly, the law had proved itself to be singularly inept in attempting to understand Britain's collective bargaining system. If an official withdraws a shop steward's credentials not only may his members still ignore his advice but the employer or workers may both sue in an attempt to prove that the steward had acted lawfully, assuming that the laws were acceptable and obeyed. Unions can no longer command unquestioning loyalty from their members, any more than employers or governments can. The law had been saved from its own inflexibility in the face of these factors only by special circumstances.

A union membership issue involving the AUEW and Mr James Goad first arose in October 1972. The latter had been expelled owing to arrears in his contributions. Both an industrial tribunal and the NIRC ruled that Mr Goad was a member of the union. If the union had chosen to defend itself, it could probably have avoided the £55 000 in fines which were eventually collected by means of sequestration. The AUEW was also involved in a very instructive and complex closed shop case, which began in 1972. Mr Joseph Langston, an employee of the Chrysler Motor Company, decided to resign from the union in order to assert his right not to be a member. Because there was a post-entry closed shop agreement in operation, his 4000 colleagues refused to work with him and he was suspended on full pay. The courts decided that only an employer could sue a union for this unfair industrial practice, which Chrysler was clearly not willing to do. Chrysler dismissed Langston and the NIRC enabled him to bring an unfair dismissal case and be compensated accordingly. Closed shop agreements were therefore not threatened by the Act and there will be a further examination of this type of agreement below.

It was during *Con-Mech (Engineering) Ltd v. AUEW* (commencing September 1973) that the Act finally became fully discredited. This recognition dispute involved

> a colourful and individualistic small employer who disliked unions; allegations that a militant philosophy graduate was stirring up trouble in the firm; the by now customary defiance of the Court by the AUEW; fines and sequestrations on the union; strikes as a result; an attack on Sir John Donaldson (President of the NIRC) by the Labour Government's Secretary of State for Employment; and anonymous benefactors who paid the AUEW's debts to the NIRC in order to prevent a national engineering strike
>
> (Moran [1977], pp. 145-6).

The fines, costs and damages to Con-Mech amounted to a total bill for the union of £147 000, although the sequestrators seized £280 000 – including the funds intended for the pay of the staff at the union's headquarters. An immediate and indefinite strike had commenced when anonymous donors produced £65 000 which was sufficient to persuade the law to withdraw and enable industrial peace to be restored (Lewis [1974], pp. 204-6). This is a moral in itself, of course, but once again it must also be emphasised that the union could have gained a recognition order, had it been registered. The CIR had made such a recommendation, although the employer was as obdurate as the union.

Conclusion

By the time the Act became law, therefore, there was little enthusiasm for its contents among employers and management. The Conservatives had disillusioned them by the same dogmatic approach to consultation which had alienated the trade union movement. Those employers who did resort to litigation were not only in a minority: they also typically sued employees of other companies. Moreover, the Con-Mech episode finally disillusioned the large employers, and the Director General of the CBI expressed the view that the Act had sullied industrial relations and should be repealed.

Even when the Act first became law, many unions, including some large ones, had not taken steps to de-register. The 1971 Congress fairly narrowly decided to instruct all its affiliates to de-register. Seven large unions were suspended from the TUC in July 1972 for not de-registering. It was only the imprisonment of the five dockers and the House of Lords' *Heatons* decision which finally persuaded all the large unions to de-register, although by now the TUC had decided that unions should be able to defend themselves before the NIRC. Nevertheless, thirty-two unions were still defiant and they were suspended at the 1972 Congress. Twenty of them were expelled in 1973, although most of them re-affiliated after the Act had been repealed.

The Trade Union and Labour Relations Act and the Employment Protection Act

The legislation

When the minority Labour government took office at the beginning of March 1974, there was a change in consultation policy. The trade unions were afforded a large degree of influence in economic policy formation in return for voluntary undertakings to exercise wage restraint – the so-called 'social contract' (see Chapter 3). In terms of collective bargaining, the Government committed itself to three stages of legislation. The first stage would be the repeal of the IR Act, followed by, second, legislative measures designed to extend employees' rights and strengthen collective bargaining. A third stage, which was not reached during the 1970s, was to consist of measures to promote industrial democracy. In 1977 the Bullock Report favoured legislation along these lines (Jenkins and Sherman [1977], pp. 148–51). During the decade workers were appointed to the Boards of the BSC and the Post Office.

The TULRA was enacted in 1974. It effectively repealed the IR Act, but also re-enacted its unfair dismissal provisions. One important feature of the IR Act which remained was the Code of Industrial Relations Practice. The Code could still be used in evidence during industrial tribunal proceedings but did not itself render anyone liable to legal proceedings

An equivocal aspect of the TULRA was the repeal of the right not to belong to a trade union but the insertion of amendments during the Bill's passage through Parliament which provided a statutory right of recourse against trade unions which excluded or expelled individuals in an arbitrary and unreasonable manner. In a contentious episode an Amendment to the Act (1976) repealed the 'arbitrary and unreasonable manner' clause and replaced it with provisions for a non-statutory review body under a legally qualified chairman whose members were to be appointed by the TUC. The only legally recognised grounds for exemption from trade union membership where a closed shop was in operation were consequently those of religious scruples.

The EP Act (1975) was the second phase of the Labour government's legislative programme – namely that of extending employees' rights and strengthening collective bargaining. Maternity pay and guaranteed weekly payments during short time became a legal requirement, along with such things as time-off with pay for union duties, retraining and the seeking of alternative work in the event of being declared redundant. Time-off work with pay at the discretion of the employer for public duties, as well as written terms for dismissal and redundancy also became legal necessities. An employer could not victimise an employee for joining an independent trade union or for taking part in its activities. If an employee were victimised on any of these counts, he could complain to an industrial tribunal and be awarded compensation.

The machinery

Some highly significant changes to collective bargaining were also made by the EP Act. Although the NIRC, CIR and Registrar were abolished, analogous institutions emerged which were to play a significant third party role. As a prelude to an analysis of this machinery, the following schematic expression may be useful:

EP Act	*IR Act*
1. Employment Appeal Tribunal (Branch of the High Court) (EAT)	1. NIRC
2. Certification Officer	2. Registrar of Trade Unions
3. Advisory, Conciliation and Arbitration Service (ACAS)	3. CIR; Department of Employment's Conciliation and Advisory Service
4. Central Arbitration Committee (CAC)	4. Industrial Board
5. Industrial Tribunals	5. Industrial Tribunals

The re-appearance of a High Court branch and the Certification Officer (Registrar) may occasion some surprise, although it must be borne in mind that all sanctions against strikers had now disappeared. Nevertheless, the EAT has functioned in manner comparable to that in most European countries. The duties of the Certification Officer included the maintenance of the list of trade unions and employers' associations required by the TULRA. Above all, he decided whether a trade union was independent and, where appropriate, issued after examination of the union's rules a Certificate of Independence.

ACAS was set up as an *independent* service in order to take over the former conciliation functions of the Department of Employment (Hunter [1977], p. 228; Crouch [1979], p. 84). Subsequently, the use made of the conciliation, mediation and arbitration services increased dramatically.

Three of the more controversial aspects of ACAS's work must be considered. First, under section 11 of the EP Act, ACAS was charged with the responsibility for adjudicating in recognition disputes. Should conciliation in such a dispute fail, ACAS can make a recommendation for recognition. Whether ACAS rules in favour of the trade union or the employer, the situation was clearly potentially explosive. Moreover, a trade union could ultimately refer a complaint arising from the failure of an employer to comply with an ACAS recommendation to CAC whose awards were enforceable at law [section 16 (EP Act)]. The well-publicised Grunwick case illustrated the potential difficulties facing ACAS in recognition disputes: a small employer determined to resist by litigation trade union pressure for recognition. An unsatisfactory ballot on the recognition issue by ACAS. Mass picketing by trade unionists not directly involved in the dispute. In short, a recipe for a prolonged dispute, given the attitudes which developed and the pressures which built up (Crouch [1979], pp. 113–15). By the end of the decade, the newly elected Conservative government viewed the situation with 'considerable concern'.

Secondly, schedule 11 of the EP Act empowered ACAS to refer to the CAC cases where it was thought that terms and conditions of employment offered by an employer were less favourable than those in comparable employment in a trade or industry. Thirdly, ACAS had the legal responsibility for up-dating the Code of Practice but here potentially controversial decisions were made without exciting controversy. Codes on the disclosure of information, disciplinary practice and procedures and time-off for trade union activities were published. These codes have encouraged a much more structured and formalised approach to collective bargaining. For example, written procedure agreements seem to have been widely introduced.

Generally speaking ACAS seems to have been a successful product of the attempts consistently mounted during the 1970s to develop third party intervention. Ultimately an impartial agency charged with generally improving collective bargaining had been welded onto a well-established conciliation and arbitration service, whereas under the IR Act they had remained separate entities. An added bonus was the dramatic growth in the number of cases in which third party intervention was voluntarily accepted.

The CAC had a somewhat more controversial reception than ACAS. This is not surprising in the sense that CAC was empowered to make legally enforceable awards on the subject matter of its reference.

By far the greatest number of references to the CAC were under schedule 11 of the EP Act. It was originally intended that schedule 11 would be a means of reducing low pay, particularly as there had been growing dissatisfaction with the Wages Council's apparent historical inability to stimulate and simulate collective bargaining. In the event it was the white collar unions which have made the most frequent use of this schedule. Another controversial area was the disclosure of information because it may involve requiring management to concede a bargaining advantage or reveal sales and other information useful to competitors. Both the EP and 1975 Industry Acts had little impact (Gospel [1976] and [1978]).

Statutory jurisdiction – or more precisely compulsory or legally-binding arbitration – is not new to the British collective bargaining system. It existed before and during the First World War, as well as during and after the Second World War, its being abolished on the apparently mistaken premise that it could cause inflation in its own right (Phelps Brown [1973], p. 331; McCarthy and Ellis [1973] pp. 126–7). Moreover, the Chairman of the CAC emphasised that his organisation had two antecedents: the Industrial Arbitration Board under the IR Act and the Industrial Court which existed between 1919 and the introduction of the IR Act. He went on to refer to the advantages of the tribunal system adopted by all three bodies: an independent chairman is joined by a CBI and a TUC nominee. History, he continued, showed that pay arbitration was important when collective bargaining did not exist or was fettered in some way by war-time control or pay policy (Wood [1979]). In this sense, therefore, the CAC displayed no radical departure from British tradition.

Industrial tribunals were first established by the *Industrial Training Act 1964* and their jurisdiction was subsequently widened gradually, for example, by the *Redundancy Payments Act 1965*. But it was the IR Act which extended the scope of the tribunals to cover unfair dismissal. The EP Act added further duties (Dickens [1978/9]). By far the largest category of claimant coming before the tribunals was in respect of unfair dismissal. Only one-third of claimants were successful. Generally, a relatively small amount of compensation is preferred by the tribunals to reinstatement.

Policy Prescriptions at the end of the decade
The leadership of the two main political parties changed during the 1970s. James Callaghan, who succeeded Harold Wilson as leader of the Labour Party, has displayed a consistent scepticism over the role of the law. As a member of both Labour's national executive committee and Harold Wilson's cabinet, he repudiated *In Place of Strife*. When Edward Heath 'sought to curb union power' by means of the IR Act, Mr Callaghan was equally opposed to the intervention of the law. His answer to the disruption caused by the transport and public workers disputes in 1979 was to rely on codes of picketing behaviour issued by the unions involved and the more general TUC–Government concordat. During the 1979 election campaign he stressed that the inability of the law to put matters right did not exempt the trade unions from the need to reform themselves. He added

that: 'It [the concordat] recommends that there would be arbitration on disputes instead of strikes. It calls for more secret ballots before the strike action and recommends limiting the powers of picketing.' (*Guardian*, 12 April 1979, p. 24). Had a Labour government been returned, it would have found itself in a political dilemma if voluntary reform along the lines of the concordat had not been introduced.

After Margaret Thatcher succeeded Edward Heath she allied herself to the views of her employment spokesman (James Prior) and promised the Conservative trade unionists' annual conference in 1976 that there would be no major industrial relations legislation such as the IR Act from any future Conservative government. She gave some indication of a hardening in her attitude during 1979. She saw trade union law as a crucial issue during the election campaign, although Mr Prior added that there would be adequate consultation with the trade unions should the Conservatives win the election. He also continued to maintain that only 'limited' changes in the law were required. The Conservative Manifesto undertook to introduce legislation to limit the right of picketing; modify the closed shop provisions of Labour's legislation; provide public money for postal votes in union elections; introduce no strike agreements into some essential public services and gradually reduce social security and other benefits paid to strikers and their families in favour of higher union strike pay. Undertakings to amend the EP Act were also given.

In July, statutory instruments were laid which increased the qualifying period of employment for claiming unfair dismissal from twenty-six weeks to fifty-two weeks and reduced the statutory period for consultation with trade unions over proposed redundancies from sixty to thirty days.

An Employment Bill duly appeared in early December. All the machinery for third party intervention which had been evolved during the decade remained in existence. ACAS was, however, relieved of its recognition duties – much to the chagrin of some smaller non-TUC unions. The Secretary of State assumed the role of issuing codes of practice with advice from ACAS and interested parties. Schedule 11 was also repealed – this time to the chagrin of the Engineering Employers' Federation whose members thought that it would undermine national bargaining. Industrial tribunals were to take the size and resources of a firm into account when assessing unfair dismissal claims. Firms employing fewer than twenty persons were to be exempted from unfair dismissal proceedings for the first two years of their existence. Provisions for maternity leave under the EP Act were also to be modified, including possible exemption for firms employing fewer than six persons.

It was further proposed that the Certification Officer would administer a new scheme providing for payments towards the cost of secret ballots held by independent unions.

Trade Union Growth, Structure and Policy

One of the most significant post-Donovan developments was the sudden upsurge in the density ratio of trade unionisation – that is to say, the proportion of the labour force organised in trade unions. This ratio had fallen from 45.2% in 1948 to 42.8% in 1967, thus reflecting the fact that the decline in manual union membership was more rapid than the increase in white collar unionisation (Price and Sayers Bain [1976]). By the end of the 1970s, however, the density had reached well over 50%. Two features of this growth should be stressed. First, the rate of growth in white collar unionisation outstripped the steady rate of growth in white collar employment. Hence by 1974, 36% of all union members were white collar employees compared with 26% ten years earlier. Secondly, the manual labour force fell 1.6m between 1964 and 1974 and although manual union membership also declined (by a smaller amount), manual union density rose from 52.9 to 57.8% over the decade – a level equalled only once before, in 1920 at the height of the short lived post-First World War boom in union membership (Price and Sayers Bain [1976], p. 345). The work of the CIR, the IR Act and its Code of Practice, and presumably ACAS and the Labour government's legislation, had all changed the recognition attitudes of employers during the 1970s.

This upsurge in middle-class militancy can also be gauged from the fact that an increasing number of white collar unions have somewhat reluctantly affiliated to the TUC. Although the total number of affiliates fell from 172 in 1965 to 112 in 1978, the number of white collar affiliates increased (TUC *Report*, 1965 and 1978). Most of the TUC's very large trade unions have a white collar membership.

Inter-union competition has been generated by the growth of white collar unionism and the recruitment opportunities afforded by this growth. As the decade opened, for example, the dust was settling on a confrontation between the largest union in the steel industry (ISTC) and two white collar unions which had detected recruitment possibilities in this re-nationalised industry. Moreover, management in the industry were encouraged to form their own union (Owen Smith [1971], pp. 42–3). Inter-union competition in steel was not confined to white collar workers. In 1975 the relatively small blastfurnacemen's union threatened a national official strike over the pay offered for operating a new generation of blastfurnaces, unofficial action having already taken place. The BSC claimed that it was constrained by the comparisons which would be generated among its other eighteen unions if the existing wage structure were disturbed. In 1979 both TGWU and ISTC members claimed jobs which were essential to the opening of the Hunterston ore terminal. There were also inter-industry comparisons. At the end of the 1970s, the ISTC was seeking the support of other steel unions for a national official stoppage in protest over the BSC's 2% offer as opposed to the miners' 20%.

Furthermore, it may appear that there are twenty-three unions in the engineering industry. However, quite apart from the relative insignificance of some of the smaller unions, each of the four major manual unions has its own white collar section. In addition there are two large, exclusively white collar unions (ASTMS and APEX).

A highly illustrative recognition issue of the 1970s is allied to the structural aspects of the engineering industry. It involved (throughout the 1970s) the United Kingdom Association of Professional Engineers (UKAPE), a body opposed to TUC affiliation. UKAPE was on one occasion in the early 1970s in alliance with two similar bodies representing scientists and executive engineers, but this survey concentrates on UKAPE as typical of a movement opposed to the TUC, until, that is, it decided to amalgamate with the electricians union in 1979. Matters were further complicated in the second half of the decade by the decision of the Electrical Power Engineers' Association (a TUC affiliate) to change its name to the Engineers' and Managers' Association (EMA) and commence recruitment and mergers which would allow it to extend beyond its traditional area of organising staff in the electricity supply to the engineering industry. All the existing unions in the industry belong to the TUC and are therefore subject to TUC's Bridlington rules which would result in their being brought before the TUC Disputes Committee if they recruited dissident members of another TUC union. UKAPE by its very nature could not recognise these rules. EMA successfully took legal action seeking to oblige ACAS to proceed with a recognition case irrespective of the progress and outcome of the TUC's deliberations in which it no longer had any confidence. ACAS was given leave to appeal to the Lords in 1979. At the time of writing (December 1979) the case had not yet been heard, but EMA had agreed to observe the TUC's rules.

Both the CIR and NIRC consistently refused to uphold UKAPE claims for recognition – on the grounds that this would result in fragmentation by increasing the number of small unions. ACAS followed a similar course to the CIR and NIRC, this time in respect of both UKAPE and EMA. But the High Court ruled in 1978 that ACAS must reconsider its advice that UKAPE be not recognised. The Court of Appeal upheld this judgement in early 1979. ACAS now reached the stage of exasperation outlined above.

A final inter-union episode of some note was when three of the four health service manual unions (COHSE, TGWU and GMWU) decided to accept the Government's pay offer during the 1979 dispute. NUPE found itself out-voted and was eventually obliged to also accept the offer and resume normal working.

Three aspects of trade union policy received increasing attention during the 1970s: strikes, the closed shop and picketing. As the decade opened, there were two conflicting views on whether Britain had a strike problem in terms of economic estimates. On the one hand, Robinson ([1972], pp. 300–1) suggested that although the trend had not markedly deteriorated during the 1960s, unofficial strikes had caused the public to conclude that there was a need for 'something to be done'. Turner ([1969], pp. 13–14 and 31–4) added that in some other countries (notably the USA on whose system the Conservatives' *Fair Deal at Work* was based) more working days per employee were lost on average through strike action than in Britain; machinery breakdowns and sickness caused greater output losses; and the more strike-prone sections of the British economy were not more backward in their rate of productivity growth. On the other hand, the Donovan Commission (para 415) had argued that the increase in both unofficial and, more particularly, unconstitutional strikes (i.e. in breach of procedure agreements) had serious economic implications and measures were needed to deal with them. These measures were principally concerned with reforming the bargaining system so that workplace relations could be more adequately controlled. Only a minority of strikes were fomented by irresponsible and subversive elements (para 475). Shonfield, in his Note of Reservation, went a stage further. He was convinced that *all* forms of industrial action, including strikes, would continue to be a necessary element of bargaining power. However, new legal powers were required to control this aspect of collective bargaining. He advocated, for example, the extension of the criminal penalties which could be imposed on employees in the gas, electricity and water industries if they engaged in lightning strikes. These provisions were repealed in the IR Act but then re-enacted so that most unofficial strikes became illegal. It was, however, the degree of support given to *official* strike action which was arguably more important. The miners' strikes of 1972 and 1974 were assisted by the refusal of lorry drivers and power workers to cross picket lines, while the defeat of the postmen in 1971 became more likely when the telephonists refused to co-operate (Burkitt and Bowers [1979], p. 15). Similarly, the largest production workers' union in the steel industry (ISTC) abandoned plans for an official national stoppage in 1979 when other unions declined to support its action over the threatened shutdown of the Corby and Shotton steel-making facilities. Support at the grass roots had been in any case sapped by the offered redundancy terms. Moreover, at the end of the decade there were a number of lock-outs. Employers were also considering a strike insurance scheme designed to compensate companies for the cost of strikes.

The growing concern with strikes, justified or otherwise, in the late 1960s and the 1970s led the Department of Employment to strengthen the empirical basis against which policy options could be evaluated. Its research team suggested that Britain's poor industrial relations image undermined the economy's internationally competitive position. Their carefully researched conclusion, based on existing data, was that British industry in general was not widely or continually affected by industrial action (Smith et al. [1978], pp. 3, 12 and 88).

It was pointed out above that the IR Act enacted the right not to belong to a union (and therefore effectively vetoed the closed shop) but that this was repealed by TULRA. However the framers of the IR Act were forced to modify their original intentions once they were made familiar with two potential anomalies. First, they modified their proposals so as to allow unions organising highly mobile groups of workers employed by small employers to continue with approved pre-entry closed shops. Hence the long-established traditions in shipping and acting were treated as exceptions. Secondly, a special register was created for the professional associations of doctors and nurses who, together with lawyers, could already practise lawful entry control. The National Union of Bank Employees was anxious to increase its membership and avoid competition from bank staff associations. It remained registered under the Act, despite the opprobrium with which its agency shop agreement was treated by other trade unions.

A traditional bargaining phenomenon was, therefore, made a legal issue during the 1970s. Total compulsion had not necessarily been practised by trade unions and management generally had no sympathy with free-riders (Weekes [1976], pp. 213, 216). There were thus two basic issues to be resolved. First, to distinguish between *eccentricity* and reasons of conscience for refusing to join a trade union. Secondly, to reconcile the unfair dismissal rights introduced in the 1970s with the old-style closed shop – a situation which the Labour government attempted to resolve by legislation which provided that a dismissal was fair when a person refused to comply with a closed shop agreement. This was to protect the employer from paying compensation to such persons. However, the Secretary of State wrote to the TUC in 1976 expressing disquiet about two persons being unfairly dismissed because they refused to join a trade union on religious grounds. The General Council of the TUC asked all affiliated to observe the law.

The Labour government and the TUC indicated in their concordat that five million of the twelve million trade unionists affiliated to the TUC were covered by closed shop agreements. Such a proportion would imply that closed shop agreements have remained stable in their coverage over the last twenty years; it was their growing formalisation into collective agreements which gave the impression of an increase. Further evidence of this growing formalisation – which occurred on a fairly dramatic scale between 1968 and 1977 – was reported by Gennard et al. ([1979], p. 1089). However, of the five million covered by closed shop agreements, only one million are subject to the pre-entry form and these workers are mainly in declining sectors such as printing and the docks. But in trying to reform the Fleet Street chapels, would-be reformers must avoid undermining the much more tenuous bargaining position of minority groups also operating pre-entry closed shops such as actors and musicians.

Public disquiet about the operation of some aspects of the closed shop, excited not least by the findings of the Leggatt report on the methods used during recruitment campaigns by one of the print unions (SLADE), undermined the work of the TUC's Review Committee on the operation of the closed shop. The Employment Bill contains proposals to extend the grounds on which dismissal for not belonging to a union would be unfair.

Because of the emotional and general political controversy surrounding picketing, it is necessary to emphasise that the law was *not*
markedly changed in the 1970s. The IR Act (section 134) and the
TULRA (section 15) were identical. Both left out the *Trade Disputes
Act 1906*'s inclusion of picketing at a person's home. It remained lawful
to attend at or a near a place for the purpose of peacefully obtaining
or communicating information. But this was not a right to picket!
It was merely an immunity from prosecution under other Acts and
the common law provided the police felt that the picketing was
'peaceful'.

During the 1972 miners' strike, the Saltley Coke depot was subjected to a mass picket. The IR Act had not come into operation
and in any case the police decided not to take any action. In 1974
the miners seemed to be more circumspect, while the 'Shrewsbury
Two' were disowned by many union leaders for physically assaulting
non-striking building workers in 1972. But the Courts passed a 'deter-
rent' sentence on a controversial criminal conspiracy charge and this
tended instead to convert them to *martyrs*. Moreover, in two other
cases brought under the IR Act (*Broome* and *Kavanagh*) the right to
address non-strikers was specifically denied by the police. This was
upheld in the Courts. Perhaps the serious secondary picketing during
the 1979 transport workers' strike, and the even more serious picketing
of some emergency services during the public workers and health
service strike in the same year, indicated a learning curve effect: trade
unionists in capital-intensive industries had gained a bargaining advantage by their ability to turn out the lights or stop the trains. Slightly
more slowly acting but ultimately equally disruptive tactics were
available to fellow trade unionists in the more labour-intensive sectors.

So much pressure built up on the subject of picketing that it was
inevitable that the Labour government–TUC concordat would contain advice on the subject. Affiliated unions were advised in general,
'and save in exceptional circumstances', to confine picketing to the
premises of the parties to the dispute or the premises of suppliers or
customers of those parties. The 1979 Employment Bill proposes to
define more strictly the place of work. Picketing would be confined
to this place of work and those involved in a trade dispute and their
union officials. Both measures are designed to reduce secondary
picketing. Employers will otherwise be able to sue for damages,
assuming that they can identify the pickets, define the place of work,
and avoid creating martyrs from amongst a fairly willing minority.

Conclusion

It has been seen that trade unions exist as collective entities to further the interests of their members. Their bargaining power is of fundamental importance in this objective. The three aspects of their bargaining power which excited considerable attention during the 1970s were strikes, the closed shop and picketing. All three of these phenomena are complex and even though the introduction of more legislation has often been advocated, the experience of litigation in the 1970s and the virtually unknown state of many aspects of the present law, give such advocacy a hollow ring. The problems – where they are not exaggerated – are unfortunately more deep seated and economic in character to be resolved by simply passing laws. Compulsory union membership and picket lines are of the essence of unionism (Olson [1974], p. 71). Collective bargaining was characterised, as were other economic policy prescriptions, by severe oscillations when new governments took office. In the case of collective bargaining the degree of immunity was the controversial issue.

On the other hand, there is agreement that further reform of collective bargaining is needed. A broad measure of agreement exists on the need for third party intervention. The progress made in this respect during the 1970s, along with the wider introduction of written procedures, indicate a degree of progress which must not be underestimated. A *further* increase in secret ballots and a more rigorous interpretation of the codes similar to those contained in the concordat on the closed shop and picketing would seem to be desirable further aims. To enact these codes in legal form, even given the general political will, appears to be a formidable undertaking unless a complete re-appraisal of the British legal system is envisaged. In short the 1970s have proved to be very instructive, but it remains to be seen whether the parties to the collective bargaining system have learned any further lessons.

References

Burkitt, B. and Bowers, D. [1979], *Trade Unions and the Economy.* London: Macmillan.
Crouch, C. [1979], *The Politics of Industrial Relations.* Glasgow: Fontana.
Donovan Report [1968], Royal Commission on Trade Unions and Employers' Associations 1965–8, *Report*, HMSO. (Most of the Evidence and Research Papers were also published by HMSO).
Dickens, L. [1978/9], 'Unfair dismissal applications and the industrial tribunal system', *Industrial Relations Journal*, Winter 1978/9, pp. 4–18.

Gennard, J. et al. [1979], 'The content of British closed shop agreements', *Department of Employment Gazette*, November 1979, pp. 1088–92.

Gospel, H. [1976], 'Disclosure of information to trade unions', *Industrial Law Journal*, Vol. 5, no. 4, pp. 223–6.

Gospel, H. [1978], 'The disclosure of information to trade unions: approaches and problems', *Industrial Relations Journal*, Autumn 1978, pp. 18–26.

Hunter, L. C. [1977], 'Economic issues in conciliation and arbitration', *British Journal of Industrial Relations*, Vol. XV, no. 2, pp. 226–45.

Jackson, D., Turner, H. A. and Wilkinson, F. [1975], *Do Trade Unions Cause Inflation?*, 2nd edn., Cambridge: Cambridge University Press.

Jenkins, C. and Sherman, B. [1977], *Collective Bargaining*. London: Routledge and Kegan Paul.

Kahn-Freund, O. [1979], *Labour Relations: Heritage and Adjustment*. Oxford: Oxford University Press.

Lewis, N. [1974], 'Con-Mech: showdown for the NIRC', *Industrial Law Journal*, Vol. 3, no. 4, pp. 201–14.

McCarthy, W. E. J. and Ellis, N. D. [1973], *Management by Agreement*. London: Hutchinson.

Moran, M. [1977], *The Politics of Industrial Relations*. London: Macmillan.

Olson, M. [1974], *The Logic of Collective Action*. Harvard University Press.

Owen Smith, E. [1971], *Productivity Bargaining*. London: Pan Books.

Phelps Brown, E. H. [1973], 'New wine in old bottles: reflections on the changed working of collective bargaining in Great Britain', *British Journal of Industrial Relations*, Vol. XI, no. 3, pp. 329–37.

Price, R. and Sayers Bain, G. [1976], 'Union growth revisited: 1948–1974 in perspective', *British Journal of Industrial Relations*, Vol. XIV, no. 3, pp. 339–55.

Prior, J. [1979], 'Some reflections on industrial relations', *Industrial Relations Journal*, Vol. 10, no. 3, pp. 9–11.

Robinson, D. [1972], in Beckerman, W. (ed.) *The Labour Government's Economic Record 1964–1970*. London: Duckworth.

Smith, C. T. B. et al. [1978], 'Strikes in Britain', *Manpower Paper* no. 15. London: Department of Employment.

Thomson, A. W. J. and Engleman, S. R. [1975], *The Industrial Relations Act*. London: Martin Robertson.

Turner, H. A. [1969], 'Is Britain really strike-prone?', *Occasional Paper* no. 20. Cambridge: Cambridge University Press.

Ulman, L. [1968], in Caves, R. E. (ed.), *Britain's Economic Prospects*. London: Allen and Unwin, pp. 332–5.

Weekes, B. et al. [1975], *Industrial Relations and the Limits of the Law*. Oxford: Blackwell's.

Weekes, B. [1976], 'Law and practice of the closed shop', *The Industrial Law Journal*, Vol. 5, no. 4, pp. 211–22.

Wood, J. [1979], 'The Central Arbitration Committee', *Department of Employment Gazette*, January 1979, pp. 9–11.

6 Industrial Policy

by Michael C. Fleming

Introduction

The term 'industrial policy' does not define an area of policy with well-defined objectives and correspondingly well-defined policy instruments. Rather it embraces a variety of different measures taken by governments to control or influence the structure or the conduct and, ultimately, the economic performance of industry. It would be more appropriate, therefore, to refer to industrial 'policies' rather than industrial 'policy'.

The development of such policies in the 1970s must be viewed against the background of Britain's economic performance and the ideological disposition of the political party in power. An outstanding feature in this period has been the extent to which both Conservative and Labour governments have adopted policies involving direct industrial intervention. At the same time, however, there has been no political consensus about the desirability of microeconomic intervention, let alone the kind of policy measures that should be taken. Labour governments, of course, are more disposed towards *dirigiste* policies involving a greater degree of economic planning and state control over industry. Conservative governments are naturally much less politically predisposed to adopt active interventionist policies and indeed were returned to power in 1970 and 1979 committed to policies of 'disengagement'. The Heath government of 1970-4, however, changed direction in this respect in 1972, half way through its term of office. The Thatcher government elected in May 1979 has moved quickly to put its policies into effect but how steadfast and how successful it will prove to be remains to be seen.

In the context of Britain's economic performance, industrial intervention must be seen as a response to a persistent failure to achieve the major objectives of economic policy (see the introduction to this work) by conventional macroeconomic policy measures. Thus while the ends of economic policy remain the same, the means used to pursue

them have been expanded to embrace micro, as well as macro, policy
instruments. The salient features of British economic performance in
the 1970s were a slow rate of economic growth, a high rate of inflation,
successive balance of payments crises and increasing difficulty in maintaining a high level of employment. At the industrial level these
problems were reflected in a slow rate of productivity increase which
has done little to offset underlying inflationary pressures or to improve
the price competitiveness of British goods on the international market.
Despite the floating of the pound, Britain's share of world trade in
manufactures fell (from 10.8 to 9.5%) between 1970 and 1978; import
penetration increased (from 17 to 25% of home demand) and the
manufacturing sector of the economy declined (from 37 to 32% of
total employment) – so-called 'de-industrialisation'.

The response of governments to these problems at the industrial
level has been to intervene in a variety of ways. Broadly speaking,
however, these may be grouped into two categories. First are those
policies which are aimed directly or indirectly at the improvement
of industry's efficiency and hence competitiveness; this must be
regarded as the main thrust of government policies and certainly their
main justification. Policies within this first group embrace competition
policy, policies aimed at influencing the structure of industry, general
and selective schemes of financial assistance and science and technology policy. Within the second group are policies which are much
less concerned with general efficiency considerations but represent
intervention measures, very often *ad hoc* in nature, aimed at alleviating
the problems of particular industries or rescuing particular firms in
financial difficulties. Government action here is motivated as much
by political and social considerations related to unemployment, particularly when it is likely to be concentrated in certain areas. Needless
to say, perhaps not all policy measures can be neatly categorised in
this way: there is an inevitable degree of overlap. It is also the case
that some policy measures taken for different reasons come into
conflict.

Given the nature of the policies towards industry adopted during
the 1970s it is not intended to consider their development in a strict
chronological sequence. A more coherent treatment may be provided
by taking each area of policy in turn. We consider first the various
measures of selective intervention developed during the period.
Secondly, we examine the operation and development of competition
policy – a continuing arm of policy. Finally we turn to various sub-

sidiary areas of policy including science and technology, small firms and industrial finance. It is emphasised at this stage that the scope of this chapter is confined to policy towards the private industrial sector.

Selective Intervention

In contrast to policies aimed at revitalising the 'invisible hand' of competition, governments of the 1970s, mainly but not solely Labour governments, have been increasingly involved with the preservation and support of individual industries or firms. Despite the commitment of the Conservative Party to market solutions to industrial problems and withdrawal from government involvement, experience in government in the 1970s showed that in particular circumstances it was prepared to intervene.

The Conservatives' period of office from 1970 to 1974 divides into two separate periods with the year 1972 marking a clear change in direction. In 1970 the incoming Conservative government proceeded to dismantle the previous Labour government's apparatus. The previous Labour government, following the collapse of its National Plan (an attempt at indicative planning) had developed instruments of a more direct interventionist kind. First it established the Industrial Reorganisation Corporation (IRC) to bring about industrial 'rationalisation' or reorganisation by encouraging mergers which were thought to be justified on the grounds of economies of scale, better management and improved international competitive strength. Secondly it took powers (*Industrial Expansion Act 1968*) to finance investment schemes in industry selectively without the need to enact separate legislation each time. Both of these key elements of Labour policy were quickly reversed by the Heath administration. The IRC was abolished early in 1971 and key sections of the Industrial Expansion Act were repealed. John Davies, the Secretary of State for Trade and Industry, talked (in a celebrated expression) of not gearing policy to 'lame ducks'. The policy was quickly put to the test, however, in the face of two major financial crises affecting Upper Clyde Shipbuilders (UCS) and the Rolls-Royce Company, the response to which marked the beginnings of a 'U-turn' on industrial policy. In brief, the outcome of the UCS case, after the Government had initially refused financial aid, was the formation of a new company (Govan Shipbuilders) out of three constituent yards – and an injection of

£35m from public funds. The Rolls-Royce crisis, brought about by technical difficulties in the development of the RB211 engine within the constraint of a fixed price contract in highly inflationary times, led to an even more unexpected outcome in the nationalisation of the company's aero-engine division. The common factor in these two episodes, it may be noted, was the unemployment that would have been the immediate consequence of non-intervention (the notable response of workers in the UCS case had been to occupy the shipyards). Unemployment was to become the focus of much of the industrial intervention that was to follow through the 1970s. The Conservative U-turn was completed with the introduction of the *Industry Act 1972*. Apart from regional provisions (see Chapter 7), this enabled the Government to provide selective financial assistance (up to £5m without parliamentary approval) and to acquire share or loan capital in an assisted firm. An Industrial Development Advisory Board (and a system of regional boards) were established to advise on the exercise of these new powers; a new Minister for Industrial Development was appointed and an Industrial Development Executive (IDE) was set up to administer the policy. We consider the legislation further in the context of the use made of it by the 1974–9 Labour government in the section about 'selective financial aids'.

Under the Act a substantial number of firms and industries received financial assistance (see Tables 6.1 and 6.2). The most succinct statement of the aims of government support at this time may be found in the report of the Trade and Industry Sub-committee of the House of Commons Expenditure Committee, namely 'the need to maintain international competitiveness; defence requirements; the balance of payments; the maintenance of an industry considered nationally essential; the special difficulties of advanced technology industries or projects; and social needs, especially the need to maintain employment' (HCP 347 [1971/2]). Needless to say, perhaps, disentangling the relative importance of these justifications for support in particular cases is not so easy. But the essential point in the present context is that it gave the government very wide powers indeed. They were described by Anthony Wedgwood Benn (Industry Minister in the succeeding Labour government) as 'the most comprehensive armoury of government control that has ever been assembled for use over private industry' (quoted in Smith [1979], p. 166), and were subsequently used by him in that office with some gusto. In summary,

Table 6.1   Aid administered under 1972 Industry Act, 1972–9
(position as at February–March 1979)

Type of aid	1972–4 (Conservative government)	1974 to February–March 1979 (Labour government)
General section 8 aid allocated to individual companies or projects, often as 'lame-duck' rescues, in grants, guarantees, loans, equity	£395m offered over the two periods including £180m to BL (which also receives NEB aid), £82m to Chrysler and £5m to Meriden co-op	
Special aid for the shipbuilding industry	£282m committed. Approximately £720m offered	
Section 8 sectoral schemes now closed for applications covering clothing, electronic components, ferrous and non-ferrous foundries, instrumentation, machine tools, paper and board, poultry and meat processing,[b] printing and textile machinery, and wool textiles	Nil	£266m aid available £71m aid spent out of £242m offered to 2604 projects costing a total of £1.1bn
Section 8 sectoral schemes still open for applications covering drop forging, footwear, micro-electronics,[a] and red meat slaughterhouses[b]	Nil	£100m aid available £1.4m aid spent out of £11.4m offered to 230 projects costing a total of £75m
Section 8 general scheme, called accelerated projects, now closed for applications	Nil	£100m aid available £36.6m spent out of £72.3m offered to 113 projects costing a total of £627m
Section 8 general schemes still open for applications including selective investment scheme, product and process development[a], energy conservation, and micro-processor application[a]	Nil	£250m aid available £3m spent out of £99m offered to 916 projects costing a total of £840m

Source: *Financial Times*, 15 May 1979.
[a] Funded wholly or in part under *Science and Technology Act 1965*.
[b] Introduced by the Ministry of Agriculture.

Table 6.2   Government expenditure on industry from 1970/1 to 1978/9

	£m at 1975 survey prices				£m at 1978 survey prices					
	1970/1	1971/2	1972/3	1973/4	1973/4	1974/5	1975/6	1976/7	1977/8	1978/9
Industrial innovation										
General industrial R and D	32.1	29.0	28.0	30.8	50	51	51	44	41	51
Department of Energy non-nuclear R & D	n.a.	n.a.	n.a.	n.a.	2	3	9	13	18	24
Technological and industrial sponsorship	6.2	2.3	4.8	4.4						
Aircraft and aeroengine general										
R and D programme	14.9	14.1	18.1	19.7	38	33	26	23	20	17
Concorde – development	103.8	93.9	69.7	49.5	81	73	58	32	25	21
production	12.0	22.5	37.1	44.4	71	60	52	28	24	19
RB211	20.9	104.8	68.5	25.0	43	88	-3	12	-6	29
Other aircraft and aeroengine projects and assistance	44.4	32.2	-2.1	39.2	31	29	93	—	5	45
Space	11.7	12.0	11.0	13.9	24	30	34	40	35	33
Nuclear	82.1	73.8	72.2	82.2	126	115	139	157	114	120
Total	328.1	384.6	307.3	309.1	465	482	459	348	275	358
General support for industry										
National Enterprise Board[a]	—	—	—	—	—	—	12	158	368	70
Selective assistance to individual industries, firms and undertakings	—	—	8.8	15.8	32	35	423	105	59	225
Promotion of tourism	10.1	17.4	24.4	42.3	63	30	22	20	20	23
Refinancing of home shipbuilding lending	—	—	78.2	135.7	207	174	152	88	-98	10
Interest support costs of home shipbuilding lending	—	—		47	57	43	54	28	33
Assistance to the shipbuilding industry	0.6	7.3	18.6	24.5	28	63	36	15	33	30
Other support services	34.0	-27.2	-26.5	-22.2	-31	-13	1	—	8	2
Investment grants	808.2	635.4	384.3	233.2	416	173	82	26	6	2
Total	852.9	632.9	487.8	429.3	762	520	771	466	427	396

Sources: Public Expenditure White Papers: Cmnd 6393 and Cmnd 7439. London: HMSO.
[a] Figures are in money terms and not at constant prices.

the significance of the period of the Heath administration from 1970–4 is that true to its political principles it set out to reduce intervention in the private sector of industry (it also hived off certain peripheral parts of the public sector – see Maunder [1979]), but it ended up facing the other way. As Mottershead concludes in his survey of the period, 'In some ways the legitimacy, and indeed the inevitability, of government intervention in the private sector was reinforced.' ([1978] p. 421).

The actual industrial policies followed by Labour governments from 1974 often reflect opposing schools of thought within the party. When in opposition from 1970–4 it is true to say that the forces of the Left in the party had the greater influence. Many of the more radical proposals (including the extension of public ownership to manufacturing industry) had been watered down by the time of the February 1974 election, however. The main industrial proposals in the manifesto were for the nationalisation of ports, shipbuilding and aircraft, a series of planning agreements to be made between the major firms and the government (rather than a full-scale national plan on the 1965 model) and, thirdly, the establishment of a National Enterprise Board.

Planning agreements and the National Enterprise Board
These proposals were set out in a White Paper, *The Regeneration of British Industry* (Cmnd 5710 [1974]) and effected in the *Industry Act 1975*. The idea behind the development of Planning Agreements had its root partly in the failure of planning in the 1960s, one cause of which, it was felt, was the lack of effective contact between the government on the one hand and actual firms on the other. The planning agreement system was envisaged as meeting this deficiency by providing for consultation between the government and individual companies leading to an agreement about strategic plans relating to investment, exports, output and employment, etc. They were also seen, incidentally, as a vehicle for furthering 'industrial democracy' in the planning of company strategy: it was envisaged that union representatives would have the right to take part in consultations and to receive all the necessary information. The question of how the plans in such agreements were to be put into effect received less attention within the party than the question of whether the agreements themselves were to be voluntary or compulsory, the issue finally being settled in favour of the Right of the party by making them voluntary. The idea itself remained essentially vague, especially as regards its implica-

tions for the conduct of companies in practice despite the publication of a separate discussion paper (DOI [1975]). In the event virtually nothing came of the idea – only one planning agreement was ever concluded in the private sector (with the ill-fated Chrysler Motor Company).

The National Enterprise Board (NEB) was originally conceived in opposition (Labour Party [1973]) as a state holding company which would 'introduce public ownership into the strongholds of private industry'. It was envisaged that it should have powers of compulsory purchase and should quickly take over 20–25 of the largest manufacturing companies. In the event, however, the *Industry Act 1975* provided for a much less powerful interventionist body. As in the case of planning agreements, there were to be no compulsory powers and there was no mention of the takeover of top firms. In brief, the functions of the Board were to control and manage existing government shareholdings; to extend public ownership into *profitable* manufacturing industry by the acquisition of shares – such holdings normally to be acquired with the agreement of the company's board – and to act as a source of advice for companies in difficulties. It could also make loans to companies or enter into joint ventures. A natural question of some contention within the government, and of some concern to industry, related to the commercial criteria on which NEB holdings were to be operated – whether commercial rates of return should be required or whether losses or below-normal rates of return should be permitted 'in the national interest' (as those on the Left of the party wished). This was settled in detailed *Guidelines* (DOI [1977]) covering this and other operational matters: commercial rates of return were required and acquisition of more than 30% of the equity of a company or expenditure of £10m required government approval. In sum, the NEB which eventually came into being was only a shadow of the one that was originally envisaged, the key elements being the lack of compulsory powers and the general requirement (except when government directed otherwise) to earn an adequate rate of return on its assets. This latter provision settled the concern of the European Commission that NEB assistance might confer an artificial advantage on some firms: only in the cases of government direction does the Commission need to be notified in advance; otherwise the submission of an annual report meets the Commission's requirements (see Chapter 11).

In the period up to the 1979 election, its influence had been limited.

Most of its resources had been tied up in the companies whose share-holdings were transferred to it by the government – mainly acquired as a result of rescue operations – the most notable being British Leyland, Rolls-Royce, Ferranti and Alfred Herbert. These companies have continued to experience difficulties and have absorbed a great deal of NEB loan finance. The extent of its activity in other areas may be gauged from the fact that its other acquisitions remained few and small (thirty-eight companies at a cost of £45m) by September 1978 and that only 3% of total loans outstanding at this time were for non-transferee companies. In general, therefore, the NEB played little more than a peripheral role, although it absorbed almost a third of total government expenditure on general aid to industry over the period from 1975/6 to 1978/9 – £608m out of £2060m at 1978 prices (see Table 6.2).

The Conservative government that returned to office in 1979, whilst not abolishing the NEB (as had been anticipated), has further reduced its role. The greater part of the NEB portfolio is to be sold as circum-stances permit (£100m target in the year 1979/80) and its powers of acquisition and investment are to be restricted. The residual role envisaged for the Board is largely as a nursery, first for the companies in its portfolio with continuing difficulties 'so long as the business concern had a prospect of viability and no solution based on the private sector was available', secondly 'for newly-established high technology companies (chiefly concerned with computer softwear, micro-electronics and their applications) in which the NEB had in-vested, until they too could be sold. It was also envisaged as having a regional policy role to play with regard to investment in small firms in the North and Northwest of England. At the time of writing (December 1979) a new Industry Bill to bring the policy into effect is passing through Parliament. In the meantime, however, friction between the NEB and the Board of Rolls-Royce has led to responsi-bility for that company being transferred to the DOI (a step which precipitated the resignation of the entire NEB board). Transfer of responsibility for British Leyland to the DOI also is being mooted. These two companies represent the major part of the NEB holdings.

The new industrial strategy

The third important arm of the 1974–9 Labour government's policy not so far discussed was the so-called 'Industrial Strategy'. Given the extent to which planning agreements and the NEB as they finally emerged were downgraded as instruments of policy, the main thrust had to come from elsewhere. Initially great use was made on a purely *ad hoc* basis of the powers given in the Conservatives' *Industry Act 1972*. Financial assistance was given to aid specific industries or projects; these are considered further below. At the same time considerable controversy was aroused by the action of the Secretary of State for Industry (Anthony Wedgwood Benn) in making finance available against the advice of the Industrial Development Advisory Board (established to advise on commercial viability) to support groups of workers who took over firms to run them as workers co-operatives.[1] These actions did much to polarise feeling and led in mid 1975 to the replacement of Mr Benn as Secretary of State for Industry and to the beginnings of an attempt at a new tripartite (management–labour–government) approach to industry problems based on agreement rather than compulsion.

Following a meeting of the NEDC at Chequers in November 1975 came a new White Paper, *An Approach to Industrial Strategy* (Cmnd 6315 [1975]). After a summary of the reasons for the country's poor performance (see the Introduction to this volume) proposals were put forward in which the Government was at pains to stress the need for a realistic and flexible framework in which a strategy could be developed. Essential elements were seen as a better co-ordination of government policies affecting industry (especially in the light of information feedback from companies via planning agreements etc.); the more effective use of the instruments of industrial policy and the deployment of financial assistance to industry (planning agreements and NEB were mentioned in this context); sufficient return on investment in both public and private sectors as a foundation and spur to·investment and innovation (the Price Code was relaxed in 1976), and a more effective manpower policy (particular importance was attached here to the recently-formed Manpower Services Commission – see Chapter 4).

Rejecting the possibility of a new national plan, an alternative was envisaged in which plans were developed in the context of a two-way flow of information between the government and individual industries within the context of government economic projections. In its turn government policy would be influenced by the information flowing up. The Economic Development Committees (EDCs) under the NEDC were seen as the machinery for this purpose. The Government also referred to the possibility of a sector-by-sector analysis to identify those sectors 'most important for achieving our economic objectives'. But in the event the course adopted was more indiscriminate. As Shanks [1977] pointed out, the intention of 'backing winners' and allowing 'losers' to fend for themselves was 'easier said than done at a time when there was general concern about employment levels and when government confidence in its ability actually to identify "winners" was less than complete'. No more striking example of this could have been given than the financial collapse of the Chrysler car company within a few weeks of the Chequers meeting which led the Government to provide £160m in the face of the prospect of 17 000 men directly unemployed and many more indirectly even though the CPRS Report [1975] published on the very same day as the rescue was announced, had indicated that Chrysler's commercial viability was doubtful.

For practical purposes the outcome was the establishment of thirty-nine Sector Working Parties (SWPs) under the aegis of NEDC. Each SWP has produced reports covering market share objectives and possible ways and means of meeting them including detailed attention to questions of capacity constraints, marketing, product development, productivity, etc. for communication to the government. Findings and recommendations are also supposed to be filtered down to the management and workforce of the companies in each sector where it is hoped they will bear fruit. At present a balanced assessment of the effectiveness of their work is almost impossible to make. Whether or not this type of highly detailed institutionalised micro approach will prove to have a lasting role to play beyond the short-term exigencies to which they have been the response remains to be seen. Certainly the question of whether or not it offers the best mechanism for maximising the country's productive potential and competitive strength internationally in the longer term is debatable. The danger is that such institutionalised attempts at problem-solving embracing the representatives of existing interests become too preoccupied with the existing organisation and pattern of production and devote little or no attention to the dynamic springs of progress (indeed they may be tempted to obstruct them) of the kind so eloquently expounded by Schumpeter [1943].

Selective financial aids

The 'new industrial strategy' was meant to provide a systematic approach to the improvement of industry's productivity and competitiveness at the most detailed micro level. Perhaps of necessity, however, it has remained essentially ephemeral and in the face of continuing and mounting problems of unemployment it is not surprising that governments have continued to respond by direct intervention of a more immediate and obvious kind. A great variety of assistance schemes proliferated in bewildering profusion throughout the 1970s under the *Industry Act 1972* and under subsequent legislation relating more specifically to employment protection and employment subsidies. The latter are dealt with separately in Chapter 4; our attention here is confined to the general (non-regional) industry aid schemes under the *Industry Act 1972*.

Section 8 of the Act provided the government with *general* powers to provide financial assistance to industry in the 'national interest' and 'likely to benefit the economy of the United Kingdom'. As noted earlier, these powers were used extensively by the Labour government from 1974 onwards and were widened still further by it in the *Industry Act 1975* by removing the requirement for the government to show a lack of existing private sector support. Assistance could be given on any terms or conditions and in any form – by grant, guarantee, loan or the acquisition of equity – and could be used to tailor assistance to the needs, as they were seen, of particular industries or industrial 'sectors', or to particular firms or for a particular purpose (e.g. a specific project or product). Apart from aid directed to individual companies a large number of 'sectoral' aid schemes were developed with the general aim of encouraging modernisation and rationalisation together with certain more generalised schemes. The 'Accelerated Project Scheme' was introduced in April 1975 as a counter-cyclical measure to encourage firms to bring forward investment projects in the recession and a successor 'Selective Investment Scheme' was introduced in December 1976 with a financial allocation of £100m (later increased) to promote investment projects which will 'through improved performance, yield significant benefits to the economy' but would not take place without government assistance. Special schemes were also developed to encourage the adoption of micro-electronics technology and energy conservation measures. A summary of the schemes and the aid provided is set out in Table 6.1. The election of a Conservative government in 1979 committed to non-intervention and the reduction of public expenditure might be thought to signal the end of these schemes; it is true that cut-backs have been made but the schemes have not been eliminated. Particular importance has been attached by the new Secretary of State (Sir Keith Joseph) to the use of selective aid to attract 'internationally mobile' investment projects into the UK, and to the desirability of support being available for 'high technology' developments such as microprocessors.

Competition Policy

Competition is generally regarded as a major force in promoting efficiency in production and encouraging innovation in products and production processes and must play a central role in any policy concerned with the performance of industry in a market economy. The term 'competition policy' is used as an omnibus expression to refer to separate policies relating to monopolies, mergers and restrictive business practices. British policy in this area was developed in stages – by both Conservative and Labour governments in a substantially bipartisan approach – over the postwar period and by 1970 its essential features had already been firmly established. Briefly these were that monopolies (defined as situations where at least one-third of the supply or processing of goods was in the hands of one firm or group of firms) and mergers that created or enhanced a monopoly situation (or if the value of assets taken over exceeded £5m) could be referred to the Monopolies Commission (MC) for investigation. It was the task of the MC to decide whether the monopoly situation or the behaviour of the firm(s) operated or could be expected to operate against the public interest and likewise whether a proposed merger was likely to operate *against* the public interest. Subsequent action, which was solely at the discretion of the Minister, could involve the dissolution of the monopoly, or the regulation of its future conduct, and the prevention of the merger. Unlike monopolies and mergers, restrictive practices, operated by agreement amongst otherwise independent firms to fix prices and regulate production and marketing of *goods*, were in general presumed to be against the public interest, but the parties to such agreements could argue a case for exemption before the Restrictive Practices Court on certain specific grounds defined in the law. No such presumption applied to the supply of commercial and professional *services*, but they could be investigated (under 1965 legislation) selectively by the MC.

Of the three elements of competition policy there is no doubt that restrictive practices policy has made the greatest contribution towards increasing competition but the effects of this policy were mostly felt in the period before 1970. Case studies of the effects of the legislation have shown that it certainly operated in the ways expected, bringing about price reductions in some cases and contributing towards improved efficiency and technical innovation (Swann et al. [1974]). Since 1970 the major issues in this area have related to the enforcement of the legislation and the enlargement of its scope. A major development has been its extension in the *Fair Trading Act 1973* to make commercial services subject to the restrictive practices regime, but at the time of writing (December 1979) no cases had been heard by the Court. The 1973 Act also transferred responsibility for the registration of agreements and enforcement of the law to the Director General of Fair Trading (DGFT) – a new office created by the Act – but did nothing to deal with the difficulty which had been faced by his predecessor of detecting unregistered agreements.

Another issue is the extent to which various types of uncompetitive practice have escaped control. These were discussed in an official review of policy set up by the Labour government in 1978 (Cmnd 7512 [1979]) and this has now been followed by proposals in a Competition Bill introduced by the incoming Conservative government in 1979 to enable the DGFT to investigate and control such activities or to refer them to the Monopolies and Mergers Commission – the Monopolies Commission as renamed in 1973 – (MMC). As far as the improvement of competitive forces is concerned, therefore, the developments represent prospective rather than actual improvements. During the 1970s the main thrust has come from the enforcement of the existing legislation. Despite the detection difficulties referred to above, a number of unregistered agreements in important industries have been uncovered and terminated.[2]

Before turning to the other arms of competition policy it is important to note a counter argument. There is not universal agreement that the removal of restrictive agreements has been wholly beneficial. To the extent to which this is the case, then the failings of British industry may be held to have arisen, at least in part, because of, rather than in spite of, the operation of restrictive practices policy. It has been suggested, for instance, that the decline in the profitability of British industry in the 1960s (a decline which continued into the 1970s) could be attributed to some extent to the operation of the policy and that this in turn had a deleterious effect on industrial investment. Statistical studies by O'Brien et al. [1979], however, indicate that profitability was not seriously impaired ('or its instability increased') by the opera-

tion of competition policy. It has also been argued (NEDO [1978])
that competition may work to ensure not the survival of the most
efficient firms but rather those who are simply financially strong and
the case is advanced for co-operation rather than competition, especially in the context of the then Labour government's 'industrial
strategy' (see above). The main danger of co-operative agreements,
of course, is that they in themselve do nothing to improve efficiency
and may sooner or later do the reverse. British experience in the past
would bear witness to this view (Swann et al. [1974]). However,
agreements are not banned *per se*. The restrictive practices legislation
does provide for the exemption of agreements with demonstrable
benefits for the economy and consumers.

We turn now to policy towards market dominance as operated via
monopoly and merger policies. We examine merger policy first. It
is fair to say that the 1970s were notable for the concern aroused
by the high level of industrial concentration achieved in much of
British industry, by its continued growth and especially by the contribution made by an unprecedented merger 'boom' that occurred
from the 1960s into the early 1970s. By 1970 the 100 largest firms
accounted for about 40% of manufacturing net output (Prais [1976])
and high levels of concentration had been reached in a substantial
number of separate markets. It also appeared that concentration in
British industry was higher than in the USA, West Germany and
other industrialised countries (Cmnd 7198 [1978]). The attitude of
successive governments towards mergers has been essentially benign
reflecting the view that there were benefits to be gained in terms of
economies of scale and better management and that larger size improved a company's strength on international markets.

No changes in merger policy took place during the 1970s but disquiet over the effects of mergers and the operation of policy grew.
From 1965 (when merger legislation was enacted) to the end of 1978,
1791 mergers *qualified* for reference to the MMC but of these only
53 were in fact referred – just under 3%. The vast majority of mergers,
therefore, have been allowed to proceed without investigation – other
than a brief informal screening carried out by the Mergers Panel (a
non-statutory inter-departmental group of civil servants chaired by
the DGFT) which advises the Secretary of State, whose prerogative
it is to decide whether or not to make a reference. Thus references
remain essentially political decisions and it is reported that the advice
of the Mergers Panel is not always followed. The burden of responsi-

bility and work that thus falls on the Mergers Panel is considerable: the number of mergers that have to be screened has risen consistently each year from 1970, almost trebling in the period to 1978 when they exceeded 200 (Graham [1979]). The vast majority of these mergers have been horizontal mergers in which the dangers of increased market power are greater than in the case of vertical or diversified mergers. For its part the MMC in judging the public interest in particular cases has been bound by the legislation which has required it to decide whether or not the merger operated or could be expected to operate against the public interest rather than show positive net benefits. The disquiet has been intensified further by a number of studies of the post-merger performance of firms which have shown that most mergers have not proved economically beneficial – post-merger profitability is shown to have declined and efficiency gains do not seem to have been realised (see Singh [1971]; Utton [1974]; Meeks [1977]; and the discussion in Cmnd 7198 [1978]).

Perhaps the most that can be said for merger policy as it has operated during the 1970s is that it may have been beneficial to the extent that some detrimental mergers may have been prevented. In the light of the economic evidence, many now argue that policy has not been forceful enough and that reforms are necessary. The review body on policy set up by the Labour government has recommended that policy should be shifted to a 'neutral' position (in contrast to the present favourable attitude) by ensuring that all mergers that have a significant effect on competition or economic power receive more critical attention (Cmnd 7198 [1978]). These recommendations, however, are still under review. The evidence on the effects of mergers naturally also prompts the question of whether or not it would be desirable for some of them to be reversed. This raises questions about monopoly policy, to which we now turn, but it is interesting to note that late in 1979 the new Conservative government set in train an inquiry into the obstacles which confront firms wishing to 'de-merge' with a view to making it as easy as possible for firms to do so voluntarily.

The prosecution of monopoly policy during the 1970s showed no significant change. It has had no direct effect on concentration, for dissolution has never been recommended by the Commission (though it may have had indirect effects inasmuch as some firms may have been deterred from growing beyond the market share criterion for fear of provoking a reference to the MMC). Its main focus has remained, as before, on uncompetitive activities of firms. The Labour government in 1970 had planned to strengthen the law in this area; its proposals came to nothing because of its defeat in that year but many of them were carried forward by the incoming Conservative government in the *Fair Trading Act 1973*. This strengthened policy in a number of ways. The criterion for a monopoly reference to the Commission was widened from a one-third market share to one-quarter and the Commission itself was enabled to concentrate its attention on specific issues in contrast to its normal wide-ranging monopoly inquiries. The scope of the law was also widened to bring oligopoly situations within its scope by defining a new category of so-called 'complex monopoly' situation, i.e. situations where several firms behave in such a way as to restrict competition but without entering into a registrable agreement under the restrictive practices legislation. In practice, however, this provision proved difficult to operate. A further significant change was a revision of the public interest criteria so that for the first time they referred to competition as the means of achieving the ends of efficiency and technical progress. A major institutional change was also made by the establishment of an Office of Fair Trading headed by the DGFT, (referred to earlier) with the responsibility of monitoring industrial developments on a wide front including competitive and non-competitive practices, negotiating undertakings with firms about their behaviour and with the power to make references of monopoly (but not merger) situations to the MMC and to refer trading practices to a new Consumer Protection Advisory Committee (CPAC) (see below). A fuller description of the Fair Trading Act in the context of previous policy will be found in Fleming [1974].

Looking at the effect of monopoly policy during the 1970s, it is difficult to conclude that it has had a significant influence in creating a more competitive environment and improving efficiency. Little distinction can be made between the attitudes of successive Conservative and Labour governments in the period either with regard to the making of references to the MMC (indeed after 1973 this was largely the independent responsibility of the DGFT) or to the action that has followed adverse findings by it. The number of references increased significantly during the period – over forty references or double the number made in the 1960s – but a good number of these were concerned with restrictions in the supply of professional services that had become referable to the MMC for the first time in 1965. In market dominance situations it is difficult to detect any notable change in the attitude of the MMC despite the new emphasis on competition in the 1973 Act. It still emphasises behaviour, rather than structure, and this fact coupled with an approach in which each case is taken on its merits has meant that its findings in monopoly cases – unlike the findings of the Restrictive Practices Court in restrictive practices cases in the 1950s and 1960s – have had seemingly little effect in the wider field of industrial behaviour beyond the specific sphere of any one investigation.

Competition and prices and incomes policies

As we noted earlier, oligopoly situations have proved difficult to tackle and new proposals have now been made (Cmnd 7198 [1978]). One aspect of monopoly and oligopoly which has been the subject of special attention, however, has been its role in the battle against inflation. The co-incidence of higher rates of inflation and higher levels of industrial concentration may be nothing more than coincidence, but failure to control inflation by other means has led both Conservative and Labour governments to intervene to control prices directly at the micro level. Labour governments in particular have made moves to tie the work of the MMC more closely to agencies concerned with prices and incomes policies.

Before its defeat in the general election of 1970 the Labour government had announced its intention to merge the MC with the National Board for Prices and Incomes (NBPI), a body established by the Labour government in 1965 to investigate claims for wage increases in particular sectors and the scope for productivity improvements to offset the inflationary effect of granting such claims, to form a new body to be called the Commission for Industry and Manpower. It was argued that situations where competition was not effective provided scope for firms to grant 'excessive' wage increases and raise prices and thus frustrate prices and incomes policy. The proposal did not proceed because the Labour government lost the general election in 1970 and the incoming Conservative government abolished the NBPI entirely. After its return in 1974, however, the Labour government once again moved in the same direction. In 1973 the Conservative government had established a Prices Commission to operate a 'Price Code' regulating industrial prices and after its return the Labour government brought the activities of this body into closer association with competition policy by enabling it to examine proposed price increases in the context of the competitive situation of firms and their efficiency. It was felt that a body able to operate more swiftly than the MMC in such cases was necessary and the Price Commission was therefore reconstituted for this purpose in 1977 (Gribbin [1978]). A rapid succession of reports followed – over forty in the period to mid 1979 compared with fewer than ten from the MMC. A subsequent proposal was that the Price Commission and the MMC should be merged, but again the Labour government left office before the proposal could come to fruition. The incoming Conservative government, committed to non-intervention, quickly moved to abolish the Price Commission but at the same time has proposed to take powers in the 1979 Competition Bill, which would allow prices or charges 'of major public concern' to be investigated by the DGFT at the instigation of the Secretary of State.

Consumer protection
Consumer protection, of course, has a long legislative history in a great variety of Acts of Parliament on specific matters, e.g. the composition of food and drugs, misrepresentation to the consumer, etc. Limitations of space again preclude any detailed comment here but the 1970s were notable for the extent to which the matter became a focus of policy in its own right rather than the occasion for *ad hoc* legislation as the need arose. The most important development was the establishment of the DGFT at the head of the Office of Fair Trading with a general duty to keep under continual review the effect upon consumers' interests of trading practices and commercial activities of all kinds with the power to take action to remedy abuses either by obtaining assurances from the parties concerned or by making recommendations for statutory action. He may also refer trade practices which adversely affect the economic interests of consumers to the newly-established Consumer Protection Advisory Committee for investigation. Consumers' interests are also represented by the National Consumer Council which was set up in 1975. Although its members are appointed by the government it is an independent body whose function is to act as the voice of the consumer. This body is a successor to the Consumer Council set up in 1963 but dissolved as an economy measure by the Conservative government in 1970. At the same time major new legislation to protect the consumer was enacted, particularly important being the *Supply of Goods (Implied Terms) Act 1973*, the *Consumer Credit Act 1974* and the *Unfair Contract*

Terms Act 1977. For further details of the legislation and a full appraisal of developments in this field see Smith and Swann [1979].

Subsidiary Aspects of Policy towards Industry

In this section we group together a number of other aspects of policy towards industry which have not been separately treated above.

Science and technology policy and industrial development

The level of government involvement in scientific research and development is substantial (see Table 6.2) and, given the importance of such activities in the development of new products and processes, they may play, at least in principle, an important part in policies aimed at improving industry's efficiency and competitiveness. Labour governments in the last half of the 1960s had attached great importance to 'stimulating a major national effort to bring advanced technology and new processes into British industry' and had established a special Ministry of Technology for the purpose. At the end of the period, however, the Permanent Secretary of the Ministry felt that 'it could not be claimed that the Ministry had succeeded in its original assignment' (Clarke [1973]). The 1970 Conservative government instituted a review of government support for research and development by the Central Policy Review Staff. In their report (Cmnd 4814 [1971]) it was argued that 'applied R & D, that is R & D with a practical application as its objective, must be done on a customer–contractor basis. The customer says what he wants; the contractor does it (if he can); and the customer pays'. The government accepted this principle. In many areas of research support, however, it is not possible to identify a customer as such because the research is of a general kind and in response to this problem a number of Requirement Boards were established to exercise general responsibility for research in their respective areas and to examine proposals from firms and research associations.[3] The Government also instituted a review of the technical services to industry which they provided. The purpose of these reviews, however, were limited: they were more concerned with achieving value for money rather than deeper questions about the appropriate level of expenditure or its allocation. Not surprisingly perhaps, in view of the employment situation, the return of a Labour government in 1974 saw no resurgence of faith in a technological revolution of the kind exuded in the 1964–70 period. Although emphasis has been placed on specific technical advances (particularly in the micro-electronics field) and a new Advisory Council on Applied Research and Development (ACARD) was set up in 1976 to advise on the application of research and development in accordance with national needs and the future development and application of technology, it is not true to say, in the context of industrial policy, that a well-articulated general policy towards science and technology emerged (see Pavitt [1976]).

Throughout the 1970s then, neither party developed a distinctive policy in this area. It is notable in fact that the major part of the government's scientific research and development budget regularly goes on defence (CSO [1976] and [1979]). Of the rest most of industry-related research and development throughout the 1970s (and earlier) was regularly on so-called high technology projects: aerospace and energy programmes (see Table 6.2) which, as it turns out, have involved the expenditure of vast sums of public money with very little return either in ordinary investment terms or in terms of export earnings.[4]

Investment and industrial finance

Successive governments throughout the whole postwar period have operated investment incentive schemes in various forms but (apart from their regional differentiation in pursuit of regional policy objectives – see Chapter 7) they were essentially part of macro demand management policies and they are not, therefore, considered here. But, as noted earlier, the size and quality of industry's capital stock and of current investment expenditure naturally figure in any diagnosis of Britain's relatively poor industrial performance and the selective measures of financial assistance discussed earlier were directly aimed at improving industry's capital base. All these aspects of policy relate to the demand side of investment expenditure. At the same time the possibility of inadequacies in the supply of finance, coupled with an often overt suspicion in the Labour Party of the financial activities of the City of London, combined to focus attention on the capital market.

Criticism of the financial institutions, insurance companies and pensions funds for not playing a big enough role in providing capital funds for industry was expressed in 1975 (Labour Party [1975]). In the following year proposals were put forward for the extension of public ownership to banks and insurance companies. Within the City itself the early 1970s saw a succession of company scandals and financial crises which both strengthened criticism and aroused action by the City institutions themselves. In particular, concern about the supply of investment finance was the background to the establishment of a working party by the Bank of England in 1974 and the creation of a so-called equity bank, Equity Capital for Industry, in 1976. This was a kind of private sector equivalent of the NEB, except that its relatively small funds (£40m) were provided by the insurance companies and pensions funds. Earlier, however, (in 1974) the Bank of England had been instrumental in persuading the institutions to offer a much larger sum (£1bn) to Finance for Industry (FFI), a holding company incorporating two bodies, Finance Corporation for Industry (FCI) and the Industrial and Commercial Finance Corporation (ICFC), which themselves had been set up by the Bank of England and the clearing banks in 1945 to assist large and small firms respectively. At the same time the finance issue was explored by a joint NEDO–Bank of England Committee on Finance for Investment under Sir Eric (later Lord) Roll in the context of the New Industrial Strategy. The year 1976 also saw the establishment of an official Committee to Review the Functioning of Financial Institutions under former Labour Prime Minister Wilson, the immediate background to which had been the proposals put forward in the Labour Party for bringing banks and insurance companies into public ownership. This Committee has not yet produced a final report, but in a progress report (Wilson Committee [1977]) it seemed to offer little support for the view that industry's investment record had been supply, rather than demand, determined.

Small firms

Concern about the problems of small firms, particularly their financial problems, has a longer history than many of the other issues discussed above. This concern seems to have intensified during the 1970s, partly for economic reasons related to industrial performance, but partly also for social reasons associated with a reaction against some of the social and economic consequences of large-scale modern industry – summed up by the expression 'small is beautiful'. Policy towards small firms brings together a number of strands from other areas of policy. On an economic plane, particular importance is attached to small firms as representing the seed-bed from which future industrial leaders grow to challenge existing firms, as an important source of technical innovation, as important sources of competition, as efficient sources of supply and as an important outlet for entrepreneurial energies.

The Labour government in 1969 had appointed a special Committee of Inquiry which reported in 1971 (Bolton [1971]). This Committee emphasised the important functions performed by the sector as outlined above, stressing in particular the preservation of dynamism in the economy. The Committee rejected policies of discrimination in favour of small firms largely because 'any action by government would have to be on a massive scale to offset the enormous market forces which are bringing about the decline [of the sector] and would necessarily lead to inequities and distortion' (para 19.7). It did not identify any gap in the sources of finance that required any further institutional innovation but stressed the need for better advisory services for small firms and for explicit recognition by the government of their interests in the formulation of policies. These recommendations were carried into effect by the Heath administration: a Small Firms Division was established under a junior Minister in the DTI and the *1972 Industry Act* made provision for the creation of regional advice centres to assist small enterprises. It has been argued (Johnson [1978]) that the Labour government's industrial strategy policies operated in practice with an inherent bias against small firms (see too Wilson Committee [1979]). Whether because of a recognition of this or not, small firms found new favour with the Labour government in 1977 when Harold Lever was given special responsibility to help their 'regeneration'. There followed tax concessions and other measures in the 1978 Budget. The Wilson Committee [1979] made a number of recommendations for assisting the sector further and, although these have not as yet been implemented, the new Conservative government has also taken steps to aid the sector. It appears (Wilson Committee [1979]) that the decline of the sector may have been halted by the early 1970s but what the current situation is, is not yet known.

Appraisal and Conclusion
The decade of the 1970s has been remarkable for the extent to which governments have intervened selectively in the private sector, a development which has aroused considerable controversy. By contrast, competition policy, which is far more concerned with the

removal of impediments to the operation of market forces, has received much less emphasis. In this concluding section we turn to consider the effectiveness of these policies and some of the basic issues that arise.

The conventional justification for intervention in a market economy rests on an analysis of market failure arising from market imperfections and a divergence between private and social costs and benefits. The interventionist measures of the 1970s, however, cannot readily be examined in this context. Section 8 of the *1972 Industry Act* which provided the basis for national selective assistance contains no criteria other than 'the national interest' and 'benefit to the UK economy'. In practice, the kinds of situation justifying intervention are defined in terms of the social, commercial and other *consequences* rather than in terms of economic justification. An attempt to devise criteria for the purposes of administering the legislation has been made (DOI [1976]) but the difficulties of replacing discretion with clear-cut guidelines are manifest. Importance is attached to the 'viability' of firms (*after* the receipt of aid) but these considerations may be overridden by arguments relating to the unemployment consequences of a firm's collapse and balance of payments considerations – as in the case of the rescue of Chrysler UK (HCP 596 [1975/6]). Thus attention may be focused on short-term considerations – the preservation of jobs in existing firms and industries – at the expense of longer-term considerations which may require industrial adaptation and change, particularly in the light of changing pattern of world demand for our goods. But of course more distant horizons of this kind are rarely likely to coincide with the horizons of governments contemplating the next election. Many decisions, therefore, are best explained in terms of an economic theory of democracy rather than an economic theory of resource allocation. An illuminating account of the difficult position of the official economic adviser in these circumstances has been given by the former Chief Economic Adviser at the Department of Industry in the mid-1970s (Peacock [1977]).

Apart from the possibility that desirable change may be retarded, intervention may also have the perverse effect of retarding, rather than improving, the economic performance of existing firms themselves. The danger has been well expressed by the Permanent Secretary to the former Ministry of Technology from 1966 to 1970:

> Once the company begins to determine its policy by what it has to do in order to continue to get money from government, its

national value in the widest sense is already beginning to disappear: it looks to the department for guidance and for decisions, and the top management find it easier to seek the company's income by bringing pressure to bear on the department instead of by developing the competitive power of the business.

(Clarke [1973], p. 151)

The scale of intervention as it developed under the Labour government during the 1970s suggests that it saw little faith in the ability of market forces to solve industry's problems. On the other hand, despite the wishes of the Left of the party, it was not prepared to replace market forces entirely by taking industries into public ownership (except in the case of aircraft and ships). With no agreed diagnosis either about the basic causes of industry's decline (or about the relative importance and inter-relationship of the suggested factors – see the Introduction to this volume) or about the efficacy and rapidity of proposed remedies (see Peacock [1977]), policies became focused on the alleviation of the symptoms.

In considering the effect of competition policy in the 1970s, it is perhaps not surprising that, given the economic circumstances, neither party saw competition as having a major role to play. The Conservative Party, despite its ideological commitment to market forces, did not use this arm of policy with any vigour during its term of office from 1970 to 1974. The legislation introduced in 1973 in the Fair Trading Act which, *inter alia*, changed the public interest criteria used by the MMC to refer to the maintenance of 'effective competition' for the first time, may perhaps have heralded a different future if the party had stayed in power, but it is idle to speculate. The attitude of the Labour Party may be characterised perhaps as one concerned less with the promotion of competition as with the prevention of the abuse of monopoly power in profiteering and in furthering inflation.

To what extent the high levels of industrial concentration attained in the UK by 1970 increased further throughout the following decade is not yet clear. It is clear, however, that the number of mergers qualifying for reference to the MMC did increase and that most of these, being horizontal mergers, will have contributed, other things being equal, towards greater market concentration. Both parties when in power have taken a benign view of mergers and have also shown no inclination to favour a policy of dissolution of monopolies even if the MMC were to go so far as to recommend it. The question of whether the great size of many corporations and their dominance of individual markets are at least a contributory factor in Britain's lack of competitiveness and relative decline is still a question which needs to be asked (see Prais [1976]) and a question which is strongly reinforced by the results of recent studies of firms' post-merger performance. Similarly new evidence that indicates the much higher incidence of industrial disputes in large, as opposed to small, plants (Prais [1978]) raises important questions about the appropriate scale of operations as well as about the conduct of industrial relations.

Other areas of policy have had a very subsidiary role to play and we comment here on two of the more important: small firms and science and technology policy. It is clear that industrial policy has tended to discriminate against the small firm. It would seem desirable that such measures should at least be neutral by presumption. A case can also be made for the need for further positive support to remove other disabilities (Wilson [1979]). In the science and technology policy field, basic questions about the role, appropriate size and deployment of government support for industry-related research and development seem not to have been asked at all and certainly not clearly enunciated.

Finally, to look ahead, the interesting question is whether or not the degree of state microeconomic intervention which has been the most notable feature of government–industry relations in the 1970s will become a continuing feature of British economic policy – and, if it does, whether such intervention will be compatible with the survival of a private sector as such – or whether, from a future vantage point, it will be seen as a short-term response to severe short-term economic difficulties.

Notes

1. These were Norton Villiers Triumph–Meriden Co-operative; Scottish News Enterprises and Kirkby Manufacturing and Engineering Ltd.
2. It may be noted that a Restrictive Trade Practices Act, a Restrictive Practices Court Act and a Resale Prices Act (relating to the maintenance of resale prices) were passed during the period (in 1976), but all these measures were simply consolidating measures and therefore do not require discussion here.
3. Requirements Boards were established for ship and marine technology, engineering materials, mechanical engineering and machine tools, metrology and standards, chemicals and minerals, computer systems and electronics, and fundamental standards (later wound up). Subsequently boards for garment and allied industries, and electrical technology were established together with a Chief Scientists Requirements Board.

4. Two of the major projects undertaken, the development of the Concorde Supersonic Airliner and the Advanced Gas Cooled Reactor have the doubtful claim to fame of being 'two of the three worst civil investment decisions in the history of mankind to date' (Henderson [1977a], p. 530; see also Henderson [1977b]).

References

Bolton Committee [1971], *Small Firms. Report of the Committee of Inquiry on Small Firms*. Cmnd 4811. London: HMSO.

CPRS [1975], *The Future of the British Car Industry*. Central Policy Review Staff. London: HMSO.

CSO [1976], *Research and Development: Expenditure and Employment*. Central Statistical Office, Studies in Official Statistics no. 27. London: HMSO.

CSO [1979], 'Research and Development: Expenditure and Employment', *Economic Trends*, no. 309, July 1979, pp. 100–24.

Clarke, Sir Richard [1973], 'Mintech in Retrospect', *Omega*, Vol. 1, pp. 25–38, 137–63.

Cmnd 4814 [1971], *A Framework for Government Research and Development*. London: HMSO.

Cmnd 5710 [1974], Department of Industry, *The Regeneration of British Industry*. London: HMSO.

Cmnd 6315 [1975], Treasury, Department of Industry. *An Approach to Industrial Strategy*. London: HMSO.

Cmnd 7198 [1978], *A Review of Monopolies and Mergers Policy, a Consultative Document*. London: HMSO.

Cmnd 7512 [1979], *A Review of Restrictive Trade Practices Policy, a Consultative Document*. London: HMSO.

DOI [1975], *The Contents of a Planning Agreement, A Discussion Document*. London: Department of Industry.

DOI [1976], 'Criteria for assistance to industry', in *Industry Act 1972, Annual Report for the year ending March 31, 1976*, Appendix A. House of Commons Paper 619 Session 1975/6. London: HMSO.

DOI [1977], *The National Enterprise Board. Guidelines*. London: The Department of Industry.

Fleming, M. C. [1974], *The Fair Trading Act 1973*. Loughborough Papers on Recent Developments in Economic Policy and Thought. Loughborough: Department of Economics, University of Loughborough.

Graham, J. [1979], 'Trends in UK Merger Control', *British Business*, 14 September 1979, pp. 525–8.

Gribbin, J. D. [1978], 'The United Kingdom 1977 Price Commission Act and Competition Policy', *Anti-Trust Bulletin*, Vol. 23, no. 2, pp. 405–31.

HCP 347 [1971/2], Sixth Report of the Expenditure Committee, 1971–72, *Public Money in the Private Sector*. House of Commons Paper 347, Session 1971/2. London: HMSO.

HCP 596 [1975/6], *Eighth Report from the Expenditure Committee, Session 1975/6. Public Expenditure on Chrysler UK Ltd, Vol. 1: Report*. London: HMSO.

Henderson, P. D. [1977a], 'Two costly British wars', *The Listener*, 27 October 1977.

Henderson, P. D. [1977b], 'Two British Errors: their probable size and some possible lessons', *Oxford Economic Papers* 29 July 1977, pp. 159–205.

Johnson, P. [1978], 'Policies Towards Small Firms: Time for Caution?', *Lloyds Bank Review*, no. 129, July 1978, pp. 1–11.

Labour Party [1973], *The National Enterprise Board, Labour's State Holding Company*, London: The Labour Party.

Labour Party [1975], *Labour and Industry: The Next Steps*, London: The Labour Party.

Maunder, P. (ed.) [1979], *Government Intervention in the Developed Economy*. London: Croom Helm.

Meeks, G. [1977], *Disappointing Marriage: A Study of the Gains From Merger*. Cambridge: Cambridge University Press.

Mottershead, P. [1978], 'Industrial Policy', Chapter 10 in Blackaby, F. T. (ed.), [1978], *British Economic Policy 1960–74*, Cambridge: Cambridge University Press, pp. 418–83.

O'Brien, D. P., Howe, W. S., Wright, D. M. and O'Brien, R. J. [1979], *Competition Policy, Profitability and Growth*. London: Macmillan.

NEDO [1978], *Competition Policy*. London: National Economic Development Office.

Pavitt, K. [1976], 'The Choice of Targets and Instruments for Government Support of Scientific Research' in Whiting, A. [1976], *The Economics of Industrial Subsidies*. Department of Industry. London: HMSO, pp. 113–38.

Peacock, A. [1977], 'Giving economic advice in difficult times', *The Three Banks Review*, no. 113, March 1977, pp. 3–23.

Prais, S. J. [1976], *The Evolution of Giant Firms in Britain*. Cambridge: Cambridge University Press.

Prais, S. J. [1978], 'The Strike Proneness of Large Plants in Britain', *Journal of the Royal Statistical Society, Ser. A*, Vol. 141, no. 3, pp. 368–84.

Schumpeter, J. A. [1943], *Capitalism Socialism and Democracy*. London: Allen and Unwin.

Shanks, M. [1977], *Planning and Politics, The British Experience 1960–76*. Political and Economic Planning. London: Allen and Unwin.

Singh, A. [1971], *Takeovers*. Cambridge: Cambridge University Press.

Smith, P. and Swann, D. [1979], *Protecting the Consumer, An Economic and Legal Analysis*. Oxford: Martin Robertson.

Smith, T. [1979], *The Politics of the Corporate Economy*. Oxford: Martin Robertson.

Swann, D., O'Brien, D. P., Maunder, W. P. J. and Howe, W. S. [1974], *Competition in British Industry*. London: Allen and Unwin.

Utton, M. [1974], 'On Measuring the Effects of Industrial Mergers', *Scottish Journal of Political Economy*, Vol. 21, pp. 13–28.

Wilson Committee [1977], Committee to Review the Functioning of Financial Institutions. *Progress Report on the Financing of Industry and Trade*. London: HMSO.

Wilson Committee [1979], *The Financing of Small Firms*. Cmnd 7503. London: HMSO.

7 Spatial Economic Policy

by Kenneth J. Button

Introduction

Spatial economic policy is concerned with the geographical distribution of economic activities. Until comparatively recently spatial policy was clearly divided into two distinct areas of concern. There was regional policy which attempted to alleviate economic disparities, and in particular spatial variations in unemployment levels, between the main regions of the United Kingdom (eight standard regions in England plus one each for Wales, Scotland and Northern Ireland) and there was urban economic policy which tended to emphasise the role structural planning can play in tackling urban decay and similar problems. For a variety of reasons, which are discussed below, this distinction between regional and urban policy has become rather blurred in recent years with interest now focusing on a comprehensive approach to policy. Indeed, towards the end of the decade it became clear that thinking had begun to move away even from spatial policies to broader industrial strategies.

In addition to the gradual merging of regional and urban questions, the 1970s also witnessed considerable switches of emphasis not simply in terms of the importance attached to spatial policy but also in the instruments employed to achieve policy objectives. Broadly, the decade began with a weakening in political commitment to spatial policy which was short-lived and rapidly followed by an expansion of government involvement. The end of the decade, however, witnessed a dimunition in the scale of regional aid and a movement away from specifically spatial policies. A superficial view would be that these changes in policy coincided with changes in the political persuasions of the government in power, but this is too simplistic an explanation. Certainly the Conservative administration achieving office in 1970 was much less committed to regional policy than its predecessors. Nevertheless, it was this Government which introduced the *1972 Industry Act* which formed the basis of policy for the remainder of the decade. Similarly, the weakening of regional policy towards the end of the period can be traced back to expenditure cut-backs in 1976 and, more specifically, the ending of the regional employment premium (REP) in 1977 by the Labour administration then in office.

Obviously the type and scale of spatial policy adopted is not independent of the ideological views of the Government in power, but ideologies have frequently tended to be tempered according to the wider economic conditions prevailing. A number of economic and institutional factors led to the quite significant changes in policy which the different administrations of the 1970s adopted. The state of the national economy is of considerable importance in influencing spatial policy. With a buoyant economy there are, as we see below, both re-distributional and efficiency grounds for adopting spatial policies but, more importantly, there are resources available to transfer to the more depressed areas. Even with a short-lived depression in the economy, it may be felt desirable on distributional grounds and, if a future shortage of capacity and manpower during the eventual upturn is anticipated, efficiency grounds to assist the industry of depressed regions. It gradually became apparent, however, through the later years of the decade that the historically low levels of both unemployment and inflation experienced until 1974 were unlikely to return in the foreseeable future. Further, the higher levels of unemployment were now affecting traditionally prosperous regions, negating many of the arguments favouring specifically spatial assistance to industry. In addition, the emerging monetarist approach to the higher levels of inflation and the relatively weak balance of payments situation tended to encourage reductions in public expenditures, including those designed to help the depressed areas (Chisholm [1976]).

Not unrelated to the complexion of the national government is the influence that new emergent political forces have had on regional policy. In particular, the growth in strength of the Welsh and Scottish national parties in the mid 1970s and the attempt to devolve economic powers to regional assemblies reflects a new dimension in the approach to British regional policy. Whether devolution would provide a partial solution to the regional problems of Scotland and Wales is debatable (see Moore and Rhodes [1978] and Firn and Maclennan [1979]) but the political strength of the nationalist parties has certainly been influential in the direction of economic resources.

External factors have also influenced the shape of spatial policy and membership of the European Economic Community (EEC) since 1973 has been of particular importance (see Chapter 11). Briefly, membership of the Community has created new regional problems by widening the scope of competition facing the staple industries of the depressed areas and also dragging the areas of greatest comparative advantage in production farther south to areas adjacent to good transport links with the Continent. The development of a Community Regional Policy counteracts this to some extent by offering new sources of regional aid to depressed areas of the Community (Armstrong [1978]) but at the same time imposes restrictions upon the national government as to the policy tools that they may employ. As a member of the Community, Britain obviously plays an important role in formulating EEC regional policy but nevertheless the political compromises necessary in such a heterogeneous Community suggest that domestic regional policy in the later 1970s has been influenced by the combined views of the EEC.

A further influence on policy decisions must have been the effectiveness of the policy instruments themselves. The 1970s saw interest grow considerably in the empirical assessment of regional policy and, in particular, the effectiveness of various policy measures in job creation and industrial relocation. Academic studies attempting to assess the economic, as opposed to accounting, costs of regional policy were also pursued (e.g. Moore and Rhodes [1975]). Although changes in detailed objectives and the recognition of the new national economic situation, which places greater emphasis on industrial efficiency and less on geographical redistribution, have led to variations in approach to regional policy, the major object has remained job creation. The new research findings provide hitherto unavailable guidance to the possible rates of return (in terms of reduced unemployment) associated with alternative regional policies. It was clear to the Trade and Industry Sub-Committee of the House of Commons Expenditure Committee [1973] which reported in October 1973, that such research was essential if a rational and efficient regional policy was to evolve. Of previous policy it rightly said 'Much has been spent and much may well have been wasted. Regional policy has been empiricism run mad, a game of hit-and-miss, played with more enthusiasm than success (p. 72)'. It seems reasonable to assume that the additional information on the effectiveness of policies, which filtered through to decision-makers, however imperfect it may have been, influenced the packages of instruments which were combined to form overall spatial policy.

The remainder of this chapter is divided into four main sections which attempt to explain the evolution of regional and urban economic policy in the 1970s and to assess its effectiveness in meeting government objectives. The first three of these sections correspond to the periods of different governments. This division is purely for expositional convenience and, as pointed out above, does not strictly reflect major phases of policy. The final main section looks at the overall effectiveness of spatial policy in meeting the objectives of government during the decade and the role which separate policy instruments have played. Although some brief comments will be directed at the EEC dimension of the policy this is covered more fully in the chapter dealing with the overall effect of Community membership on the British economy. Additionally, it should be said that because of the unique political situation in Northern Ireland and the almost independent regional policies operational there, this chapter confines itself almost exclusively to British spatial policy. Readers interested in the problems and economic performance of Northern Ireland are referred to Davies and McGurnaghan [1975], Davies, McGurnaghan and Sams [1977] and Moore, Rhodes and Tarling [1978].

The Conservative Administration: 1970–4

The 1960s had been a period of experimentation and innovation in spatial economic policy following a decade (from 1947 to 1958) of almost total inactivity. Initially, the Conservative government of Harold Macmillan had introduced a series of acts designed almost entirely to tackle unemployment problems. Small Development Districts had been favoured to replace the long-standing broad Development Areas; schemes for retraining labour and encouraging resettlement were implemented; a number of standard grants and tax incentives introduced to stimulate investment. Such measures were seen as short-term solutions to essentially localised problems; indeed the Development Districts were designated on fixed criteria and boundaries automatically changed as jobs were generated. In contrast, the Wilson government elected in 1964 had seen a much more positive role for regional policy and, in particular, it was seen as an aid to national economic planning (Hardie [1972]). It was felt that the economic growth anticipated as part of the National Plan could only be achieved if the resources of the depressed areas of the country were fully utilised. It was envisaged that national labour shortages would gradually emerge as economic expansion accelerated beyond the capacity of the more prosperous South East and Midlands and, without the depressed areas taking some of the inflationary pressure, balance of payments constraints would rapidly become binding and limit further growth. As an additional factor, voting behaviour in the 1964 election showed a pronounced shift to Labour in the depressed areas of the country giving political strength to an invigorated regional policy. The failure to achieve the desired growth in the economy later gave justification on distributional grounds for helping the depressed areas further. The Labour administration of the 1960s both geographically broadened regional policy by introducing large Development Areas and institutionally broadened the agencies of policy by initiating various planning agencies. It also placed more emphasis on direct financial subsidies than the previous administration, both in the form of capital grants and a labour subsidy (REP), and took some notice of the role service industries can play in regional policy (see McCrone [1969] for details).

It was thus against this background of a strong regional policy that the Heath administration took office in 1970. Ideologically the new government was opposed to excessive aid being given to what it considered inefficient industry ('lame ducks') and consequently began reducing regional assistance. To some extent this apparently abrupt reversal in policy was less dramatic than it was argued at the time. Already by the late 1960s there was a growing feeling that the £300m then being spent annually on regional policy was excessive in relation to the results obtained. Indeed, there was a change of emphasis by the Labour government towards the close of the decade which may be seen as illustrative of this concern. It, for example, gave a decidedly cool response to the recommendations of the Hunt Committee which had in 1969 looked into the problems of Intermediate Areas, and had recommended additional policy initiatives (Department of Economic Affairs [1969]).

Conservative thinking manifested itself almost immediately in the October mini-budget of 1970 (see Department of Trade and Industry [1970]). Investment grants, which formed a major component of the previous government's policy, were abolished and replaced by tax incentives which permitted free 100% accelerated depreciation for plant and machinery in Development Areas compared with only 60% initial allowances elsewhere in the country. Differential initial allowances for industrial buildings were offered to Development and Intermediate Areas in contrast to the rest of the country while building grants, which were directly related to the provision of additional employment, were raised by 10% for the severely depressed Special Development and Development Areas. There was also a substantial relaxation of Industrial Development Certificate (IDC) and Office Development Permit (ODP) controls and a promise that REP would not be continued after 1974 when the original seven-year commitment expired. The package reduced the total amount of assistance available quite considerably. Additionally, the change in emphasis, from direct grants to tax incentives, was clearly intended to favour those firms which were commercially successful. To achieve the necessary profitability to reap the benefits of tax incentives an expanding national economy was necessary. Unfortunately the recession which afflicted the economy during the early 1970s (unemployment reached the emotive figure of one million during the winter of 1971–2) depressed the motivation to invest throughout the country. It became apparent that the switch to tax incentives had been mis-timed and had actually worsened the regional problem; at times of excess idle capacity, poor returns and reduced liquidity, capital grants were likely to have encouraged investment while tax concessions are, at best, ineffectual. Attempts to mitigate the effects of the depression on the assisted areas by initially extending the areas with Special Development status and incorporating service industries into the free depreciation grouping were insufficient and, anyway, were partly offset by other measures designed to stimulate investment nationally which reduced the differential advantages enjoyed by the assisted regions. It was clear by 1972 that a much stronger regional package was necessary if unemployment in the worst hit of the depressed regions was to be contained.

The result was the publication of *Industry and Regional Development* (Department of Trade and Industry [1972]) which set out the Government's objectives for a revised policy. The intention was not simply to narrow regional differentials for distributional reasons but also to modernise and increase the productivity of industry in general and so permit the economy to grow at the same rate as competitors.

Regional policy was seen as complementary to the general reflationary measures contained in the March budget. The actual policy contained in the consequent Industry Act was a reversal of the Government's previous thinking. It represented, however, not a revolutionary break in approach but rather a return to the strategies of the late 1960s (see Nuttall [1973]). In detail the standard grant system, which had initially been favoured in Labour's *Industrial Development Act 1966*, was reinstated with regional development grants to be paid at differential rates, dependent upon the type of region, for investments by the non-service sector in plant, machinery and industrial building. Modifications to the original system included the availability of grants to firms already in assisted areas, rather than simply to migrant or new firms, and some tax relief on a portion of the grants. The formerly favourable tax concessions enjoyed by assisted areas were extended throughout the country making them a tool of general reflation rather than a specific instrument of spatial policy.

The *Industry Act 1972* also extended the Intermediate Areas so that some 65% of the land area of Great Britain and 44% of the population were now deemed in need of assistance. To ensure that aid was available in particularly difficult areas the Act, under the famous section 7, also dealt with the selective financial assistance which had formerly been available under Local Employment Acts (the *Local Employment Act 1972* concerned itself primarily with industrial estates and government factory construction). Decisions on selective aid became more decentralised as regional offices of the Department of Trade and Industry (DTI) were established. The assistance was also to be given where projects helped to maintain existing levels of employment or led to modernisation rather than under the older criteria of job creation. Further the need for IDCs was abolished in Special Development and Development Areas, although the raising of the limits beyond which IDCs were required in the remainder of the country tended to outweigh any beneficial effects this may have had to the assisted regions – particularly since IDCs were very freely available in such areas prior to 1972. Finally, announcements were made that REP would not now be immediately removed in 1974 but would be gradually phased out from that time.

The framework initiated by the Industry Act was to form the foundation for much of the regional policy of the remainder of the decade. A number of deficiencies, however, soon became apparent. There was excessive concentration on the manufacturing sector and an almost total neglect of service industries – they only benefited from selective assistance and training grants. This, in part, reflected the Kaldorian theory of regional growth which argues that a region's exports, both to the rest of the national economy and to overseas markets, are the major determinant of its prosperity (Kaldor [1970]). Because manufactured products are obviously more exportable than services, it is the sector engaged in their production which should be stimulated to assist a depressed area. However, it was becoming clear in the early 1970s that nationally the service sector was both growing more rapidly in employment terms than manufacturing (indeed the latter declined by 8% between 1965 and 1971) and, because of high rents and labour costs in the South East, was becoming increasingly mobile (see Nuttall [1973] and Manners [1976]). Further, the Assisted Areas had a disproportionately small share of the total service employment in the economy and considerable scope for expansion existed.

The Labour Government 1974–9
The Labour government was elected in 1974 on a platform which, among other things, argued for the pursuit of an active regional policy. The similarity of the *Industry Act 1972* to the type of measures favoured by the 1964–70 administration provided the Government with an acceptable basic statute and eliminated the need for major changes in legislation. One important modification to policy, however, was the announcement that REP was to be retained and that the rate of subsidy was to be doubled. Direct labour subsidies of this kind were seen to give depressed areas the same benefits as a devaluation of the currency does to a national economy with the added advantage that the actual cost of the measure is borne by the tax-paying community at large rather than by residents of the region. (In the case of a national devaluation, higher import prices are imposed on those living in the devaluing country.) Further, even if the subsidy did not immediately create employment, but leaked away into profits or higher wages to the existing labour force, it may well still be beneficial to a region if the effect of higher profits was to attract more investment into the area or the influence of higher wages kept skilled labour, which would otherwise have migrated, in the region. The difficulty of retaining REP indefinitely, however, was that it tended to stifle dynamic change by propping up existing firms rather than

offering cost advantages to new ones (Wilson [1979]). In particular, although the devaluation effect of employing the REP is achieved without placing any excessive burden on the recipient region, this type of burden itself often stimulates the increased efficiency, and hence greater competitiveness, which is often seen as one of the main benefits of a devaluation. Given these conflicting views of REP it was not surprising that it became something of a political football in the 1970s. The greater emphasis placed on economic efficiency by the Conservatives between 1970 and 1974 clearly tended to result in considerable opposition to a measure which may restrict long-term growth in the economy.

The new Wilson government also favoured giving greater power to local Department of Industry offices (the Department of Industry now having lost its trade functions) in the approval of selective assistance. It was also felt necessary to extend and modify the bound-aries of the assisted areas with Chesterfield being incorporated as an Intermediate Area, Edinburgh and Cardiff being given Development Area status and Merseyside, Special Development Area status. Further, a substantial number of civil service jobs were to be dispersed from London, a number well in excess of those suggested in the Hardman Report (Civil Service Department [1973]). IDC controls were also tightened by lowering the limits for which a certificate was required to 5000 sq. ft. in the South East, 10 000 sq ft. in other non-assisted areas and 15 000 sq. ft. in Intermediate Areas. Com-plementary to this, office development in Central London was con-siderably restricted, in part to encourage dispersal of the service sector but also in response to public disquiet over the 'property boom' which had been a feature of the expansionary macroeconomic policy of the early 1970s.

Before these measures could have effect, another general election was fought (October 1974) which was notable for the comparatively strong showing of the nationalist parties. Their obvious concern with the state of their regional economies clearly required the government to react to the unemployment problems facing Scotland and Wales. Specific bodies, the Scottish and Welsh Development Agencies, were thus established in 1975 and 1976 respectively with power to intervene in local industry and, by taking over the Scottish and Welsh Industrial Estates Corporation, to become involved in land clearance activities. These agencies were essentially regional versions of the National Enter-prise Board (NEB) which had been established under the *Industry Act*

1975 as part of the new industrial strategy. It was intended that they would invest in industry, build and lease advance factories, create new companies and generally increase government involvement in industry. At the same time political events indicated a need to give Scotland and Wales even greater autonomy (Cmnd 6348 [1975]). A Scottish Economic Planning Department was set up in 1973, and in 1975 the Scottish and Welsh Secretaries took over, from the Department of Industry, powers to administer selective assistance within their areas. From 1977 the Scottish office was also given responsibility for labour retraining and other functions of the Manpower Services Commission. Clearly, this period marked a change in overall policy. Regional assistance was now to be administered locally with the English assisted areas being treated differently from Scotland and Wales. These changes inevitably caused some friction in the English depressed regions which felt at a disadvantage in attracting mobile industry. In effect Scotland (and to a much lesser extent Wales) had become almost as powerful as a state in a federal system, a position not enjoyed by other regions. Attempts at further devolution of power in 1979 were prevented by the results of the Welsh and Scottish referenda.

Nationalism was then one important new element affecting spatial policy in the mid 1970s. Another equally forceful influence was the gradual recognition that traditional approaches to regional problems were rapidly becoming inappropriate. Although substantial regional differences in unemployment had certainly not been alleviated, it became clear that *intra*-regional disparities were becoming even more pressing (Gripaios [1978]). In particular, unemployment tended to be concentrated in the main conurbations and, at a more micro level, within the older inner areas of these 'city regions'. However, the inadequacies of statistical sources prevented the growing depth of the Inner City Area Problem being recognised until the situation had become extremely serious. It was not until 1976 that details of the 1971 census of population became readily available, and it was made clear that there had been an accelerated outflow of manufacturing industry from inner city areas since the early 1960s leaving substantial pools of unemployed and unskilled labour. In inner Birmingham, for example, 38% of the labour force was unskilled or semi-skilled, in Liverpool it was 39% and Glasgow 34%; these figures can be compared with the national average in 1971 of 23% (see also Gripaios's [1977] work on Greater London). Until this time emphasis had been placed on policies of decentralisation away from the old inner city areas to new and expanded towns at green field sites. Unfortunately a combination of circumstances, some the result of changes in economic conditions, others the actions of central and local government, created cumulative pressures which led to an excessive outflow of employment from central areas. Part of the difficulty lay in the national decline in manufacturing (employment in the sector falling by 14.8% between 1966 and 1971), combined with gradual changes in industrial technology which have resulted in a trend towards higher land–output ratios and the need for greater skills from labour. Although regional policy, with its emphasis on broad geographical areas and attempts to attract industry from some of the major urban areas (especially London and the West Midlands) played some part in exacerbating the inner city situation, it seems likely that local land use planning and housing policies created greater problems. Comprehensive structure planning resulted in many small hand-craft firms being uprooted from cheap urban sites while financial restrictions prevented many local authorities from carrying out proposed redevelopments. Where new workshops were constructed, rentals tended to be high and the quality of facilities excessive for the requirements of small firms. While industry has moved out, unskilled workers, who are dependent upon council housing for accommodation, have been tied in, unable to move because of rigidities in council house allocation procedures. (Gleave and Palmer [1979]).

The Labour government's reaction to the problems of inner urban areas was initially to seek more details of the real nature of the crisis by instigating a series of studies into the economies of the number of affected areas. In the short term, measures to tackle the social effects of the problem involved some stepping up of the Urban Aid Programme (which had been initiated to tackle purely local difficulties in 1968). Additionally Comprehensive Community Programmes were established in an attempt to develop a unified and co-ordinated approach to urban deprivation. These measures were intended to treat the symptoms of the problem while stronger policies were being devised to get at its root causes. The Government also began in early 1977 to relax physical controls on office development in inner city areas with ODP limits being raised and small employers becoming exempt entirely. The Location of Offices Bureau, which had previously had a remit to encourage office dispersal out of London, was now given the task of bringing jobs to the capital. Additionally, the gradual dispersal of civil service employment was allowed to 'slip'. Eventually, with the publication of *A Policy for the Inner Cities* (Department of the Environment [1977]), the Government officially announced its intention of reversing previous policy and that serious attempts would be made to attract manufacturing industry back to central city areas. Financial aid was made available for the financing of both capital and current outlays on industrial, environmental and recreational projects as well as for social need. Part of the money was to come from a contraction in New Town growth. The actual level of assistance, in the context of cut-backs being made elsewhere in the economy, was not large, however, and the emphasis on locating new small-scale industry in inner city areas may have been misguided given both the reliance of small firms on large local customers and the fact that there is ample evidence that much modern industry is more suited to peripheral locations (Foreman-Peck and Gripaios [1977]).

The inner city area problem was only one of two major inter-related changes in the geographical distribution of unemployment which became apparent in the mid 1970s. From 1974 to the beginning of 1976 the national rise in unemployment manifested itself most strongly in the traditionally prosperous areas of the country rather than in the assisted regions. The South East and the West Midlands were particularly badly affected with the respective unemployment rates rising during this period by 153 and 170%. Of course, the low base level of unemployment in these regions tends to exaggerate the growth in numbers of unemployed but there was still, nevertheless, a general levelling up of unemployment rates throughout the country. Part of this new situation can be explained in terms of the unemployment concentrated in the larger conurbations of the South East and the West Midlands but, in addition, there was an uncharacteristic depression in the engineering sector where car manufacturing was hit particularly severely. At the same time the Labour government's thinking was turning away from specific regional aid to aspatial assistance designed to restructure and improve the overall performance of the British economy. To this end (see Chapter 6), the industrial strategy was initiated in 1975 and it became clear that conflicts with regional policy were likely to develop if there existed substantial differences in productivity between the assisted areas and the rest of the country. The subsequent aid given via the NEB, and to British Leyland and the aerospace industry in particular, represented a complete change of emphasis in selective policy away from geographically based aid to assistance to particular industries whose location was of secondary importance. It was becoming clear, even in the early 1970s, that the incidence of previous regional assistance had not been as favourable to the traditional problem regions as had sometimes been suggested, and the introduction of industrial aids must have worsened further the relative position of the traditionally assisted areas towards the end of the decade (e.g. see McCallum [1979] for some basic calculations).

The aid differentials among the regions were also eroded in the mid 1970s with the abolition, in 1977, of REP in Britain (although the Selective Employment Premium was retained in Northern Ireland). In part the ending of the direct labour subsidy can be explained in terms of the financial cut-backs announced in the December 1976 mini-budget. It was, in public sector terms, a huge outlay amounting in 1975/6 to about one-third of public expenditure on regional policies. Equally important, however, was a new element in the formulation of policy, namely membership of the EEC. The European Community was attempting to formulate a regional development programme and REP contravened the basic formula. In particular, it could not easily be translated into an investment grant equivalent (in the jargon of the EEC it was not 'transparent'), nor was it conditional upon any investment activity. Further, the Commission had an implicit feeling that the REP tended to keep afloat firms which would otherwise have closed down and hence was diverting funds from more productive activities. It was also suggested that aid of this type aimed at reducing operating costs, may not produce a sustained increase in output unless the subsidy was continued indefinitely.

By 1979, therefore, there were already clear signs that the traditional forms of spatial policy had changed quite dramatically from the standard approach to regional problems which had been broadly accepted, albeit on different scales, by governments earlier in the decade. In particular, a combination of internal and external considerations had led to a much wider view of economic welfare being developed which places more emphasis, in the short term at least, on efficiency (and, on occasions, political expediency) to the comparative neglect of geographical distribution. The trend was clearly visible in the later years of the Labour administration and to become much more explicit with the return of Mrs Thatcher's Conservative government in early summer 1979.

The Second Conservative Phase, 1979

A Conservative government was returned in 1979 on a programme which involved promises of very substantial cuts in public expenditure and a reduction of political involvement in British industry. The long-term objective was seen to be the restoration of international competitiveness and an improvement in industrial productivity. As part of their policy, both in terms of a reduction of public expenditure for macroeconomic reasons and a reduction of official involvement in industry for microeconomic reasons, the Conservatives instigated a run-down of regional related aid. In July 1979 the new package of regional assistance was made explicit. The general form of the *Industry Act 1972* was retained, but its influence weakened considerably. Over a three-year period the traditional regional aid programme was to be gradually cut accelerating to a reduction of some £233m from the £609m projected for 1982/3. Special Development Areas were still to receive 22% regional development grants for capital expenditure incurred in the provision of new plant and machinery, buildings and works, but the grants were to be reduced from 20 to 15% for Development Areas (saving the exchequer some £19m). The Intermediate Areas were no longer to be eligible for automatic regional development grants but instead must rely upon discretionary aid to attract new industry. In all cases the threshold size of projects eligible for assistance was increased so that the emphasis was concentrated on larger-scale investments. In addition to the monies saved by altering the level of grants, further savings (some £58m) were to be obtained by reductions from 1980 in the geographical size and status of some of the assisted areas. The aim was to introduce greater selectivity into the areas to receive aid. This again reflects the growing movement in regional policy away from a blanket approach. The origins of this particular feature of the new strategy can be traced back to the downgrading of status of some Development Areas to Intermediate Areas under the Labour administration in 1977. The new boundaries introduced in July 1979 meant that despite some new areas being added and some upgrading of areas, only some 25% of the employed population were resident in some form of assisted area in contrast to over 40% under the previous administration.

In addition to the explicit effects of the new regional policies on depressed areas there were the consequences of other economic policies pursued by the new government. The new industrial strategy involved a substantial reduction in general aid to industry, while cuts in public expenditure outlays on social services and transport affect the assisted areas relatively more harshly. Work by Short [1977], for example, looking at a wide selection of public expenditures, suggests that in the period 1969–73, Scotland, Wales and the Northern regions were net beneficiaries from budgetary activities compared with the West Midlands, East Midlands and Yorkshire and Humberside. Because public expenditure covers a wide range of activities and cut-backs have been selective, it is possible that the likely adverse effects may be less than broad national data suggests. However, the withdrawal or contraction of financial support from several large undertakings, for example in the steel and shipbuilding sectors, is likely to result in a concentration of unemployment in pockets within some of the traditional problem areas.

Administrative changes proposed by the new Thatcher administration also emphasised the movement away from spatially based policy. The controls over industrial location were to be relaxed and the IDCs were to become freely available in Intermediate Areas. The actual effects of relaxing IDC controls further is not likely to be great for although, as we see below, they may be a potent tool of regional policy they had only been relatively sparingly and spasmodically used throughout the 1970s compared with the later years of the previous decade. Although no firm decision was announced at that time regarding various development agencies which had come into being in Scotland, Wales and certain rural areas of England (e.g. the Highlands and Islands Development Board, the Council for Small Industries in Rural Areas, the Welsh Development Agency, etc.), the general reduction in official intervention and cut-backs in administrative expenditure which were to take place led to the recommendation that their future should be examined if their responsibility covered non-assisted areas. The Conservative government's dislike of 'quasi autonomous non-governmental organisations' (quangos), however, subsequently resulted in the removal of a number of other agencies with decidedly spatial responsibilities. Together with the eight Regional Economic Planning Councils, the Location of Offices Bureau was among fifty-seven organisations from which the DOE withdrew support. Further, the Centre for Environmental Studies, which has in the past undertaken considerable research work on urban economic problems, has had government finance withdrawn. Although the exact result of such measures is difficult to assess, clearly the main effect is likely to be on the longer-term information flows between government and industry concerning the types and scale of incentives available. One point to note is that some new quangos have emerged, notably the urban development corporations in London and Merseyside to organise the redevelopment of derelict dockland.

The Effectiveness of Spatial Policies

The effectiveness of the regional and urban policies pursued in the 1970s is far from easy to assess. Three factors explain why recent measures have had uncertain results. Firstly, although the *Industry Act 1972* formed the legislative basis for policy, the detail and scale of policy was frequently changed, making it impossible to trace out the specific effects of any policy phase, let alone assess the effect of individual component policy instruments within a package. Indeed, the continuing interference with policy is itself likely to have reduced the efficiency of many measures by greatly increasing the uncertainty with which potential investors and employers (and also, with retraining schemes, workers) could view different incentives. Although all industrial decisions must, by their nature, involve a degree of risk and uncertainty, frequent changes in attitude and policy by government greatly increases the tendency towards inertia.

Secondly, not only did policy change but, as has been frequently emphasised in the chapter, government's objectives also changed periodically for a variety of political and economic reasons. This makes it even more difficult to assess the effect of policy, for not only did frequent legislative changes make it almost impossible to trace out the effects of official measures but, in addition, the actual targets being aimed at were also changing. Many of the switches in objectives were changes in emphasis or degree and, in particular, many involved shifts in priorities between the regional welfare distribution and the national level of economic efficiency. In broad terms one might say that until about 1976 the traditional problem of reducing disparities in unemployment dominated official thinking (with occasional comments on migration, income, social welfare, etc. appearing in policy statements) and the object of policy was, in the main, seen in terms of moving work to the unemployed workers. The retraining and relocation of labour was very much a secondary issue. The realisation that slow national growth restricts the number of mobile firms available for geographical redistribution led, in the late 1970s, to greater emphasis being placed on revitalising ailing but potentially dynamic indigenous firms in the worst affected areas as part of an aspatial industrial strategy. While some evidence may be drawn upon to assess the effect of policy in the earlier phase, little information is available on the latter.

Thirdly, assessment of new or modified policy involves the need to be able to say what would have happened if either no positive policy had been adopted (which is essentially a policy option in itself) or if no change in the existing policy had been made. It is of little value simply to compare the before with the after situation because the former totally ignores the independent and external changes which would have occurred anyway even if no policy had been introduced. This is one of the reasons, for example, that the Department of Industry gives little significance to the fact that many of the new jobs forecast by applicants from aid given under section 7 of the *Industry Act 1972* have not materialised (HCP 173 [1979]). Forecasting the probable course of events if no active intervention had taken place is the most difficult and unreliable part of any policy assessment. The situation is further complicated when considering regional policy because of the lack of reliable information about the existing situation, let alone, details of the likely state of affairs which would have occurred if no government action had been taken. The sudden discovery of the inner city problem highlights this. One of the more notable aspects of spatial economics in the 1970s was that some attempt was initiated to improve and expand official statistical sources (e.g. regional accounts became available, see Kent-Smith and Hartley [1976]). Despite important steps forward there is still a considerable dearth of basic raw data available at the regional level and, more importantly, given the increased recognition of more localised problems, at the sub-regional and urban level.

Accepting the above caveats we can now make some general comments upon the suitability of spatial policies adopted in the 1970s and, in particular, consider whether they made a significant contribution to the containment of unemployment. While unemployment was not the sole focus of attention, its reduction does form an important component of most regional policies of the 1970s and is, also, a useful tangible measure against which success or otherwise can be gauged. It is clear from Table 7.1 that both the overall trend in the level of unemployment in the economy and, specifically, the level of unemployment in the assisted areas have risen quite dramatically over the decade, although the latter has not increased to the same extent as unemployment in the traditionally prosperous regions.

Table 7.1   Unemployment rates in UK regions

	1971	1973	1975[a]	1977	1979[b]
North	5.7	4.6	5.9	8.4	7.9
Yorkshire and Humberside	3.8	2.8	4.0	5.8	5.3
East Midlands	2.9	2.0	3.6	5.1	4.5
East Anglia	3.2	1.9	3.4	5.4	4.3
South East	2.0	1.5	2.8	4.5	3.8
South West	3.3	2.4	4.7	6.9	5.5
West Midlands	2.9	2.2	4.1	5.8	5.1
North West	3.9	3.5	5.3	7.5	6.6
Wales	4.4	3.4	5.9	8.1	7.4
Scotland	5.8	4.5	5.2	8.3	7.3
Northern Ireland	7.9	6.1	7.9	11.2	10.4
UK	2.3	2.7	4.2	6.2	5.4

[a]Industrial action at the Department of Employment resulted in an eleven month average being used.
[b]Second quarter figures, seasonally adjusted.

Migration and changes in activity rates make it difficult to assess the success of spatial policies in containing unemployment in the assisted areas. Empirical studies suggest that regional policy in the late 1960s generated some 72 000 or so new jobs per annum in the Development Areas (Brown [1972]), shifted industrial building completions in their favour (Hart [1971]), diverted investment to them (Buck and Lowe [1972]), slowed the rate of plant closure (Sant [1975]) and increased national output by £500m in 1970 (Moore and Rhodes [1973]). Of course, these studies, which adopted a variety of econometric and normalising procedures, are not definitive but they do suggest that policy in that period was comparatively influential. Unfortunately, the useful switch from a passive to an active phase of policy which occurred in the mid 1960s, and which supplied a useful yardstick upon which most of the studies gauged policy effectiveness, did not recur so clearly in the 1970s. Attempts have been made to trace the likely trends if the passive phase of the early 1960s had continued into the 1970s, but such a base obviously becomes increasingly remote and its role as a numeraire, against which subsequent policies can be measured, increasingly doubtful. A somewhat more extended analysis by Moore, Rhodes and Tyler [1977] suggests that there is evidence that manufacturing employment in the assisted areas continued to benefit from regional policy up until 1976 (when their data series ends) with some 240 000 jobs being created from 1960. Further Tyler, Moore and Rhodes [1979] find that policies over the period increased manufacturing output in the Development Areas (the Scottish economy, for instance, may have benefited by up to 20%) above the likely outcome in the absence of such policies. Further, evidence is presented that this regional growth in output was not at the expense of productivity and hence efficiency in the economy as a whole.

While the exact overall result of the job creation packages has been difficult to ascertain, the importance of individual policy tools – because they tend to interact with one another – creates even greater problems. There is support for A. J. Brown's minority view expressed in the Hunt Report (Department of Economic Affairs [1969]), although firm empirical measures are scant, that differential spending on infrastructure does little to help the assisted areas: generally their problems do not stem from a shortage of infrastructure but rather an under utilisation of what they have. Although there is no evidence on the effectiveness of the 1970 measures to replace investment grants with free depreciation, studies have been done on the tax allowance scheme which operated in the 1960s under the *1963 Local Employment Act*. Unfortunately the findings are inconclusive; MacKay [1972] finds evidence of the superiority of the tax allowances in comparison with grants, but Brown [1972] disagrees with this.

In considering the three main components of spatial policy in the 1970s, REP, investment grants and IDC controls, the evidence is perhaps slightly less blurred. IDC controls have never been popular with industry, but several academic studies suggest that they have been a strong influence in directing industry to the depressed areas although, again most of the evidence tends to relate only to the early years of the decade. Bowers and Gunawardena ([1977] and [1978]) suggest that IDC controls were the most effective measures for diverting industry to the assisted areas between 1963 and 1970 and provide some fairly firm support to the earlier findings of Moore and Rhodes [1976] and Ashcroft and Taylor [1977] on this. If this were so why were IDC controls progressively relaxed in the 1970s? Firstly, membership of the EEC widened the potential locations open to industrialists and, increasingly fears were expressed that firms not permitted to establish themselves in their first choice site, say in the South East or West Midlands, would move to the Continent in preference to an assisted area or even not build new plant at all. It is perhaps no accident that Italy, the EEC country with the most pronounced regional disparities, only employs positive incentives to encourage firms to the south, fearing industry will move out of the country if negative controls are introduced in the north. Secondly, locational controls only direct investment, they do not encourage extra investment (indeed at the extreme if firms choose not to invest rather than go to an assisted area they may discourage it). As it became increasingly recognised towards the end of the decade that the economy was moving into a prolonged period of slow growth so the emphasis switched to more positive investment generating policy instruments. Finally, the more even regional spread of unemployment, with substantial intra-regional differentials, made it difficult to discourage any firm from establishing itself in a region if it generated employment even if historically the area had been seen as prosperous. The growth in concern over inner city economies was an important element in this new situation. Because of these changes it is not surprising that attention has switched to measures which are likely to stimulate extra jobs rather than simply relocating those that would appear anyway.

The REP, being a direct labour subsidy, was intended both to create new jobs and to encourage the retention of existing employment. The effectiveness of the instrument in the 1970s is not altogether clear, however, although it is a subject which has attracted considerable interest amongst economists. The bipartisan Trade and Industry Sub-Committee of the House of Commons Expenditure Committee [1973] were particularly keen to retain REP arguing that 'Our evidence ... left us in little doubt that the withdrawal of REP without comparable replacement could create operating difficulties for many firms. (p. 75)' Quantitatively, because of the problems of deciding upon lag structures, it has proved difficult to isolate the exact cost-effectiveness of REP in terms of job creation for the assisted areas, although Moore and Rhodes [1976] estimated that it produced about 50 000 jobs per annum in 1968–70 falling to some 20–30 000 when its real value was substantially reduced between 1971 and 1973. Thus they estimated that 10–15% of new jobs resulting from regional policy in the Development Areas over the period can be attributed to REP. Even if this figure is accepted (and MacKay [1976] and Ashcroft and Taylor [1977] have offered quantitative evidence that Moore and Rhodes overstate the effects of REP by ignoring important parallel policy changes and understating the pressure of aggregate demand in their equations), it suggests that the overall result of the labour subsidy was not large. But could one have expected more? Given the actual quantitative level of subsidy, and despite the guaranteed period of provision, which was thought a major innovation at the time of introduction, it seems unlikely that it would ever dominate regional policy. When introduced in 1967 it reduced labour costs by at most 3.9%, a figure eroded in the early 1970s by inflation to about 1.5%. In 1971, for example, the typical migrant firm settling in a Development Area only gained a 2% reduction in labour costs from REP contrasted to an 11% gain in capital costs. Despite this comparatively small effect, the willingness of Labour administrations, in particular, to persist with the REP in the early 1970s is easy to understand. It was a direct labour subsidy and, hence, appeared to strike at the core of the regional problem as then perceived and, despite its high budgetary costs, there were definite and substantial claw-backs in reduced unemployment payments and increased income tax revenue which could be pinpointed. It was only abandoned when both the nature of the unemployment problem had been reassessed and replacement aid, in the form of the EEC Community Regional Policy, had become available.

While both IDC and REP policy were comparatively new instruments in the 1970s, regionally differentiated investment and capital grants have a much longer history. Changes in the rate of capital subsidy and the criteria of allocation formed a central part of regional policy in the 1970s. Comparisons between the grants and tax incentives policies of the early 1960s offer, as we saw above, no conclusive results. Capital grants in the later years of the 1960s and the early 1970s seem to have had a substantial effect on the movement of industry to assisted areas (Ashcroft and Taylor [1977]) and to have had a strong positive effect on the completion of projects once initiated (Bowers and Gunawerdena [1978]). Perhaps the strongest criticism of investment subsidies is that they tend to encourage capital intensive projects rather than those with a high labour-output ratio. It is difficult, therefore, to see how they are likely to have favourable effects, especially in the short term, on unemployment. This is misleading, however, because the main problem in the depressed areas is that capital is relatively expensive compared with labour, and thus it is logical to reduce the capital shortage by cutting its cost with subsidies. Further, as the emphasis has shifted towards efficiency criteria in the late 1970s there is a rationale in increasing the amount of capital utilised in the assisted areas if the productivity resulting exceeds that elsewhere in the economy. Counter to this, however, and a partial explanation of the reduction in spatially differentiated grants towards the end of the decade, is the new situation which began to develop after 1974 where labour is relatively abundant throughout the economy.

Given our knowledge of the strengths and weaknesses of different policy options it appears that in general the types of packages evolved corresponded broadly to the aims of the government of the day. It is impossible, however, to say whether the scale of intervention and its timing could have been substantially improved. Certainly, many of the measures seemed to be treating maladies which already existed (e.g. the role of the inner city areas and the overall industrial strategy) rather than be part of a long-term policy to alleviate serious regional disparities.

Conclusions

The 1970s has witnessed what has probably been the most dramatic and important reconsideration of spatial economic problems since the inception of an official regional policy in the early 1930s. Although the containment of unemployment within the national economy has remained a major policy objective the changing economic circumstances of the later years of the decade have resulted in an entirely new attitude towards the problem arising. No longer are spatial variations in unemployment among large administrative regions seen as the main area of concern; rather the more concentrated geographical unemployment associated with specific inner city areas or industries has come to the forefront of official thinking. The emphasis has switched from regional problems to urban policy and industrial strategy.

Of course, the new situation did not develop overnight and throughout the decade there were conscious attempts to modify traditional policy to tackle the new types of problem. Indeed, even the final phase of policy under the Conservative government still relied heavily upon the framework established under the *Industry Act 1972* although the emphasis had quite clearly switched from blanket aid to greater spatial and industrial selectivity. Because of the anticipated slow rate of economic expansion forecast for the next decade, it seems likely that even greater emphasis will be put on the selective improvement of industrial efficiency at the expense of distributional considerations. The exact details of the likely policy to emerge are impossible to predict. The new approach is so radically different from previous regionally-based measures that inevitably a period of experimentation and change must occur.

References

Armstrong, H. W. [1978], 'Community regional policy: a survey and critique', *Regional Studies*, Vol. 12, pp. 511–28.

Ashcroft, B. and Taylor, J. [1977], 'The movement of manufacturing industry and the effect of regional policy', *Oxford Economic Papers*, Vol. 29, pp. 84–101.

Bowers, J. K. and Gunawardena, A. [1977], 'Industrial development certificates and regional policy, part 1', *Bulletin of Economic Research*, Vol. 29, pp. 112–22.

Bowers, J. K. and Gunawardena, A. [1978], 'Industrial development certificates and regional policy, part 2', *Bulletin of Economic Research*, Vol. 30, pp. 3–13.

Brown, A. J. [1972], *The Framework of Regional Economics in the United Kingdom*. Cambridge: Cambridge University Press.

Buck, T. W. and Lowe, J. F. [1972], 'Regional policy and the distribution of investment', *Scottish Journal of Political Economy*, Vol. 19, pp. 253–71.

Chisholm, M. [1976], 'Regional Policies in an era of slow population growth and higher unemployment', *Regional Studies*, Vol. 10, no. 2, pp. 201–13.

Civil Service Department [1973], *The Dispersal of Government Work from London*. Cmnd 5322. London: HMSO.

Cmnd 6348 [1975], *Our Changing Democracy: Devolution to Scotland and Wales*. London: HMSO.

Davies, R. and McGurnaghan, M. A. [1975], 'Northern Ireland: the economics of adversity', *National Westminster Bank Quarterly Review*, May 1975, pp. 56–68.

Davies, R., McGurnaghan, M. A. and Sams, K. I. [1977], 'The Northern Ireland economy: progress (1968–75) and prospects', *Regional Studies*, Vol. 11, pp. 297–307.

Department of Economic Affairs [1969], *The Intermediate Areas*. Cmnd 3998. London: HMSO.

Department of the Environment [1977], *A Policy for the Inner Cities*. Cmnd 6845. London: HMSO.

Department of Trade and Industry [1970], *Investment Incentives*. Cmnd 4516. London: HMSO.

Department of Trade and Industry [1972], *Industrial and Regional Development*. Cmnd 4942. London: HMSO.

Firn, J. R. and Maclennan, D. [1979], 'Devolution: the changing political economy of regional policy' in Maclennan, D. and Parr, J. B. (eds.), *Regional Policy: Post Experience and New Directions*. London: Martin Robertson, pp. 273–96.

Foreman-Peck, J. S. and Gripaios, P. A. [1977], 'Inner city problems and inner city policies', *Regional Studies*, Vol. 11, pp. 401–12.

Gleave, D. and Palmer, D. [1979], 'Mobility constraints and unemployment mismatch: an analysis of structural changes in the housing market and their consequences on job migration' in *Papers of the Urban Economic Conference*. London: CES.

Gripaios, P. [1977], 'The closure of firms in the inner city: the south east London case 1970–5', *Regional Studies*, Vol. 11, pp. 1–6.

Gripaios, P. [1978], 'Spatial employment in England: an urban and a regional problem', *British Review of Economic Issues*, Vol. 1, pp. 25–35.

Hardie, J. [1972], 'Regional policy' in W. Beckerman (ed.), *The Labour Government's Economic Record 1964–70*. London: Duckworth, pp. 218–46.

Hart, R. A. [1971], 'The distribution of new industrial building in the 1960s', *Scottish Journal of Political Economy*, Vol. 18, pp. 181–97.

HCP 173 [1979], House of Commons Committee of Public Accounts, *First Report from the Session 1979/80*. London: HMSO.

Kaldor, N. [1970], 'The case for regional policies', *Scottish Journal of Political Economy*, Vol. 17, pp. 337–48.

Kent-Smith, D. and Hartley, E. [1976], 'United Kingdom regional accounts', *Economic Trends*, no. 277, pp. 78–90.

McCallum, D. [1979], 'The development of British regional policy' in Maclennan, D. and Parr, J. B., *Regional Policy: Post Experience and New Directions*. London: Martin Robertson, pp. 3–42.

McCrone, G. [1969], *Regional Policy in Britain*. London: Allen and Unwin.

MacKay, R. R. [1972], 'Employment creation in the Development Areas', *Scottish Journal of Political Economy*, Vol. 19, pp. 287–96.

MacKay, R. R. [1976], 'The impact of the Regional Employment Premium' in Whiting, A. (ed.) *The Economics of Industrial Subsidies*. London: HMSO., pp. 225–42.

Manners, G. [1976], 'Reinterpreting the regional problem', *Three Banks Review*, no. 111, pp. 33–55.

Moore, B. C. and Rhodes, J. [1973], 'Evaluating the effects of Britain's regional economic policy', *Economic Journal*, Vol. 83, pp. 87–110.

Moore, B. C. and Rhodes, J. [1975], 'The economic and exchequer implications of British regional economic policy' in Vaizey, J. (ed.), *Economic Sovereignty and Regional Policy*. Dublin: Gill and Macmillan, pp. 80–102.

Moore, B. C. and Rhodes, J. [1976], 'A quantitative analysis of the effects of the Regional Employment Premium and other regional policy instruments' in Whiting, A. (ed.), *The Economics of Industrial Subsidies*. London: HMSO, pp. 191–219.

Moore, B. C. and Rhodes, J. [1978], 'Economic and financial implications of devolution' in Nevin, E. (ed.), *The Economics of Devolution*. Cardiff: University of Wales Press, pp. 56–82.

Moore, B. C., Rhodes, J. and Tarling, R. [1978], 'Industrial policy and economic development: the experience of Northern Ireland and the Republic of Ireland', *Cambridge Journal of Economics*, Vol. 2, pp. 99–114.

Moore, B. C., Rhodes, J. and Tyler, P. [1977], 'The impact of regional policy in the 1970s', *C. E. S. Review*, no. 1, pp. 67–77.

Nuttall, T. [1973], 'The Industry Act and regional policy', *National Westminster Bank Quarterly Review*, November 1973, pp. 55–68.

Sant, M. C. [1975], *Industrial Movement and Regional Development: the British Case*. Oxford: Pergamon.

Short, J. [1977], *The Regional Distribution of Public Expenditure in Great Britain 1969/70–1973/4*. University of Durham (mimeo).

Trade and Industry Sub-Committee of the House of Commons Expenditure Committee [1973], *Regional Development Incentives – Report*. House of Commons Paper 85, London: HMSO.

Tyler, P., Moore, B. C. and Rhodes, J. [1979], 'Regional policy and growth in the Development Areas', *Paper presented to the S.S.R.C. Urban and Regional Economics Seminar Group*. Newcastle.

Wilson, T. [1979], 'Regional policy and the national interest' in Maclennan, D. & Parr, J. B. (eds.), *Regional Policy Past Experience and New Directions*. London: Martin Robertson, pp. 81–108.

8 The Nationalised Industries: Changing Attitudes and Changing Roles

by T. G. Weyman-Jones

Introduction

At the outset of the 1970s, the role of nationalised industries both as providers of public services and as vehicles for improving the overall allocation of resources seemed established beyond doubt. The predominant problems of the decade: the fight against inflation, and the response to a world-wide imbalance in energy markets, have resulted, however, in a serious revision of this role, and the emergence of a new set of attitudes about how the industries should operate and how their long-term strategies are to be determined.

In these years, new industries have been nationalised, and this has re-opened the debate on why an industry or collection of companies should or should not be brought into the public sector. Along with this, there was a general expression of discontent with the guidelines for nationalised industries (Cmnd 3437 [1967]) that operated from the beginning of the period until 1978; these guidelines were eventually replaced by Cmnd 7131 [1978]. Finally, government began slowly to respond to demands for policies designed to apply to a whole sector of the economy; this has been most noticeable in the energy sector, the focus of one of the decade's 'crises'; statements of government policy on energy (Cmnds 3438 [1967] and 7101 [1978]) were and are exactly contemporaneous with the nationalised industry White Papers mentioned above. All of these policy statements have been introduced by Labour governments, but none was amended by subsequent Conservative governments.

The discussion in this chapter is structured as follows. The next section reviews, briefly, the position of the nationalised industries in the public sector; for reasons of space, and because a wealth of factual detail is available in the background papers to NEDO [1976], a detailed description and chronology of the industries' activities over the decade is omitted. Rather, the subsequent sections examine the primary policy issues that have emerged in the period, beginning with a consideration of the re-opened arguments on the proper scope of nationalisation in the economy: what has been termed by one commentator, Wiseman [1978] as 'the political economy of nationalised industry'. Following this, two broad conceptions of policy are discussed, borrowing a useful distinction from Bates and Fraser [1974], between price-signalling policy and sectoral guidance policy. In the case of the latter, attention is focused on the most developed, and at the same time, most topical area: energy policy.

Organisation of the Nationalised Industries in the Public Sector

Over the period of the 1970s, the nationalised industries can safely be called major users of national resources, employing, on average over the period, about one-twelfth of the labour force, producing about one-tenth of GDP and accounting for slightly under one-fifth of investment. Nevertheless, they form a heterogeneous collection of organisations ranging from the traditional public utilities – gas, electricity, posts – to commercially based competitors in international markets – steel, air, transport, etc. In turn, they form only a part of the public sector's collection of enterprises and are distinguished by the following characteristics according to NEDO [1976]: their assets are in public ownership and vested in a corporation; their board members (not civil servants) are appointed by a Secretary of State; employees are not civil servants; they are engaged in industrial activities and are differentiated from other public corporations by the degree to which they engage in sale of goods and services, and raise revenue from their customers.

Table 8.1 provides a list of the main nationalised industries in 1979, categorised as 'major' and 'other' (following NEDO [1976]) on the basis that a 'major' employs at least 50 000 people. Two 'industries' were nationalised in the 1970s: shipbuilding and aerospace, and BNOC, a small operator in world oil markets, was formed chiefly on the basis of the North Sea oil assets previously owned by the

National Coal Board and The British Gas Corporation. They are said to 'dominate four strategic sectors of economic activity: energy, public transport, communications and iron and steel' though this overstates their ability to act outside competitive forces.

Table 8.1   The nationalised industries

Major industries	Date of nationalisation, if during the 1970s	Sponsor department
British Aerospace, BAs	November 1976	Industry
British Airways, BA		Trade
British Gas Corporation, BGC		Energy
British Railways Board, BR		Transport
British Shipbuilders, BS	November 1976	Industry
British Steel Corporation, BSC		Industry
Electricity industry in England and Wales: Central Electricity Generating Board, CEGB, the Electricity Council, EC and Area Boards		Energy
National Bus Company, NBC		Transport
National Coal Board, NCB		Energy
National Freight Corporation, NFC		Transport
Post Office-Telecommunications, PO(T), Posts, and Girobank		Industry
Other nationalised industries		
British Airports Authority		Trade
British National Oil Corporation BNOC	January 1976	Energy
British Transport Docks Board		Transport
British Waterways Board		Environment
North of Scotland Hydro-electric Board		Scottish Economic Planning Department (SEPD)
Scottish Transport Group		SEPD
South of Scotland Electricity Board		SEPD

Each industry must contend with two Ministries: its sponsor department, in which the civil servants can be expected to have a detailed knowledge of and sympathy for the industries' operations, and the Treasury, which is responsible for overall guidelines of behaviour, and for allocating the external finance (i.e. other than retained profits) of the industries.

The role of the Treasury as 'banker' to the nationalised industries became increasingly pivotal during the 1970s. This was firstly as a result of price restraint policies at the beginning of the decade which resulted in substantial losses and a shift away from internal funding by the industries of their investment programmes. Secondly a preoccupation with the monetary consequences of the public sector borrowing requirement became prominent in stabilisation policy.

In obtaining external finance, the industries rely mainly on either fixed-interest loans from the National Loans Fund (NLF) or, in some cases, on public dividend capital (PDC), i.e. a form of equity finance on which the industries pay to the government a variable dividend based on their profits. Quite deliberately, access to PDC is restricted to those nationalised industries 'which are expected to be both fully viable, and also especially subject to cyclical fluctuations in their returns as a result of their trading conditions and the nature of their assets' (Cmnd 7131 [1978]). This applies to the international competitors (whose market opponents will also be chiefly reliant on equity capital for external finance) and at the beginning of the 1970s included only BA and BSC; subsequently BAs, BS and PO–Giro have also had access to PDC.

The bulk, therefore, of external finance is borrowings through NLF, where the maturity of the debt is normally made to correspond to the life of the assets being accumulated: gas pipelines, electricity generating sets, etc., and on which the actual interest payments are comparable to the interest rates on gilt-edged securities; for substantial parts of the 1970s this meant negative real fixed interest payments. The changes in the Treasury–industries–sponsor departments relationship will be one of the themes discussed in detail below.

The industries' main channel to Parliament over the 1970s has been the Select Committee on Nationalised Industries (SCNI), and this has proved a both valuable and informative forum for airing the views of the nationalised industries' boards. It is before SCNI that some of the chief policy issues – particularly the role of the Treasury guidelines for nationalised industries' operations (Cmnds 3437 [1967] and 7131 [1978]) – have been examined in detail. Occasionally, some of the industries are involved in public inquiries into environmental and other objections to proposed investments. It is here that ordinary citizens may have the greatest opportunity to scrutinise their behaviour; it is notable that sponsor departments (e.g. Energy in the case of the Windscale inquiry) deliberately distance themselves from the industries in such public inquiries.

The Role and Control of Nationalised Industries

In 1976, the National Economic Development Office completed a large study of UK nationalised industries (NEDO [1976]), which crystallised many of the feelings of discontent, which had grown up in the 1970s inside and outside the industries, about their role and their relationship with Government. Sir Ronald McIntosh, the Director General of NEDO, believed four main problems had been revealed. First, there was a lack of trust and mutual understanding between those who ran the industries and the government. Second, there was a confusion about roles; so that accountability was blurred. Third, there was no systematic framework for reaching agreement on long-term strategy and no assurance of continuity. Finally, there was no effective system for measuring performance of nationalised industries and assessing managerial competence.

The overriding cause of these problems, in the opinion of the board chairmen of the nationalised industries was the tendency of government to intervene with short-run, *ad hoc* policy measures, such as price restraint in inflation, to the detriment of long-term plans.

The historical perspective on these problems takes us back to the foundation of many of the nationalised industries after the Second World War. NEDO [1976] points out that the fundamental approach, associated with Herbert Morrison, was to keep the industries at 'arm's length' from government or Ministerial actions; that a nationalised industry board's policies 'would embody the public interest, and that conflict with government on the interpretation of national interest would be very exceptional'. NEDO [1976] believed this argument was based on a 'false analogy with the private sector'; it argued that the 'financial structures and disciplines in the public and private sectors are very different – not least because the ultimate sanction of liquidation is, in practice, absent in the major nationalised industries'.

The answer, NEDO believed, was a radical change in government–industry relationships towards a more 'concerted' approach. It suggested that instead of a single board there should be a policy council and a corporation board for the industry. The policy council would include the corporation board chairman, civil servants from the

Treasury and sponsor department, representatives of trade unions and consumer groups. It would be responsible for the long-term strategy of the industry and for finally deciding on a corporate plan – and would involve a great deal of co-operative decision-making by the industry and the sponsor department. The corporation board, on the other hand, was to be the executive authority, staffed from the industry. The overall aim of these recommendations was to re-establish a 'sense of purpose and commitment' in relationships between government and industries on the so-called commanding heights of the economy.

Simultaneously with this study, there was a similar diagnosis of nationalised industry performance among some academic economists and parts of the Conservative Party, then in opposition. The remedies suggested however were vastly different. Wiseman [1978] and Little-child [1978], for example, both reconsidered the supposed fundamental reasons for nationalisation. In essence, they argued these amounted to the view that certain industries would operate more efficiently under state ownership than under private ownership. Certainly, as we shall see below, the policy guidelines for nationalised industries that operated during this period involved the arguments about economic efficiency familiar to economists.

In this alternative diagnosis, these efficiency arguments were rejected on the grounds that nationalised industries lacked the stimuli of 'feedback and competition' (Littlechild [1978]) that operated on private firms in the free-market mechanism. As Wiseman [1978] put it, there was no one who had a direct interest in the fruitful use of the assets of a nationalised industry. On the other hand there was clearly burden of risk of losses placed on the tax-payer, and Heath [1978] argued that the only means of reducing this unsought risk was emigration. The remedy might consist of emphasising the burden of risk to managers in the industries, within an overall concerted approach (Heath [1978]) or, alternatively, opening up the industries to competition (Littlechild [1978]; Wiseman [1978]). This led to demands for 'hiving off' profitable parts of the public sector to private ownership, and towards the end of the decade, the prime candidates for this became telecommunications – PO(T) – and the North Sea assets of BGC.

The reaction of the industries was full agreement that relations and performance had deteriorated drastically, but they completely rejected the 'concerted' remedy of NEDO.[1] Any attack on the 'arm's

length' philosophy was an anathema, and the mixed membership
Policy Council was entirely condemned. Not unexpectedly, the competition was also distrusted, as an attempt to separate the commercially successful parts of the corporations from those in which their
function was to provide a social service, for example rural post
deliveries. In a sense, this latter reaction confirms an argument of
Wiseman and Littlechild that all individuals – even chairmen of
nationalised industries – acted as individual decision-makers pursuing
their own interest.

As a contrast to the theory, the aerospace and shipbuilding industries provide practical examples of private corporations which were
nationalised during the period. In proposing their nationalisation in
1975 the Secretary of State for Industry, Mr Benn, did not use the
economist's arguments about efficiency; indeed the aerospace industry's performance in private hands had not been bad, in the view
of some commentators,[2] nor was it expected to improve under state
ownership. The case for nationalisation of aerospace was simply that
the industry already, through grants and favourable contracts, was
effectively part of the public sector and its policies could be more
easily rationalised with those of its main customer, BA. In the case
of shipbuilding, nationalisation was regarded purely as a defensive
measure in the face of a looming slump in demand; under state control
the pace of decline could be more easily planned.

The Government replied to the mounting criticism of its relations
with the corporations in its 1978 White Paper *The Nationalised Industries*
(Cmnd 7131 [1978]). It rejected NEDO's idea of a Policy Council,
but was prepared to adopt some of the detailed proposals. For example
it was ready to consider appointing union-member employees and
civil servants from the sponsor department and Treasury to corporation boards and was prepared to tackle the problem of continuity
through the establishment of medium and long-term corporate plans,
which would be published. The power of ministerial intervention was
strengthened by enabling the Minister 'to give a board either general
or specific directions on matters which appeared to him to affect the
national interest', and compensation would be paid to cover the extra
cost, if any, of these directives.

The problem of monitoring and incentives in relation to industries'
operations was left open by Cmnd 7131 [1978]. As we shall see below,
it was proposed that there would be strict targets for financial performance and these would be examined, but no form of incentives

or penalties for good or poor out-turns (say in the form of Littlechild's suggestion of managerial bonuses in proportion to financial surpluses) was even considered. We turn now to look at the detailed framework under which the industries operated in the 1970s.

Nationalised Industry Price Signals

As we saw in the previous section, the original and prevailing conception of Government–nationalised industry relationships was the 'at arm's length' idea – in economist's jargon, the pursuit of decentralised decision-making. In this context, we can use the ideas of welfare economics about how information is signalled to consumers by means of price structures. If we are able to assume (i) that there are no external effects in consumption or production; (ii) there are competitive forces operating outside the public sector; (iii) there are no important indirect taxes driving a wedge between producers' and consumers' prices; and (iv) the existing distribution of income and wealth is deemed satisfactory, and if our objective is an allocation of resources such that no one can be made better off without making anyone else worse off (the Pareto criterion), then an instruction to base price signals on marginal costs will be socially optimal.

Several comments are immediately in order. Firstly, calculation of marginal costs – which must be based on changes in future output plans – and design of marginal cost reflecting price schedules is time-consuming. Secondly, the assumptions listed above are probably never likely to hold, so that marginal cost pricing is no longer socially optimal (the problem of second best). Thirdly, pricing on the basis of future output changes, leaves open the question of whether current costs are covered and profits or losses are made. Finally, there are a great many objectives – provision of social services, redistribution of income, stabilising the economy – which the ordinary voter or members of SCNI may regard as more pressing than the Pareto criterion.

Two attempts at formulating price structures were in operation in the 1970s: Cmnds 3437 [1967] and 7131 [1978], and these need to be clarified.[3] Take our model nationalised industry to be a large, capital-intensive organisation, forecasting and planning for demand on an interconnected 'system' of plant and equipment over many periods. If it has just installed plant to meet an output target for some years ahead, but which is currently underused, it will achieve the socially optimal use of resources by charging short-run marginal cost – here the running cost (r) of a unit of output on the current system; initially, price is

$$p_0 = r_0. \tag{1}$$

However, as time passes and demand expands beyond the currently available system size, it may be rationed by charging a sufficient excess over running cost; subsequently, price is

$$p_t = r_t + k_t \tag{2}$$

where k_t is the excess over running cost required to restrict demand to capacity output in period t. Both (1) and (2) exemplify the idea of short-run marginal cost pricing. However k_t also indicates the amount that consumers are willing to pay over r_t, in order to have a larger system in period t. Summing over all periods and using the discounting procedure, suggests that a unit expansion of system size is warranted on cost–benefit analysis grounds if

$$\sum_{t=0}^{t=T} k_t (1+i)^{-t} > c \tag{3}$$

where c is the cost of installing an extra unit of capacity on the system. Thus, the instruction to use short-run marginal cost prices, (2), should imply that the industry simultaneously undertakes investment appraisals using (3). To do so it must receive Government instructions about the 'test discount rate', (TDR), to be used to allocate future and current resources.

An alternative way to look at (2), is to regard k_t as a (socially optimal) capital charge, so that if (3) holds with exact equality, then (2) is saying price equals running plus capital costs in each period; i.e. long-run marginal cost. In essence, short-run marginal cost-pricing using (2) and investment policy using (3) is equivalent to long-run marginal cost pricing.

In discussing (2) and (3), we are not limited to yearly time periods. A large part of the supply problem of many nationalised industries (telephone calls, electricity, gas; bus and rail transport) is meeting demands which fluctuate in a regular peak and off-peak manner. At the trough of the demand cycle, marginal cost may be no more than the additional fuel and labour costs on an underutilised system, while at the peak (system maximum demand) marginal cost can include a large part of the capital costs of the system – in other words to supply additional output at the peak may require a capacity expansion. The principles embodied in (2) and (3) remain true: different prices are charged according to the strength of demand in different periods, i.e. marginal cost-pricing implies 'time-of-day' pricing to meet the peak loading problem because there is a different marginal cost for every identifiable sub-period of a system's life in which demand varies.

Going a step further, (3) can also act as a guide to which type of plant should be a candidate for investment choice. The current system will usually consist of both old and new equipment. At the margin of use will be the oldest, most expensive to run, plant, whose capital costs are long since sunk. If it is deemed just economic to use, then this oldest plant running cost, say m_t, will also represent short-run marginal cost on the system, and will equal price, so that we can write:

$$k_t = p_t - r_t = m_t - r_t. \qquad (4)$$

In other words the benefit in year t of new equipment is the difference between its running cost (r_t) and the running cost on the oldest plant in use. If there are two types of plant, A and B, available to replace old equipment then we would prefer type A if

$$\sum_{t=0}^{t=T_A} (m_{At} - r_{At})(1+i)^{-t} - c_A > \sum_{t=0}^{t=T_B} (m_{Bt} - r_{Bt})(1+i)^{-t} - c_B \qquad (5)$$

where m_{At} is short-run marginal cost on a system including type A, r_{At} is running cost on type A, T_A is its economic life, and c_A its installation cost, and similar definitions hold for type B.

These ideas underlie some of the guidelines in Cmnd 3437 [1967], by which nationalised industries operated between 1967 and 1978. The statements in this White Paper on marginal cost-pricing (para 21) and choice of test discount rate as the shadow price of low risk private sector capital in real terms (para 9), in themselves are quite unequivocal. However, the level of profits or losses resulting from the application of these rules is merely accidental. Suppose for example that future demand expansion is grossly overestimated, and demand never needs to be rationed to capacity; then, optimal use of fixed resources will require $p_t = r_t$, and prices will not recover capital charges. Clearly there is a relation between accurately forecasting an uncertain future (especially where demand may be contracting) and the avoidance of financial losses when marginal cost pricing is adopted. Cmnd 3437 [1967] seems in part to have realised this, and laid down financial targets for the industries arguing that those served 'as an incentive to management and as one of the standards by which success or failure in a period of years may be judged' (para 33). At the same time, application of the guidelines was further constrained by allowing the industries to depart from them and the financial targets 'for social or wider economic reasons' (para 13).

In practice, the industries seem to have found these guidelines difficult to operate – indeed the NEDO [1976] study concluded, from an investigation of the application and limits of the guidelines in BGC, PO(T), BR and BSC, that none of these industries based prices on marginal costs, although they felt the reasons were different in each case. PO(T), for example, argued that (i) marginal cost prices would not differ from average cost based prices and (ii) calculation of marginal cost was too difficult anyway; however, because these arguments flatly contradict each other, a more accurate reason may be that the principles involved were simply not understood, and the sponsoring department did not pursue their application. In the case of BR and BSC, the argument was that they were price-takers in competitive markets and hence marginal cost pricing was irrelevant.

BGC in fact replied to SCNI requests for comments[4] on the NEDO study by declaring itself satisfied with the Cmnd 3437 guidelines in principle, adding however that their failure to be widely practised was 'due more to the superimposition of price controls and other government intervention than to any shortcomings of the White Paper itself'. (We return to this below).

The industry which is generally agreed to have gone furthest in using marginal cost pricing is electricity. The CEGB declared that its bulk supply tariff (BST) (which includes several time-of-day rates) is wholly based on marginal cost principles, and points to the substantial increases in system load factor over the 1970s as evidence of improved efficiency in resource allocation. However, as the SCNI noted in investigating gas and electricity prices in 1975/6, the marginal cost complexities of the BST are not reflected in the area boards' retail tariffs. The obstacles to this are that simplicity is a desirable feature of retail tariffs, and in a large sample survey over the years 1969–74, the Electricity Council found that the welfare benefits of emphasising marginal cost signals in retail tariffs did not outweigh the additional metering costs associated with several time switches.[5]

The NEDO study also found that the investment criterion using the TDR was applied to only a small proportion of the industries' capital expenditure, the bulk of it being regarded as inescapable in order to maintain existing standards of service, and hence not to be evaluated on a cost–benefit basis. Rees [1979] and, to a certain extent, Heath [1978] have suggested the following analysis of this apparently curious reasoning. Clearly the TDR criterion [e.g. equations (3) and (5)] applied to 'choice of technique' decisions, i.e. what type of plant to choose for a given expansion. However, the most pressing practical constraint on capital expenditure was the *actual* interest repayment on borrowed funds, and this was what was reflected, through the financial target, in the actual level of prices and consequently in determining demand. Because the actual interest charged to the industries was usually lower in real terms than the TDR (which was 10% throughout the period up to 1978), the industries made their choice of overall scale as if capital were cheap, while they still compared plant types as if capital were expensive. Briefly, choice of scale decisions were implicitly made at lower interest rates than choice of technique decisions. Because the industries are instructed to maintain standards of reliability and service, they could argue that the *scale* of the system ought not to be contracted in principle and hence replacement investment could largely be decided without reference to TDR. There is a difficulty in finding evidence for this argument so we can only accept it as a persuasive conjecture – nevertheless, Webb [1977] has argued that the 'standards of service' criterion could be tested in the marketplace to discover consumer trade-offs between arbitrary standards and lower prices.

Our factor does seem to stand out as an obstacle to the guidelines: government price restraint policies. Millward [1976] shows that government had a strong incentive to hold down nationalised industry prices relative to the private sector (i) to lead by example in price restraint, (ii) to reduce inflationary expectations, and (iii) to cushion the undesirable income distribution effects of rapid inflation. He provides statistical evidence of lower price inflation in public corporations than in the private sector in the early 1970s, despite little difference in cost changes and argues that the closer scrutiny of nationalised industries' prices as they went through the formalised process of seeking price rises allowed much more behind the scenes arm-twisting than could be applied to the private sector.

This factor, more than any other, seems – if the evidence of the board chairmen to SCNI is correct – to have led to the breakdown of Cmnd 3437 [1967]. In any case, it led to large financial deficits in the industries and fostered the need for a new set of guidelines in the wake of NEDO's evidence. By 1976 the Treasury was admitting to SCNI that even the income distribution argument for price restraint was unsound, although there had been many demands (for example from the National Consumer Council) for holding down gas and electricity prices. It calculated that it would cost eight times as much to reduce the retail price index by 1% by restraining gas and electricity prices, as it would to raise social security benefits by 1%.[6]

In response to the criticisms from the industries, SCNI, and finally NEDO, the Government reviewed in Cmnd 7131 [1978] the financial and economic framework under which the nationalised industries operated. (We have already examined, above, the institutional proposals of this White Paper).

As Orson (Treasury [1979]) remarks, it is difficult to obtain from the White Paper a 'completely comprehensive message' – partly because it is addressed not only to nationalised industries, but also to central and local government, Parliament, and, finally, professional economists. Nevertheless the Treasury, in explaining the background to its publication (Treasury [1979]), believes that its new approach is not concerned with the issues of principle of Cmnd 3437 [1967], but with making them effective in the real world.

There are four principal ingredients in Cmnd 7131's new framework: the required rate of return (RRR), pricing policy, financial targets and cash limits. We begin with RRR, designed, according to Byatt (Treasury [1979]) to achieve the modest purpose of linking 'resource allocation and national economic policy to financial disciplines and the corporate planning of individual nationalised industries'.

On investment appraisal, Cmnd 7131 argues that the 'opportunity cost of capital should be brought to bear on the industries' investment programmes as a whole, not only on individual projects' and that this opportunity cost of capital would be represented by a 'required rate of return (RRR) which the industries would be expected to achieve on their new investment as a whole' (para 60). RRR then is the rate which 'public investment would have to earn in order to justify committing resources to that sector rather than using them in other ways (for investment or consumption)' (Smith, Treasury

[1979]). The underlying theme, therefore, is that the Treasury is reinforcing the 'arm's length' idea; its main signal to the industries is the social opportunity cost of capital (rather than specific price guidelines), and how the industries meet this is largely left to them. The choice of the RRR was 5% in real terms before tax; this was largely based on the achieved pre-tax real returns in the private sector in the 1970s, (see Appendix 1 to Cmnd 7131 [1978]).

The Treasury, with this overall shadow cost of capital in mind, believed that RRR should become a factor in pricing policy, the scale of new investment and financial targets. The relationship with pricing policy however needs to be spelt out, and Appendix 1 of Cmnd 7131 and Short indicate that it is 'essentially a long-run marginal cost approach' (Short, Treasury [1979], p. 35).

To see this consider equation (2) again and now interpret k_t as the optimal capital charge, so that:

$$p_t = r_t + k_t = \text{LRMC}_t.$$

Equation (3) provides the link between the capital charge element in LRMC and the opportunity cost of capital. If equation (3) holds exactly, we can solve for any one of the ks, e.g. k_n:

$$\dot{k}_n = (1 + i)^n \left(c - \sum_{t \neq n} k_t (1 + i)^{-t} \right) \tag{6}$$

where we would interpret i as RRR.

Clearly there is a strong forecasting element here because for any investment programme, it is still necessary to forecast k_t ahead for each year of the project. All that has changed in principle from Cmnd 3437 [1967] is that the LRMC becomes the focus of attention. For some industries, e.g. electricity, the investment policy can be programmed as a divisible economic model, the overall pricing results appear to be unchanged. However, Cmnd 7131 [1978] is anxious to provide a model for *all* types of nationalised industry investment, and consequently needs to be applicable to industries where a new project cannot be separately identified.

Some industries, therefore, will only be able to approximate equation (6) very crudely, for example by ascribing a level annual capital charge to each year of an increment in output:

$$k = \frac{ic}{1 - (1 + i)^{-T}}$$

In summary the industries should calculate LRMC (however approximately) using $i = $ RRR. One difficulty arises where the output increment is not small in the textbook economic sense, but the Treasury accepts this and would be content simply with identifying what Short calls the 'full cost of supplying the tranche of output associated with the investment programme'. Rees [1979] describes this as the average cost over the large output *increment* and believes it may not be at all a bad approximation to LRMC.

This emphasis on approximate LRMC is believed by the Treasury to be a more workable concept than the approach via SRMC and TDR embodied in Cmnd 3437 [1967]. Nevertheless, where the pricing model of (2) and (3) above is feasible, it is not to be ignored and Cmnd 7131 [1978] emphasised that the industries should ensure that 'charges for peak and off-peak usage are properly related to the relative costs of supply' and 'arbitrary cross subsidisation between different consumers ... should be avoided' (para 68).

Subject to this analysis, the government believes that it is primarily for each nationalised industry to work out details of its prices 'with regard to its markets and overall objectives, including its financial targets'. We consider financial targets below, but this statement seems to recognise the problem of 'second best pricing'. The government has stopped short of a blanket order to use marginal cost pricing, although LRMC remains as the vital cost calculation. Partly this recognition of the second best problem arises out of a recently evolved distinction between nationalised industries which are 'price-makers' (the traditional utilities: gas, electricity, etc.) and those which are 'price-takers' (i.e. those competing in international or domestic markets: steel, shipbuilding, transport, banking and so forth). Given the competitive structure of the 'price-takers' markets Cmnd 7131 [1978] recognised that while LRMC should be covered in looking at future programmes, individual output of different products at different times may need to respond to externally determined price changes. BSC is recognised as the body to whom steel pricing should be left, just as BNOC is best able to judge current and future oil prices and so on. This willingness to leave decision-making to the industries applies not only to detailed price schedules but also to individual project appraisal.

The TDR concept of Cmnd 3437, while downgraded, is not completely defunct. The primary responsibility for appraisal of individual projects is left to the industries, but they would be expected to evaluate some *revenue raising* projects individually at a TDR higher than RRR, so that these can carry non-revenue raising projects (such as Head Office expansion) within an overall investment programme earning RRR. For choice of technique decisions, however, RRR would be the appropriate discount rate.

In Cmnd 7131 [1978], the financial target is given a central role as the primary expression of the financial performance which the government intends the industries to achieve. This means that it cannot be independent of the use of RRR and LRMC pricing, and this is clearly recognised in the White Paper, although the translation into accounting terms is not direct. Suppose that prices necessary to cover the approximate LRMC of an overall programme have been worked out on the basis of $i = $ RRR. These are translated into a probable cash flow over the next three to five years, given output forecasts at these prices, i.e. $(p_0 x_0, p_1 x_1 \ldots)$. Adopting the accounting conventions peculiar to each industry, this produces a *forecast* of accounting profits, AP_t^*, in each year, before interest:

$$AP_t^* = p_t x_t - OC_t - D_t$$

where OC_t is operating costs and D_t is depreciation according to the convention in operation. This forecast – for instance expressed as a percentage of the asset value of the industry – would then be the basis of its financial target for the next three to five years. It has to be tailored to each industry, and will differ according to depreciation conventions, while maintaining the essential idea that prices will at least cover LRMC.

These depreciation conventions have themselves been the object of some debate, and the government wishes the industries to adopt an inflation accounting standard and hopes to put the financial targets on 'some suitable inflation-adjusted basis' as soon as possible. In the absence of an agreed inflation accounting standard amongst the accountancy profession, some of the nationalised industries have adopted a variety of *ad hoc* methods of accounting for the replacement cost of their assets; as Wright [1978] has pointed out these have not always been comprehensive and the lack of unanimity has made comparisons of financial performance difficult. BGC, in particular, started from 1975 to make very large supplementary depreciation provisions with the result that it was accused of using unrealistic accounting techniques to disguise its profit position and forestall demands for lower gas prices. Nevertheless, BGC would argue that part, at least, of its capital stock consists of non-renewable energy sources and the implicit cost of replacing these is probably very high indeed – certainly far in excess of their original capital cost. For these and other reasons, the full set of nationalised industry financial targets remains to be settled.

If this framework were all, the White Paper system would be consistent and self contained. But Cmnd 7131 [1978] went on to impose several qualifications. Social or sectoral objectives, or public sector borrowing requirement implications, might be brought to bear on the final level of the financial target. This equivocation makes it lose part of its impact as an indicator of how well an industry is forecasting its demand and measuring LRMC.

Perhaps most important in practice will be the cash limits system; under this, the amount of borrowing from the NLF to top up revenue-financed programmes is agreed in advance with the Treasury, along with public dividend capital and grants, and if an industry faces the need for an increased, unforeseen, borrowing requirement, there will be 'no presumption that the government will agree to this being met by a further injection of external finance and an increase in the cash limit, as opposed to other action which the industry can take. . . .' (para 81). Indeed Likierman [1979] believes that the Treasury is 'using cash as first-line control rather than the integrated framework which the White Paper sought to provide' (p. 32).

A Case Study in Sectoral Guidance: Energy Policy

We have emphasised, so far, the Treasury–nationalised industry relationship, but the industries themselves have deeper connections with their sponsor departments. Over the late 1960s and 1970s, the idea of having a policy towards a whole sector, part of which was nationalised, gained momentum, and two obvious candidates were the transport sector and the energy sector.

It is most useful here to use energy as a case study of sectoral guidance policy. It is in the energy sector that many of the problems of nationalised industries: price signals, subsidisation, relationship with macroeconomic trends have been highlighted, and no survey of the 1970s would be complete without a recognition of the effects of energy crises.

From its beginnings in the Ministry of Power in the 1960s, Energy emerged, via the giant 'Mintech' of the second Wilson government, as a sponsor department with large responsibilities in the 1970s. It has close relations with all the fuel industries: coal, gas and electricity via the NCB, BGC and CEGB–EC utilities, and, since 1976, with oil through BNOC. At the beginning of the period, price signalling and sectoral guidance policy went very clearly hand-in-hand; the energy sector's development was planned in Cmnd 3438 *Fuel Policy* [1967], issued simultaneously with Cmnd 3437 [1967], and providing the first application of the ideas of marginal cost pricing and TDR.

One of the architects of Cmnd 3438, M. V. Posner, has described the following model of making energy policy:

> the object is merely to minimise the total cost, in some year, (far enough into the future for decisions taken today about the energy industries to have some effect on the actual outcome), of producing a required total output of primary energy, which is achieved by allowing the output of all home industries to increase until either some physical constraint is reached, or until the 'marginal' ton of home-produced coal or gas equals the cost to the community of purchasing energy from overseas.
>
> (Posner [1974], pp. 3–4)

It is this model (not unlike the marginal cost pricing model of Cmnd 3437 [1967]) which underlay energy policy at the beginning of the 1970s. The crucial policy issues which the decade was to resolve concerned firstly the paced rundown of the NCB, secondly the exploitation of North Sea Gas by BGC, and thirdly the switch to nuclear electricity using the Advanced Gas Cooled Reactor (AGR) by CEGB. Quite clearly the nationalised fuel industries had to be the vehicle for policy in the energy sector.

What was the rationale for these policies? In 1970, three years after Cmnd 3438, it was still possible to view Middle East oil as the cheap energy source of the rest of the century; its shadow marginal cost to the UK was only high because of our chronic balance of payments difficulties. The traditional fuel, coal, could not compete with oil and its production had to be phased down on efficiency grounds, although such were the social costs of unemployment in mining communities, that this phased decline was delayed by instructing CEGB to maintain an uneconomic level of 'coal burn' in electricity generation. The cheap fuels for the UK were natural gas, discovered in large quantities in the Southern Basin of the North Sea in the mid 1960s and responsible for the resurgence of the UK gas industry and nuclear electricity. The forecasts of low, stable oil prices which underlay Cmnd 3438

[1967], combined to suggest a growth in premium demand for gas that was below the forecast offtake from the North Sea (an offtake that had been pitched at a relatively fast level to guarantee large early cash flows at a low price for the operating oil companies). All the signs, therefore, pointed to a necessarily low gas price with rapid depletion, and penetration of the home heating market. The nuclear side also suggested the 1970s would be an era of cheap energy as the much-vaunted AGR programme reached completion.

In the event, all the assumptions of Cmnd 3438 [1967] went drastically awry; from 1973 the price of oil began to escalate and OPEC achieved a 500% rise in about eighteen months.

Table 8.2 shows how the primary fuel mix in the UK altered over the period. The decline of coal began to be halted after 1975 as it partly regained its competitive position in relation to oil; the depletion of natural gas went ahead but the planned virtual doubling of nuclear capacity did not come about. The one offsetting factor for the UK was the discovery and exploitation of North Sea oil – not a cheap fuel as its price is set by world markets – but a welcome release from balance of payments constraints.

Table 8.2   Inland energy consumption of primary fuels
(million tonnes of coal equivalent (*mtce*))

	1970	1975	1978
Coal	157	120	120
Oil	150	137	139
Natural Gas	18	55	65
Nuclear and Hydroelectric	12	13	16
Total	337	325	340

Source: *Department of Energy Digest* [1979], p. 12.

Let us consider how the sponsor department, Energy, and the nationalised fuel industries responded to these developments. An immediate, and obvious reaction was that energy would become a much more expensive commodity and that this was to be the basic assumption of policy. Curiously, though, this message has not so far appeared in price signals. Table 8.3 indicates, on the very crude basis of unit values of energy consumption, that, relative to all other prices, the price of energy has not risen steeply for final UK consumers.

Table 8.3   The price of energy in the UK

Year	Unit values for total final consumption of energy (p/therm)	Index (1975 = 100)	GDP deflator (1975 = 100)	Index of real price of energy (1975 = 100)
1970	8.78	43.00	51	84
1971	9.77	47.86	57	84
1972	10.37	50.79	62	82
1973	10.87	53.24	67	79
1974	15.79	77.30	78	99
1975	20.42	100.00	100	100
1976	23.91	117.38	113	104
1977	27.37	134.04	127	106
1978	28.82	141.15	140	101

Sources: *Department of Energy Digest* [1979] and *Economic Trends* (various).

There seem to be two reasons for this: (i) the restraint on coal, gas and electricity prices already discussed in the previous section; and (ii) the decision to offset the deflationary impact of the 1973 oil price rise by permitting increases in government spending so that the unemployment level did not seriously worsen.

Nevertheless, a rising real price of energy became a part of the Department of Energy's future assumptions in its 1977 Energy Policy Review, and this has re-opened the case for an expanded coal industry. Such a view first emerged from the tripartite 'Plan for Coal' (1974), one of the few cases in which a nationalised industry's policy has been settled by including the industry's trade union, NUM, as an equal partner in the discussion between industry and sponsor department. The Department agreed to a large capital investment in new pits at Selby and the Vale of Belvoir (at the time of writing (December 1979), subject to a local planning inquiry) and accepted that there would have to be substantial rises in miners' real wages to recruit a younger skilled labour force.

A second characteristic problem of energy policy over the decade has been the debate on nuclear power. One of the classic examples in 1967 of an investment appraisal using TDR, was the evaluation of the advanced gas cooled reactor (AGR). The appraisal used the methodology of equation (5) above, in which the cheaper running costs of nuclear capacity provided benefits over coal and oil-fired alternatives for generating electricity. The running and capital costs of the AGR programme were catastrophically underestimated, and it can be seen from Henderson's [1977] retrospective cost–benefit study that the programme was a major error, which ought not to have been undertaken. Burn [1978] suggested that the history of the AGR had shown that the CEGB had accepted over-optimistic projections from the Atomic Energy Authority, of the potential of the UK-designed, but untried, AGR system, over the more proven cost levels of the US-designed pressurised water reactor (PWR).

History partly repeated itself in 1974 when the decision by the Secretary of State for Energy, Mr Varley, on a third generation of nuclear reactors was made – after overruling CEGB preferences for PWR – in favour of another, relatively untried UK design (the steam generating heavy water reactor, SGHWR). This was also opposed by the construction consortium, a partially publicly-owned corporation. Once more, the programme faltered and SGHWR was abandoned.

New forces joined the nuclear debate at this time, as world-wide political opposition to nuclear power developed. This came to the fore in the UK in 1978 when British Nuclear Fuels Ltd (BNFL), a public company wholly owned by the Atomic Energy Authority on behalf of the Secretary of State for Energy, sought permission, through a local planning inquiry, chaired by Mr Justice Parker, to expand its nuclear fuel re-processing facilities at Windscale. Though BNFL received support from the CEGB, the sponsor department, Energy, deliberately remained aloof from the proceedings, which eventually overruled the environmentalist objections in favour of BNFL. Pearce [1979] argued that the local planning inquiry method of opening up the debate on energy policy to outside parties, besides the Department of Energy and the CEGB, has little to recommend it. It fails to provide the freedom of information about decisions available, for example, in the US.

Part of the energy sector remained outside the Department-nationalised industry nexus at the beginning of the decade: oil. As North Sea oil replaced imports, the Department gained access to this part of the energy sector through the compulsory participation of BNOC in new North Sea licences. The eventual aim, at present under discussion, was to have BNOC as majority participator in all offshore oil operations. This policy, if continued by the Conservative government of 1979 can be accomplished only relatively slowly.

While the preparation of Cmnd 7131 [1978] on the new nationalised industry guidelines was in progress, the Government issued (February 1978) a green paper on *Energy Policy: a consultative document* (Cmnd 7101 [1978]). This sets out the assumptions and possible evolution of the nationalised fuel industries and the whole energy sector until the year 2000. While recognising that energy conservation and alternative energy sources (wind, wave, solar, etc.) may have a limited contribution to make to energy supply, it emphasised two key areas of expansion: coal (aims to reach output of 137 and 173 million tonnes by 1985 and 2000 respectively) and nuclear (aims to reach capacity of 25 and 97 million tonnes of coal equivalent by 1985 and 2000 respectively). From consulting Table 8.2, we can see that these, especially nuclear, are massive programmes of expansion. Given the demoralisation of the nationalised fuel industries in the 1970s which we have discussed, it is apparent that such plans are extremely optimistic – even then, there remains an ominous 'policy gap' between indigenous supply and projected demand in 2000. From the point of view of the industries, the Department of Energy appears to have absorbed two welcome messages however. It is prepared to see substantial rises in the real price of energy – in other words large rises in gas and electricity tariffs – and it seems prepared to at least investigate the CEGB's preference for US PWR reactors over the tarnished reputation of the AGR.

What remains doubtful is how the public at large will accept the imposition of large nationalised industry price increases, and the rapid expansion of a fuel source which appears to carry awesome long-term risks. If the 1970s saw a great deal of thought about the Treasury–nationalised industry–sponsor department interrelationship, the 1980s may witness a strenuous debate about the nationalised industry–ordinary citizen relationship. Certainly in energy policy, the ordinary people of the UK are going to become increasingly aware of how the decisions of some of the nationalised industries can affect much of their lives.

Notes

1. In evidence to SCNI [1976/7].
2. For example, *The Economist*, 18 January 1975, p. 74.
3. The analysis of this section relies heavily on Turvey [1971].
4. Published as SCNI [1976/7]; see also industries' evidence to SCNI [1973/4].
5. See Electricity Council [1975].
6. Evidence to SCNI [1975/6].

References

Bates, R. and Fraser, N. [1974], *Investment Decisions in the Nationalised Fuel Industries.* Cambridge: Cambridge University Press.

Burn, D. [1978], *Nuclear Power and the Energy Crisis.* Macmillan for the Trade Policy Research Centre.

Cmnd 3437 [1967], *Nationalised Industries: a review of economic and financial objectives.* London: HMSO.

Cmnd 3438 [1967], *Fuel Policy.* London: HMSO.

Cmnd 7101 [1978], *Energy Policy: a consultative document.* London: HMSO.

Cmnd 7131 [1978], *The Nationalised Industries.* London: HMSO.

Department of Energy [1979], *Digest of United Kingdom Energy Statistics.* London: HMSO.

Electricity Council [1975], 'Domestic Tariffs Experiment'. Load and Market Research Report no. 121. London: The Electricity Council.

Heath, J. B. [1978], 'Comments' in SCNI (1977/8) Select Committee on Nationalised Industries' Sixth Special Report, *Comments by Nationalised Industries and others on the Government White Paper on the Nationalised Industries.* HCP 638. London: HMSO.

Henderson, P. D. [1977], 'Two British Errors: their probable size and some possible lessons', *Oxford Economic Papers*, 29 July 1977, pp. 159–205.

Likierman, A. [1979], 'The Financial Framework for Nationalised Industries', *Lloyds Bank Review*, October 1979, pp. 16–32.

Littlechild, S. C. [1978], *The Fallacy of the Mixed Economy.* London: Hobart Paper 80, Institute of Economic Affairs.

Millward, R. [1976], 'Price Restraint, Anti-inflation Policy, and Public and Private Industry in the United Kingdom 1949–1973', *Economic Journal*, Vol. 86, June 1976, pp. 226–42.

NEDO [1976], *A Study of UK Nationalised Industries.* Report (with appendix volume and background papers) to the government from the National Economic Development Office. London: HMSO.

Pearce, D. [1979], *Decision Making for Energy Futures.* Social Science Research Council.

Posner, M. V. [1974], 'Energy at the Centre of the Stage', *Three Banks Review*, December 1974, pp. 3–27.

Rees, R. [1979], 'The Pricing Policies of the Nationalised Industries', *Three Banks Review*, June 1979, pp. 3–31.

SCNI (1973/4) Select Committee on Nationalised Industries' First Report, *Capital Investment Procedures.* HCP 65. London: HMSO.

SCNI (1975/6) Select Committee on Nationalised Industries' Fourth Report, *Gas and Electricity Prices.* HCP 353. London: HMSO.

SCNI (1976/7) Select Committee on Nationalised Industries' Second Special Report, *Comments by Nationalised Industries on the NEDO Report.* HCP 345. London: HMSO.

Treasury [1979], 'The Test Discount Rate and the Required Rate of Return'. Proceedings of a seminar at the Civil Service College, published as Government Economic Service Working Paper no. 22.

Turvey, R. [1971], *Economic Analysis and Public Enterprises.* London: Allen and Unwin.

Webb, M. [1977], 'The Determination of Reserve Generating Capacity Criteria in Electricity Supply Systems', *Applied Economics*, Vol. 9, March 1977, pp. 19–31.

Wiseman, J. [1978], 'The Political Economy of Nationalised Industry' in *The Economics of Politics*. Institute of Economic Affairs Readings 18.

Wright, D. M. [1978], 'Inflation Accounting in the Nationalised Industries: a survey and appraisal'. Working Paper no. 15, Department of Economics, University of Durham.

9　Payments and Exchange Rate Problems

by Chris R. Milner*

Introduction

Following the Group of Ten meeting in Washington on 17–18 December 1971, the new 'central rate' or 'par value' for sterling was raised from the post-1967 devaluation level of $2.40 to approximately $2.60. With the floating of sterling after June 1972, however, the dollar price of sterling fell below $1.60 during October 1976, but by mid 1979 the exchange rate had risen above $2.30. Such dramatic reversals in the external fortunes of the pound have been produced by a complex set of domestic and external factors.

The decade has witnessed the 'dollar crisis' and the suspension of dollar convertibility; the collapse of the Bretton Woods system of pegged (but adjustable) exchange rates and its replacement by the disorderly floating of the major currencies; large and divergent inflation rates produced among other factors by the large upward administration of oil prices after 1973; and the shift in status for the UK from oil importer to oil producer. Identifying and evaluating UK policies that influence the balance of international payments and/or the rate of exchange is therefore no simple matter.

Assessment of policy is in fact complicated in three ways. First, the ends and means of policy clearly overlap. The nature of balance of payments problems is defined by the form of exchange rate policy. Although sterling has not been officially pegged since 1972, it has remained a closely monitored economic variable. Second, increasing international interdependence and changing global conditions make it more difficult to establish what we are to take as 'given'. And finally, targets and instruments must be linked by means of causal relation-

* The author would like to thank Professor D. Llewellyn (Loughborough University) and Mr D. Greenaway (University College, Buckingham) for helpful comments on an earlier draft of this chapter.

ship. The link, provided by conventional models however has been challenged by 'new' economic theories.

Sterling: target or instrument?

In principle balance of payments problems are associated only with the maintenance of a 'disequilibrium' exchange rate. Although a freely floating exchange rate does not guarantee a particular composition of international payments (e.g. current balance) it does produce an overall balance on international payments. The choice therefore between a fixed and floating currency will depend, among other factors, upon the authorities willingness to sacrifice other policy objectives (and control of other instruments). Where the exchange rate is fixed, internal and external balance are defined by this 'ruling price'. Where the exchange rate is free to float, the overall balance of payments cease to be an objective of, or constraint on, policy.

In practice balance of payments problems are associated with most forms of exchange rate policy. Until June 1972 the UK authorities 'pegged' sterling to the dollar and since that time have allowed sterling to float. More precisely the former was an adjustable peg and the latter a managed (albeit intermittently) float. In assessing the efficacy of payments policies therefore we must know to what extent the exchange rate was 'adjustable' or 'managed'.

Certainly the attitude of the UK authorities to the role of the exchange rate has changed. The view that the exchange rate is sacrosanct, often for reasons of political and national prestige, was dispelled by the experience of the 1967 sterling devaluation and of the costs of international adjustment rigidity during the 1960s in general. However, apart from the relatively small re-alignments produced by the Smithsonian Agreement in December 1971, there was little official indication that the floating of sterling was under consideration. The Barber budget of March 1972 – three months before the float – contained no explicit indication of this subsequent development. Removing the external constraint on the Chancellor's expansionist plans was described as a temporary measure. Although the generalisation of the float to the major currencies mitigated against any unilateral reversal of policy by the UK, the stringency of the UK conditions for rejoining in the same year the 'snake' arrangements for pegging intra-European exchange rates demonstrates the greater commitment to 'market orientation', on pragmatic grounds at least.

During the general downward float of sterling after 1973 and until

1977 (see Figure 9.1), the intermittent management by interest rate manipulation and support buying demonstrates the authorities' unwillingness after the initial experiment to relinquish totally responsibility for the value of sterling. Fears of an inflation–depreciation cycle and of the possible depressing effects of currency variability on international trade shifted thinking back towards the benefits of currency stabilisation. The proposals for global reform and support in principle for a new European Monetary System (EMS) during 1978 are indicative of this shift. Subsequently the strong appreciation of sterling in relation to the dollar has focused some attention on the problem of export competitiveness. Confidence in sterling, attributable to the increasing value of North Sea oil but in the face of an apparently deteriorating current payments position, is a somewhat novel experience for the UK. The Conservative government's (1979) attitude to sterling as yet seems unclear; a reluctance on the one hand to discourage sterling's (initial) appreciation and a sympathy for the idea on the other of joining the EMS. The dilemma is a familiar one; if, and at what level to stabilise the pound, and at what cost.

The changing international climate

The floating of currencies during 1973 was an *ad hoc* attempt by some countries to insulate themselves from external events. Speculative attacks on prevailing par-values made monetary aggregates dependent significantly on inflows and outflows of foreign exchange. The subsequent 'non-system', involving to varying degrees the floating of major currencies,[1] has proved relatively successful in avoiding excessive depression or overt protectionism. However the UK's external policies must be judged against a background of global monetary turmoil on a scale previously unwitnessed in the postwar period: the dollar crisis, the on-set of 'managed' floating, the oil crisis, unprecedented inflation rates, and an enormous growth of private and potentially destabilising international liquidity (see Williamson [1978]).

The speculative pressures against the dollar (and in turn against the potentially upvalued currencies), which culminated in the suspension of convertibility of the dollar into gold in August 1971 and technically brought the Bretton Woods system to an end, had long been predicted (Triffin [1961]). Growing dollar balances, provided by an overall US payments deficit, inevitably threatened the bankers' liquidity position in conditions of restricted gold supplies, and reduced

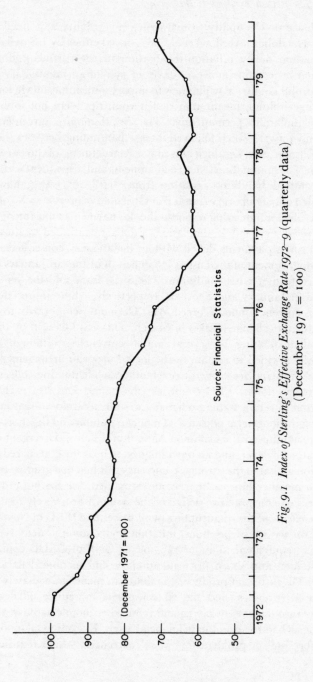

Fig. 9.1 Index of Sterling's Effective Exchange Rate 1972–9 (quarterly data)
(December 1971 = 100)

Source: Financial Statistics

confidence in US ability to maintain convertibility at a fixed gold price. The dollar 'overflow' could be reduced either by US deflation/ devaluation or by reflation/revaluation in the surplus countries. Reluctance to adjust however gave the system an inflationary bias. The surplus countries' willingness to import some inflation via foreign exchange inflows, meant that deficit countries were not forced to reduce inflation permanently. The Smithsonian Agreement in December 1971, which followed intense bargaining between the US and 'Europe', was heralded as a major restructuring of the par value system. The nominal currency re-alignments and subsequent widening of permitted bands of variation from $\pm 1\%$ to $\pm 2\frac{1}{4}\%$ however provided only temporary respite from speculative pressures. No operational rules for indicating responsibility for payments adjustment were established; external accumulation of dollars continued to allow the US to run a payments deficit without deflationary consequences.

Announcement of the largest US deficit in history in January 1973 induced further crisis conditions. The Swiss franc and the yen were floated in January and February respectively, while unprecedented foreign currency inflows forced West Germany temporarily to close the foreign exchange market in March. This was followed by the independent floating of several major currencies, although some countries decided to remain in the joint European arrangement – a 'snake' of currencies pegged to each other, while floating collectively against the dollar. EEC countries (the pound and lira excluded) preferred to retain stable exchange rates for a variety of reasons, including the long-term objective of monetary union and the short-term need to administer the Common Agricultural Policy. Divergent inflation rates, however, and an unwillingness to bear the costs of reducing inflation to that of the 'strongest' currency resulted in a gradual reduction in membership – a 'mark zone' remained (see Brittan [1979]).

The scope for grand re-design of the system was severely restricted by the effects of the quadrupling of oil prices by OPEC in November 1973, on payments positions, inflation and economic activity. The 'oil tax', equivalent to about $1\frac{1}{2}\%$ of the GNP of OECD countries, had sudden and sharp price inflationary and income deflationary effects. Given the oil producers' inability to spend immediately their increased revenues, and the oil consumers to reduce oil demand further through energy-saving and reduced economic activity, the oil producers had to accumulate financial assets. Recycling oil funds was therefore only a problem for 'weak' currencies which required an interest premium to cover anticipated depreciations.

In the event the private financial markets, rather than limited official schemes, were relatively successful in recycling without experiencing extreme instability; though the increase in private international liquidity has created a potential source of instability. Some commentators view this development and the legalisation of the various exchange rate practices after the Jamaica agreement in 1976, as an abdication of responsibility by governments to the private markets (Triffin [1978]). Given the prevailing economic conditions, inherited characteristics and bargaining positions global reform was, and remains, unlikely. In any case, the key-currency country, the US, pursued a policy until 1978 that has been imperfectly described as one of 'benign neglect'. (By leaving determination of the exchange rate to market forces, except in the event of ill-defined 'disorderly conditions', the US could adopt independent, domestic monetary policies). Piecemeal co-operation, involving the US and other major currencies, was necessary to alter this state of affairs. In November 1978 the US announced commitments to tighten domestic policies and to support the dollar, with the help of currency 'swap' arrangements including the D-mark (see Midland Bank [1979]). This shift of policy was produced by concern for increasing inflation, the threat to end the dollar pricing of oil, and pressures from the 'strong' currency countries. These countries were fearful of the inflationary consequences of reserve accumulation, and of the loss of competitiveness from currency appreciation. This and fears of deepening recession were the motives for the attempts at the end of 1978 to re-peg currencies within a new European Monetary System (see Richardson [1979]). Like all EEC members the UK was committed to monetary union in the long run, but in the short run was unwilling to return to the discipline of, or bear the costs of, a pegged exchange rate.

Questioning the conventional wisdoms
Events in the last decade have shown therefore that exchange rate flexibility alone does not guarantee current balance. Recent theoretical developments have also questioned the importance and desirability of exchange-rate induced changes in relative prices. Admittedly the prevailing orthodoxy was not that exchange rate adjustments guaranteed a particular composition of the balance of payments. It was however that, given elasticity 'optimism' and complementary policies to control domestic absorption, currency changes would produce

desired expenditure – switching effects. This view has been challenged by the monetary approach to the balance of payments and the 'new Cambridge' theories (Bispham [1975]).

As with macroeconomics in general balance of payments theory has seen a revival of interest in the role of monetary factors (Frenkel and Johnson [1976]). Rather than concentrating on relative price and income adjustment, the monetary approach views payments imbalance as the product of money market adjustment. Given stable asset preferences, current and/or capital imbalance is equivalent to stock disequilibrium in the money market, and is inherently temporary. In the absence of sterilisation policies excesses will be cleared. With a fixed exchange rate excesses are passed over the foreign exchanges on the consumption and acquisition of foreign assets. Where the exchange rate is free to move, real money balances are maintained at the desired level by exchange rate movements. According to this view devaluation is unnecessary to remove a deficit. A deficit is a once-and-for-all phenomenon, and any beneficial effects of devaluation are the product of the disabsorption effects of rising prices (i.e. cash balance effects) and not the product of relative price changes. Flexible exchange rates only offer therefore an additional degree of freedom in pursuing independent monetary policies, and not an adjustment mechanism. (The link between balance of payments flows and monetary aggregates is examined in Lomax and Mowl [1978]).

The validity of this view is dependent upon the stability and predictability of asset preferences (including the demand for money), the exogeneity of the money supply and the temporary nature of sterilisation. (For a thorough critique see Tsiang [1977]). If the authorities can sterilise foreign exchange flows for relatively long periods of time, the monetary approach is only a very long run theory and does not contradict the 'orthodoxy'. The contributory role of monetary factors in payments adjustment has long been acknowledged (see Coppock [1978]).

Although affecting policy less than 'monetarism', the 'new Cambridge' approach has directed attention to two particular issues. One is that the public sector financial deficit and the current account deficit tend to move together, causality flowing from the public to overseas sector. The other is the assertion that import controls are more effective than exchange rate adjustments in raising economic growth and removing the balance of payments constraint on growth.

There is an affinity therefore with the monetary approach. Because any increase in the budget deficit must result in a deteriorating current position, government has a direct responsibility for creating payments problems. (Early formulations of this approach therefore reversed the orthodox assignment rule by arguing that budgetary policy should be used to regulate the balance of payments). Establishing causality from accounting identities is clearly dangerous, and the accuracy of forecasts has been imperfect. Nevertheless, the Cambridge Economic Policy Group has retained its preference for import restrictions. Long term under-investment and structural rigidities are seen as making the competitive stimulus of devaluation an inappropriate tool for breaking out of the traditional 'stop–go' cycle. Demand expansion from guaranteed or protected domestic markets is by contrast viewed as a necessary condition for achieving innovation and productivity growth. Conservative and Labour governments alike, however, have remained obligated to international agreements (e.g. GATT and EEC) and aware of the threat of retaliation, as far as overt measures of protection are concerned! (For a fuller consideration of the 'new Cambridge' arguments see Greenaway and Milner [1979]).

Table 9.1   A summary of the UK balance of payments, 1960–78 (£m)

Year	Current balance (a)	Investment and other capital transactions (b)	Net transactions with overseas monetary authorities (c)	Official financing Foreign currency borrowing (d)	Changes in official reserves[a] (e)
1960	− 244	+ 286	− 116	—	− 177
1961	+ 27	− 316	+ 370	—	− 31
1962	+ 130	− 3	− 375	—	+ 183
1963	+ 129	− 100	+ 5	—	+ 53
1964	− 357	− 311	+ 573	—	+ 122
1965	− 45	− 317	+ 599	—	− 246
1966	+ 111	− 580	+ 625	—	− 34
1967	− 293	− 504	+ 556	—	+ 115
1968	− 242	− 759	+ 1296	—	+ 114
1969	+ 509	− 175	− 699	+ 56	− 44
1970	+ 776	+ 546	− 1295	—	− 125
1971	+ 1150	+ 1791	− 1817	+ 82	− 1536
1972	+ 208	− 683	+ 449	—	+ 692
1973	− 875	+ 148	—	+ 999	− 228
1974	− 3307	+ 1606	—	+ 1751	− 105
1975	− 1621	+ 126	—	+ 810	+ 655
1976	− 842	− 3016	+ 984	+ 1792	+ 853
1977	+ 293	+ 4406	+ 1113	+ 1114	− 9588
1978	+ 1032	− 2931	− 1016	− 187	+ 2329

Source: *United Kingdom Balance of Payments, 1979*, Table 1.1 (HMSO).

The sum of columns (a) + (b) does not necessarily equal the sum of columns (c) + (d) + (e), because several items are excluded from the summary.

[a]Drawings on (+); additions to (−).

Long-term Payments Targets

Up to the devaluation of sterling in 1967 it is possible to identify several broad characteristics of the UK's balance of payments (see Table 9.1). An invisible trade surplus normally more than offset a visible trade deficit. The resulting current surplus was usually coupled with a net export of long-term capital. And finally, the existence of sterling balances inadequately supported by gold and foreign exchange reserves meant that short-term capital flows were volatile and played a disproportionate role in the overall payments schema. Although the weight attached to particular problems has since altered because of changed circumstances and exchange rate policy, it was possible to identify at the outset of the 1970s certain long-term payments targets.

The current account

There had been a steady decline in the international competitiveness of UK manufacturing industry up to 1967. The UK's share of world trade had declined, and more importantly the volume of imports had tended to grow faster than exports and real GDP. (These adverse movements were not offset by the generally favourable movement in the terms of trade). Thus during years of peak growth (e.g. 1960, 1964 and 1967) sharp rises in the visible trade deficit could not be offset by invisible earnings. Although import growth was temporarily reduced by expenditure-reducing policies, permanent reversal of the worsening 'full-employment' trade deficit required measures to improve international competitiveness.

Some commentators also attribute the worsening current account position during the 1960s to the decline in the invisible surplus. The relative decline in sterling's international role, the restrictions on the export of long-term capital and the growth of government overseas expenditure, in particular military expenditure, contributed to this decline. The Labour government had committed itself in the mid 1960s to reducing its 'own' contribution to this decline and drain on reserves, by concentrating defence effort within Europe and the North Atlantic community and by seeking to 'offset' foreign exchange costs through purchases of British military equipment. (For a fuller consideration of the factors influencing the current account see Chapter 10 on trade policies).

Long-term capital flows

Up to the end of the 1960s exchange controls had sought to satisfy two major objectives: preventing reserve-loss from portfolio and direct investment overseas without discouraging capital inflows and discriminating in favour of capital flows to the Overseas Sterling Area (OSA) (see Cairncross [1973]). This discrimination, a legacy of earlier commercial and financial links, exempted the OSA from exchange controls in return for the pooling of sterling area reserves (official sterling balances) in London. Weakening economic links during the 1960s weakened the motive however for discrimination. 'Voluntary restraint' was imposed in 1966 on investment to advanced OSA countries, and in 1972, following the floating of sterling, portfolio investment to the OSA had also to go through the investment currency market.[2] The 1974 budget finally ended the discriminatory nature of exchange controls.

The aim of financing foreign investment without reserve-loss was largely satisfied in the second half of the 1960s. In fact the 25% surrender rule introduced in April 1965, which ploughed back foreign currency income from existing investments rendered a net addition to reserves. However the restrictions and the premium on investment currency appeared to have little effect on the total outflow of long-term capital. They merely encouraged more non-sterling borrowing. (For a consideration of the arguments in favour of liberalising capital flows, see Miller and Wood [1979]).

By 1970, however, the UK was no longer a consistent net exporter of private capital, and this has continued to be the case during the 1970s (until recently) as a result of capital imports associated with North Sea oil development. In fact in most years after 1971 the UK has been a net importer of capital as a result of large-scale non-sterling borrowing by the public sector. (Though the motive for this was again the protection of reserves, despite the 'floating' of sterling). With the easing of exchange controls however – the surrender rule was abolished in January 1978 as EEC membership required – there was a significant increase in the export of private capital. (This increase was likely to be sustained following the decision in October 1979 to remove all remaining exchange controls).

Liquidity and the role of sterling

A condition of UK entry into the EEC was also the gradual reduction in sterling's reserve role. The Conservative government was prepared to envisage a gradual run-down of official sterling balances after accession. The EEC states were concerned about the threat to exchange rate stability from sterling crises. The UK for its part was well aware of the costs of fulfilling the reserve currency function, with inadequate reserves.

The risk was one of illiquidity rather than insolvency. The UK acted as an international banker, consistently committing the error of borrowing short and lending long, and not having an asset structure which would prevent crises of confidence. Figure 9.2 illustrates the source of this 'confidence problem'. Following the devaluation of sterling in 1967, when private and official holders of sterling balances had been shown the risks of holding a depreciating asset, and up to 1977 official reserves of gold and foreign exchange were consistently and significantly less than potential claims on those reserves (see Llewellyn [1977]).

The maintenance of confidence in the foreign exchange value of sterling balances was necessary if crises and speculative 'runs on the bank' were to be avoided. Given the underlying weakness on current account and the expectation of profitable speculation, confidence was not easily maintained in the period before the 1967 devaluation. Temporary protection to reserves could be given by raising interest rates and forward interventions to offset anticipated losses on sterling. Similarly the immediate threat of the 'overhang' to finite reserves could be reduced by foreign exchange borrowing, or by evidence of the potential to borrow. In 1968, for example, the Labour government had negotiated a medium-term borrowing facility of $2000m – the Basle Group Arrangement – which could be drawn upon to offset fluctuations in sterling balances below an agreed base level. (Dollar guarantees on official holdings were also offered in return for guarantees to maintain specified proportions of sterling in reserves). This facility was in fact renewed periodically until 1973, when it was replaced by short-term, unilaterally agreed exchange rate guarantees with OSA countries: these proved costly after the floating of sterling in 1972.

As Figure 9.2 shows, however, sterling balances grew during the period 1968–74, and the long-term solution to the confidence problem was the reduction of the 'overhang' itself – either via reserve accumulation or reduction of the sterling balances. The latter could be achieved, in the absence of crisis conditions by their substitution. In 1971,

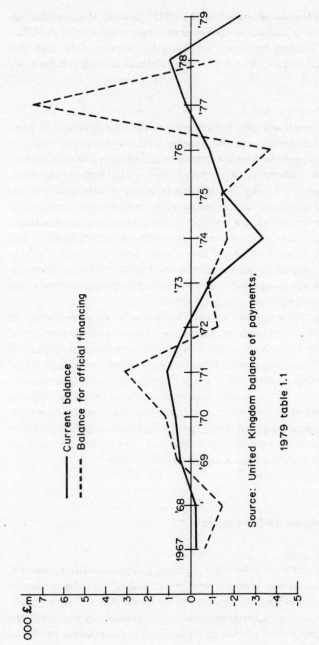

Fig. 9.2. *Official Reserves and 'Sterling Balances'*:[1] 1967–79 (annual data)

Source: United Kingdom balance of payments, 1979 table 1.1

Source: Financial Statistics (various issues).
[1] Proxied by exchange reserves in sterling, and banking and money market liabilities in sterling.

—— Current balance
----- Balance for official financing

000 £m

Chancellor Barber proposed to the IMF Annual Meeting that an international organisation take over sterling's reserve role; the UK's short-term sterling liabilities becoming longer-term debt with this international organ. (For a full consideration of such schemes, see Cohen [1971]).

Ending the 'stop–go' cycle

Improving international competitiveness and the adoption of policies more consistent with the country's relative economic status – 'British alone' policies – were means of breaking the traditional pattern of economic policy, as experienced during the 1950s and 1960s. Periodic current deficits and sterling crises were stabilised, without recourse to exchange rate adjustment, by deflationary measures to improve the trade balance and short-term interest rate manipulation to discourage short-term capital outflows. Domestic employment and growth targets were sacrificed for external ones; a 'vicious' circle in which the balance of payments operated as a constraint on stable growth and low productivity growth helped to perpetuate the trend decline in international competitiveness.

The view that demand had been consistently excessive during the postwar period, and that the balance of payments had in fact served as a desirable constraint on demand growth appeared less reasonable by the mid 1960s. After several years of demand contraction, the $2.80 peg for sterling appeared to remain incompatible with 'full employment' balance of payments equilibrium. Academic and political opinion remained divided however on the benefits of devaluation right up to November 1967, (see Tew [1978]). The final decision to devalue to $2.40 was taken in crisis conditions, but nevertheless provided an opportunity to break into a more 'virtuous' circle.

Policy Options and Measures

The 'pegged' pound

The incoming Conservative government in 1970 inherited a sharply improving payments position, and by the end of 1971 the trade and current surpluses were at unprecedented levels. Apparently devaluation had produced a fundamental transformation. In the event the improvement proved neither to be fundamental nor solely produced

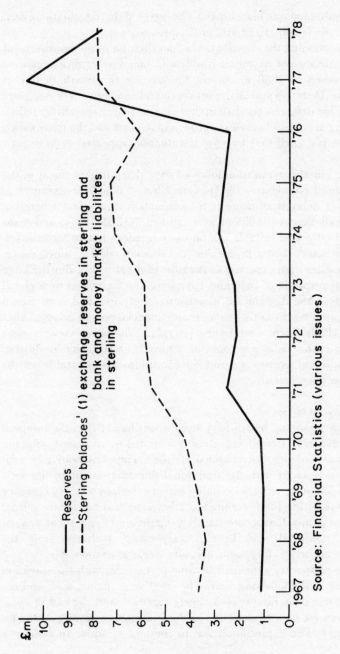

£m

10
9
8
7
6
5
4
3
2
1
0

1967 '68 '69 '70 '71 '72 '73 '74 '75 '76 '77 '78

—— Reserves

---- 'Sterling balances' (1) exchange reserves in sterling and
bank and money market liabilities in sterling

Source: Financial Statistics (various issues)

Fig. 9.3 *UK Balance of Payments, 1967–78* (annual data)

Source: United Kingdom Balance of Payments, 1979 (Table 1.1).

by devaluation (see Figure 9.3). (The extent of the 'devaluation effect' after 1967 is considered also in Chapter 10).

Apportioning the contribution of devaluation to the improvement in the balance of payments is difficult, since further measures were undertaken in 1968 to correct the adverse of growth in import volume. Deflation and an import deposit scheme were made necessary by a trade deficit larger than in the previous year. Expenditure reduction in particular checked the growth of imports and the trade deficit fell sharply, such that by 1970 devaluation appeared to have been effective.

The initial deterioration followed by a sharp improvement in the balance of payments – the 'J-curve effect' – could be explained in terms of delayed adjustment to devaluation in a world where the Marshall–Lerner conditions were satisfied. NIESR [1972] and Artus [1975] estimated suitable combined elasticities (despite inelastic import demand) and a favourable 'devaluation effect' – albeit slower and smaller than expected at the time of devaluation. But the large current surpluses of 1970 and 1971 were also facilitated by a global growth in the demand for manufactured exports, and some would argue most significantly by the stricter financial policies adopted after 1968 (Ball, Burns and Laury [1977]). Whichever view is most accurate, the $2.80 peg could only have been sustained by further international borrowing and on conditions unacceptable to the Labour government.

The decision to float

During the second half of 1971 and the first half of 1972 the competitive advantage from devaluation was eroded by increased inflation. The trade balance moved back into deficit. The Conservative government were faced with the traditional dilemma, maintain domestic expansion or protect the exchange rate. In the face of heavy currency outflows during June, sterling was allowed to float outside the official support points. Chancellor Barber's expansionist experiment was not to be sacrificed, and Britain 'temporarily' withdrew from the European 'snake' arrangements eight weeks after joining.

The temporary expedient became permanent, with the spread of floating in the following year. The effective exchange rate[3] and the dollar rate of sterling moved closely together until the end of 1972, registering a 10% depreciation on the Smithsonian parities of December 1971. The depreciation was to continue steadily, apart from a period of speculation against the dollar in May 1973, until 1977, and despite periodic support by the Bank of England.

The sinking pound

After the initial experiment, the authorities were unwilling to relinquish total responsibility for the exchange rate. The economic and political costs of depreciation meant that the balance of payments consequences of domestic policies could not be ignored. The relationship between movements in the effective exchange rate and the balance of payments was to prove complex (see Figures 9.1 and 9.3). In 1972 for instance the current account was in surplus, albeit significantly reduced, but short-term capital outflows caused sterling to depreciate despite significant use of reserves. By contrast in the following year the current balance moved sharply into deficit as commodity price rises pushed the terms of trade against the UK. On this occasion reserves grew while sterling depreciated. This was made possible by non-sterling borrowing by the public sector, which sold the foreign currency to the Exchange Equalisation Account and received forward cover from the Treasury. A similar pattern of events was repeated in 1974, except on a greater scale. The oil price rises at the end of 1973 combined with industrial problems during the winter of 1973–4 resulted in a current deficit of unprecedented scale. Increased financing by the public sector and a large-scale inflow of short-term funds in response to historically high interest rates again allowed reserves to grow while the exchange rate fell. The new Labour government, returned in spring 1974, inherited a precarious situation: growing external debt coupled with an increasing current deficit and falling production and large amounts of liquid credits received in the face of a depreciating currency.

Financing the oil deficit

In fact there was a net outflow of short-term capital during 1975 and 1976 as the fall in the value of sterling continued, and the oil producers became more reluctant to receive payment in sterling and deposit it in sterling balances in London. This shifted the burden from private to official financing of the current deficit. Because of the threat of the sterling 'overhang' to reserves and the borrowing facilities available from the OPEC surpluses, borrowing was more appropriate than reserve use. The public sector and the government directly were able to borrow OPEC funds 'recycled' via the Eurocurrency market,

and offered in the form of medium term loans. (Borrowing at commercial rates of interest, and with exchange guarantees was preferred
to the conditionality of IMF borrowing).

Thus foreign borrowing insulated the exchange rate and aggregate
demand from the full effects of the oil deficit. Active deflationary
measures would have been undesirable in circumstances of global
recession. Similarly depreciation sufficient to remove the current
deficit would have risked widespread competitive depreciations and
protection. By 1976, however, the authorities in the UK were unable
to resist a sharp depreciation of sterling or to avoid a more deflationary
stance, despite the fall in the current deficit as domestic demand fell
and the terms of trade improved. This depreciation can largely be
explained (speculative pressures apart) by excess inflation in the UK
relative to major competitors, rather than by the oil price rise (foreign
currency borrowing largely insulated the exchange rate from the
consequences of the oil deficit). Despite this depreciation the current
account remained in deficit. A current surplus was required if foreign
debts were to be repaid, but the ability of the authorities to remove
excess inflation was clearly doubted by holders of sterling. Because
official sterling balances, particularly of oil producing members of the
OSA had increased during 1973–5, the speculative threat to sterling
and/or reserves was apparent. Similarly the scope for foreign currency
borrowing from the private banking system was restricted (and cost
increased) by worsening economic conditions and prospects.

The sterling rescue

The scale of the liquidity crisis was such that the government was
faced with few options.

Figure 9.2 shows the sharp fall in sterling balances during 1976
– predominantly withdrawals from official holdings. In September
1976 the Chancellor of the Exchequer, Denis Healey, announced that
Britain would ask the IMF for a medium-term standby facility of
$3.9bn – a record request! After sterling had fallen to below $1.60, an
IMF delegation arrived in London in early November to negotiate
policy conditions attached to a loan.

After several weeks of negotiation and Cabinet drama the government accepted the policy conditions (cuts in the public sector borrowing requirement and in money supply growth) linked to the credit
line. The stand-by arrangement was officially approved in January
1977 by the IMF, which was to monitor the fulfilment of the condi-

tions. (The funds were provided mainly by the Group of Ten industrial countries and Switzerland under the General Arrangement to Borrow instituted in 1962).

In a more positive attempt to reduce sterling's reserve role, the Bank for International Settlements announced shortly after the initial package a second mesh to the 'safety net'. A further medium-term facility of $3bn was made available by a group of central banks to finance any run-down in official sterling balances below the level prevailing at the end of 1976. This was to be combined with bilateral negotiations between the UK and major official holders of sterling, to convert short-term balances into negotiable, medium-term bonds denominated in certain foreign currencies, offering a more stable value but lower rate of interest. Given the safety net however only a relatively small proportion of balances were converted. Overseas central banks presumably considered it unnecessary to convert high-interest, liquid assets into less liquid and possibly less profitable securities.

Indeed the safety net induced the desired restoration of confidence in sterling, which recovered steadily during 1977 to in excess of $1.80. Figure 9.2 shows that sterling balances actually rose during 1977 as holdings withdrawn in 1976 returned in anticipation of appreciation and high interest rates. In fact the Bank of England intervened to prevent too rapid an appreciation. The authorities wished to main-

Table 9.2   UK's outstanding official short and medium-term borrowing from abroad ($m)

| *End of | Total | IMF | Public sector foreign currency borrowing | |
			HMG	Other under exchange cover schemes
1970	3 406	2 328	—	120
1971	1 447	1 081	—	366
1972	266	—	—	366
1973	2 982	—	—	2 982
1974	7 092	—	1 500	5 592
1975	8 921	—	2 500	6 421
1976	14 160	2 051	2 500	9 609
1977	18 042	4 029	4 000	10 013
1978	15 847	2 152	4 350	9 345
1979	15 104	1 209	4 350	9 545

Source: *Bank of England Quarterly Bulletin*, September 1979, Table 16.
*except 1979 (2nd quarter).

tain the competitive advantages of sterling's earlier depreciation, which combined with tighter financial policies and wage restraint, moved the current account strongly into surplus in the last two quarters of the year. Support *selling* of sterling simultaneously provided an opportunity to dramatically increase the foreign currency reserves. Figure 9.2 demonstrates the disappearance (temporarily at least) of the illiquidity problem during 1977, without ending sterling's reserve role. The UK's external debt had however substantially increased during the 1974–8 period.

The rising pound

Outstanding official short and medium-term borrowing from abroad rose from $8.9bn in 1975 to $18bn in 1977. The burden of this external debt no longer appeared excessive in view of renewed confidence in sterling and Britain's imminent status of oil producer.

Prime Minister Callaghan claimed that domestic policy was freed from external constraints. (Arguably externally-imposed conditions had achieved a level of wage and financial discipline which would not otherwise have occurred – albeit at the expense of domestic employment). The degree of monetary independence would depend in any case upon how rapidly the government was willing to allow sterling to appreciate. Inflows of funds in anticipation of the benefits of North Sea oil could push the exchange rate up to the detriment of the manufacturing sector's competitiveness and of the non-oil trade balance.

Prospects of North Sea oil

Following the decision in autumn 1977 to break away from the dollar, the weakness of the dollar and the anticipation of increased domestic oil production helped to push sterling towards the $2 point by the beginning of 1978. This rise against the dollar was checked temporarily by efforts to stabilise the dollar, but increased uncertainty about oil prices and US policies caused a further sharp appreciation of the pound against the dollar later in the year. Throughout the period the effective rate of exchange remained much more stable than the dollar rate. In conditions of relative stability and greater financial discipline the government was able to reduce external debt – in some cases making early repayment. This resulted in a fall in reserves; though the decision in March 1979 to recognise officially the upward revaluation of gold and other currencies in terms of dollars more than offset this fall.

Estimates (NIESR [1976]) predicted that, if the non-oil current deficit remained equivalent to 1½% of GNP, the current surplus from 1979–82 would be sufficient to pay off accumulated debts incurred on current account since 1973. (These predictions would be invalidated by a continuation in the trend increase in manufactured imports). The (revised) figures for 1978 did show a large current surplus, but the appreciation of sterling after 1977 and excess inflation in the UK have however halted this improvement.

The new Conservative government in 1979 inherited an unusual situation; an appreciating currency and deteriorating current account. The steady deterioration in the UK's trade competitiveness since 1976 appears to have accelerated sharply during 1979. The invisible surplus, which had grown steadily since the 1967 devaluation with London's functioning successfully as a financial centre in non-sterling currencies, is unlikely to offset the prospective trade deficit for 1979. The view that the economy was about to break into a 'virtuous' circle, in which improved competitiveness and confidence help to strengthen sterling and weaken inflationary pressure now appears premature. Excess inflation remains and confidence in sterling was based on high interest rates and the expectation of an oil surplus and overall current surplus with which to repay external debts. The continuing gloomy prospects for industrial production and the non-oil deficit, and the likelihood of US interest rate increases following the failure to stabilise the dollar exchange rate are likely to erode that confidence. Indeed confidence was ebbing by autumn 1979. Following the abolition of exchange controls in November and the possibility of increased capital outflows, sterling fell back to below the $2.10 mark before the end of the year.

The dismantling of capital controls

The early 1970s had witnessed the dismantling of discriminatory regulations on international capital transactions. In the second half of the decade, EEC commitments in particular accelerated the process of capital liberalisation. From the beginning of 1978 the UK agreed that the surrender rule should be abolished, although the premium currency system could still be retained. The controls on outward direct investment were eased – the ceiling on the amount a British company could invest abroad (at normal exchange rates) was increased and the required pay-back period (the so-called 'super-criterion') was eased. The rules concerning personal capital movements were also made more liberal. Then in the June 1979 budget the Thatcher government took further liberalisation steps. In particular it eased the rules on outward direct investment: the 'super-criterion' was abolished on direct investments of less than £5m and in the following month currency was made available without limit at the official rate for all outward direct investment. The budget statement also included the abolition of the two-thirds rule which restricted the reinvestment of profits earned overseas. It also liberalised portfolio investment. UK residents were allowed to invest at the official rate of exchange in most securities denominated in EEC member currencies. In doing all this the Chancellor of the Exchequer noted the obligations to liberalise which fell upon the UK as a member of the community. Finally on 23 October 1979 the Government announced the end of all the remaining exchange controls.

The Efficacy of Policy

To what extent have the characteristics of the UK's external position changed since the devaluation in 1967? In five out of the last ten years (1970–9) the UK has run a current surplus, in only one (1971) a trade surplus. In contrast to the 1960s, the UK has on average been a net importer of long-term capital during the 1970s as a result of North Sea development and public sector borrowing policy. (During 1979, however, the relaxation of exchange controls was once again encouraging the net export of portfolio capital). Short-term capital flows have remained volatile during the decade. In 1974 for example external sterling liabilities increased by £1558m, while in 1976 they decreased by £1152m. Over the decade as a whole sterling balances have increased. The enormous growth of reserves during 1977 has, however, temporarily at least removed the illiquidity problem and reduced the speculative threat from the sterling balances. Removing the sterling 'overhang' and continued exchange rate flexibility provide an opportunity for lowering the external constraint on domestic policy. But for much of the decade this constraint has been significant.

On the face of it therefore there has been little fundamental change in the pattern of balance of payments problems during the last decade, except for the substantial increase in reserves in 1977 made possible by the earlier sharp depreciation of sterling and substantial foreign currency borrowing. A depreciation, which combined with the 1967 devaluation, has failed to reverse permanently the underlying deterioration in international competitiveness and upward trend in manufactured imports. We must be careful, however, not to assess balance of payments policies simply on a comparison of the raw data. The decade witnessed global monetary turmoil unparalleled in the postwar period. Traditional policy instruments (demand management and the exchange rate) could not be expected to remedy quickly the oil deficits after 1973. Also balance of payments and exchange rate policy cannot be divorced from a whole gamut of policies (incomes, industrial, etc.) which directly and indirectly affect trade performance and the balance of payments (see Chapters 3 and 6). A more flexible exchange rate alone cannot be expected to remedy several decades of relative economic decline (see also Major [1979]).

In assessing the efficacy of policy it is also important to distinguish between policies to stabilise payments imbalances in the short term, and policies to remove 'disequilibrium' in the longer term, i.e. to distinguish between financing and adjustment. The precise distinction between the two is somewhat arbitrary because it is difficult to define precisely external equilibrium or balance (see Milner and Greenaway [1979]). In any case the authorities' actual target may well differ from the normative definition. Ignoring long-term private capital, it may be reasonable on pragmatic grounds to argue that the government viewed adjustment policies as being directed at the current account and financing measures (induced short-term capital flows, borrowing and reserve use) as being directed at certain transactions 'below the line' of the current account in the overall accounts.

Stabilisation and 'recycling'

The criteria against which the efficacy of financing policies should be measured include the appropriateness of the distribution between adjustment and financing, and between private and official financing, and the relative costs and benefits of alternative forms of borrowing as opposed to reserve use. In the absence of social welfare and time preference functions the assessment can only be intuitive.

Adjustment requires that a country in deficit reduce real absorption relative to real income, and receives a smaller proportion of global output than previously. Attempts after 1973 to adjust the non-oil trade balance sufficiently to compensate for the oil deficit would have required a massive deflation and further unemployment, and risked the outbreak of overt trade wars between industrial countries anxious to run trade surpluses with each other. 'Recycling' of OPEC surpluses was largely unavoidable therefore, given the oil producers inability to immediately absorb all the surpluses. (Their ability to absorb has subsequently increased as development and military programmes expanded).

Recycling was therefore relatively successful in avoiding extreme recession. However a substantial part of the recycling was via the intermediary of the Eurocurrency markets rather than official international agencies. This growth of 'offshore' banking has given rise to concern on two grounds. It has reduced central bank control over credit creation and also permitted a potentially destablising expansion of the credit pyramid (short-term lending from the oil producers and medium-term borrowing by the oil consumers). The commercial prudency of this international bank lending is particularly important in the case of lending to the non-oil developing countries, whose debt burden has increased sharply during the last decade. This is however an issue of supra-national concern. The UK authorities choice was between 'official' borrowing and the encouragement of private borrowing.

Short-term capital flows are sensitive to interest and exchange rate movements and expected movements. Dependence on such flows requires the maintainance of confidence and increases the speculative threat to the exchange rate. In 1976, for example, despite historically high interest rates, the inflow of short-term capital was reversed. After initial success in 1974 in using high interest rates to attract funds, raising interest rates even higher was not sufficient to offset the anticipated depreciation of sterling. The higher rates may, however, have discouraged even larger outflows – but at what cost to the domestic economy? Double figure interest rates after 1973 (except for a period from April 1977 to April 1978) have been produced in part by tighter control after 1976 of the money supply in an inflationary state, but also by increased international competition for funds. This external orientation of interest rates for financing purposes may have discouraged investment and encouraged misallocation of resources. (These economic costs are difficult to measure, but the political costs, e.g. of higher private housing costs, are more evident).

As the burden shifted after 1974 to official financing (see Table 9.2) the government had to consider the relative merits of reserve use and borrowing. Although reserve holding involves an opportunity cost, in the British case reserve use was potentially destabilising, given excess sterling balances. Borrowing, on the other hand, has imposed a burden on future output and on the management of the public sector deficit. Although the real value of debt would be reduced by inflation, financing current consumption on the collateral of North Sea oil revenues has reduced the government's ability to use those oil revenues to finance domestic investment and/or tax cuts in the future. (Table 9.2 demonstrates the importance of public sector borrowing under the exchange cover scheme; foreign currency acquired without policy conditions on the government).

Adjustment and the floating experience
Advocates of more flexible exchange rates before the floating era claimed that the viewing of any parity as sacrosanct gave rise to adjustment, allocative and liquidity problems. Under a pegged rate, the downward rigidity of wages and prices results in balance of payments adjustment falling on domestic incomes and employment. The maintenance of a non-equilibrium rate is also likely to result in a loss of economic welfare from resource misallocation (Johnson [1966]). And finally, the more rigid the exchange rate, the greater in general is reserve requirement and the reserve loss constraint on domestic policies.

Sterling's float since 1972 has, however, been a managed float. Assessment of the floating experience is further complicated because the degree and duration of intervention has been inconsistent, and imperfectly co-ordinated with domestic and other countries' policies. There was for example a marked improvement in the competitiveness of UK products from the beginning of 1975 to late in 1976, as a lower level of pay settlements reinforced a 25% depreciation in the effective exchange rate. This trend was reversed in 1977 as confidence returned to sterling, and the Government shifted priority to avoiding the inflationary consequences of depreciation. At the same time the relaxation of wages policy during 1978 and 1979 has allowed labour costs to grow more quickly.

Changes in competitiveness have not (but were not expected to be) been sufficient criteria for achieving balance of payments adjustment. Evaluation of actual trade performance over the decade supports the view that 'floating' has not provided a panacea solution to adjustment, allocation and liquidity problems. The external constraint on policy has been loosened but not removed, and there is little evidence to suggest that resource mobility has increased. Indeed longer-term movements in the effective exchange rate have to a large extent moved in response to the UK's excess inflation, rather than adjusted relative prices sufficiently fundamentally to alter trade performance. By the end of 1978 the effective exchange rate had fallen by about 34% below its December 1971 Smithsonian value, but relative export prices were at similar level to the pre-devaluation level in 1967. Indeed it may be that domestic inflation was not independent of depreciation; the price of raw material and component imports increasing as sterling depreciated and fuelling the wage–price spiral (see Goldstein [1974]). Thus over the decade as a whole the penetration of imports of manufactures into the home market has continued to increase, and the UK's share of world exports has declined.

Opponents of flexible exchange rates prior to floating argued that freely floating rates were likely to increase speculation, instability, uncertainty, policy indiscipline and inflationary pressures. Again, testing this view is difficult because sterling has not been allowed to float freely. There is some evidence that depreciation has fed inflationary pressures and that the diminished external constraint has – in the short term at least – permitted greater economic mismanagement. The boom strategy during 1971/2 and inflationary wage settlements during 1974/5 give some support to this view (see Thirlwall [1978]). It is also evident that fluctuations in the exchange rate have been substantial, and that the stabilising role of the speculator is far from proven (see Hirsch and Higham [1974]). It must be stressed however that fluctuations in sterling in the early stages of floating were also aggravated by incompatible domestic policies and unco-ordinated international management. Clearly this initial period involved a learning process, and there have been some subsequent moves towards 'managing the managed float' (Ethier and Bloomfield [1975]). The IMF have for instance adopted guidelines for managing floating currencies, and central bank co-operation during 1978 helped to stabilise the dollar. (The failure of active intervention in the autumn of 1979 to discourage short term capital flows and the depreciation of the dollar, re-emphasises the need for compatible financial policies in surplus and deficit countries).

There is less evidence however to suggest that the tendency for currency markets to overcorrect and thereby reduce certainty in trading transactions has had a significant influence on the volume of trade. Clearly it is difficult to measure the impact of exchange rate variability, but the downturn in world trade during the period 1973–5 for instance could largely be explained by the downturn in world output. The protracted nature of the global recession, however, since 1975 has led politicians and central bankers at least to argue in favour of returning to greater exchange rate stability and certainty in trade relations (see Richardson [1979]).

The Future?

There has therefore been some shift of attitude from 'a competitive to a stabilising exchange rate' (Emminger [1979], p. 17). Lessons have been learned from the floating 'experiment' of the 1970s. A floating rate is not sufficient to adjust fundamental current imbalances (i.e. to shift resources and change real wages). Exchange rate variations have been slow to adjust the current account and quick to influence domestic prices. In fact the fight against inflation has reduced concern for the competitive effects of exchange rate policy, and highlighted certain benefits of a higher rather than lower exchange rate. The 'virtuous circle' enjoyed by the persistent surplus countries has helped to reinforce this view.

In isolation therefore UK governments may be attracted in the 1980s to the idea of 'stabilising' via a strong exchange rate. However, as with the competitive benefits of depreciation, the stabilising benefits of a strong pound can only be achieved by supporting exchange rate policies with other appropriate economic and financial policies. They are also more likely to be achieved if policies are internationally compatible – not all countries can have an appreciating currency! The domestic political pressures for price stability (from consumers) and competitiveness (from exporters) and international political pressures (for European unity and stability) may spur the UK to join the EMS. The longevity of EMS will depend however on a greater willingness to adjust exchange rates than was demonstrated under the Bretton Woods system. This may be particularly important for the UK once the 'temporary' benefits of North Sea oil to the current account have been lost.

The influence of North Sea oil on the state and composition of the balance of payments, the exchange rate and external constraint on domestic expansion during the 1980s will be significantly affected by the decision at the end of 1979 to abolish remaining exchange controls. North Sea oil on the one hand provides an opportunity to pursue domestic policies less constrained by concern about the balance of payments. This constraint could reappear on the other hand, however, if the authorities choose to return to a pegged exchange rate within the EMS at a parity incompatible with the 'post-oil' payments position. Speculating about either possibility must be conditional upon the effect of the liberalisation of capital flows upon the exchange rate. (See also Forsyth and Edwards [1979]).

Consider the following scenario. The abolition of capital controls will result in the consistent net export of long-term capital. A net outflow of capital, which matches the current surplus, would allow the authorities to avoid a choice between either a sharp appreciation of sterling or monetary expansion produced by reserve accumulation. A sharp appreciation of sterling may be detrimental to the non-oil trade balance and result in entry to EMS at a parity incompatible with the competitiveness of much of the UK's manufacturing sector. Avoiding appreciation in the North Sea era, without offsetting capital outflows, would undermine attempts to pursue counter-inflation, monetary policies.

Arguments of philosophy (and political commitments to the EEC) apart the Conservative government's decision to abolish exchange controls may therefore have been motivated by a desire to avoid both monetary expansion and currency appreciation. Indeed the initial fall in the exchange rate, following the abolition of exchange controls, may permit entry to EMS at a more competitive and durable parity (conversion to the stable or strong pound is far from complete!). Opponents of the decision to abolish exchange controls would argue however that there are other real costs of permitting the export of long-term capital. They view the export of long-term capital as a drain of funds which would be used for domestic investment purposes, and as a return to the dangerous strategy of lending long while simultaneously encouraging short-term inflows of funds. Some investment and employment may be transferred abroad, but foreign investment and domestic investment may be complimentary as well as substitutes. As for the traditional confidence problem, the large increase in reserves during 1977 has lessened the immediate speculative threat of the sterling balances. In any case long-term confidence in sterling will be influenced by the competitiveness of the UK economy, the current account position and the efficacy therefore of many policy decisions besides the removal of exchange controls. Investment transferred abroad certainly would not improve competitiveness, but acquisition of foreign assets can provide a future stream of income (which will benefit the current account) after the benefits of North Sea oil have been lost.

The feasibility of returning to a stable exchange rate era will not be influenced however only by the efficacy of domestic policy actions. Within the EMS itself, a greater willingness to adjust parities and to co-ordinate domestic policies will be required than was the case during the 'snake' arrangements of the 1970s. The stability of European currencies is in turn also contingent upon important exogenous factors: the extent of further oil price increases and the success of tighter US monetary policies in stabilising the dollar. Given these uncertainties, continuing inflation at divergent rates and the prospects of deepening world recession at the end of 1979, UK payments and exchange rate policies in the next decade may well be subject to the type of reversals of direction as was experienced in the 1970s.

Notes

1. A majority of currencies have remained pegged to other currencies, e.g. the dollar, or a basket of currencies, e.g. the SDR, but the floating currencies dominate world trade and financial transactions.
2. Following the budget of April 1965, 25% of the proceeds of all sales of foreign currency securities had to be sold on the official exchange markets. The remaining investment currency earnings were therefore available for reinvestment or for sale at a premium.
3. A trade-weighted measure of the average movements in the sterling exchange rates with other currencies.

References

Artus, J. R. [1975], 'The 1967 devaluation of pound sterling', *International Monetary Fund Staff Papers*, Vol. 22, pp. 595–640.

Ball, R. J., Burns, S. T. and Laury, J. S. E. [1977], 'The role of exchange rate changes in balance of payments adjustments: the United Kingdom case', *Economic Journal*, Vol. 87, no. 345, pp. 1–29.

Bispham, G. [1975], 'New Cambridge and monetarist criticisms of conventional economic policy-making', *National Institute Economic Review*, no. 74, pp. 39–55.

Brittan, S. [1979], 'EMS: a compromise that could be worse than either extreme', *The World Economy*, Vol. 2, no. 1, pp. 1–30.

Cairncross, A. K. [1973], *Control of International Long-Term Capital Movements*. Brookings Institution.

Cohen, B. J. [1971], *The Future of Sterling as an International Currency*. Macmillan.

Coppock, D. J. [1978], 'Some thoughts on the monetary approach to balance of payments theory', *Manchester School of Economics and Social Studies*, Vol. 46, no. 3, pp. 186–208.

Emminger, O. [1979], 'The exchange rate as an instrument of policy', *Lloyds Bank Review*, no. 133, pp. 1–22.

Ethier, W. and Bloomfield, A. I. [1975], 'Managing the managed float', *Essays in International Finance*, no. 112. Princeton University.

Forsyth, J. and Edwards, F. [1979], *A Policy for Sterling*. Royal Institute of International Affairs.

Frenkel, J. and Johnson, H. G. (eds.) [1976], *The Monetary Approach to the Balance of Payments*. Allen and Unwin.

Greenaway, D. and Milner, C. R. [1979], *Protectionism Again. . . ? Causes and Consequences of a Retreat from Freer Trade to Economic Nationalism. Hobart Paper*. Institute of Economic Affairs.

Hirsch, F. and Higham, D. [1974], 'Floating rates – expectations and experience', *Three Banks Review*, no. 102, pp. 3–34.

Goldstein, M. [1974], 'The effect of exchange rate changes on wages and prices in the UK: an empirical study', IMF Staff Papers, Vol. 21, November 1974, pp. 694–739.

Johnson, H. G. [1966], 'The welfare costs of exchange stabilisation', *Journal of Political Economy*, Vol. 74, October 1966, pp. 512–18.

Llewellyn, D. T. [1977], 'The UK's Overseas Assets and Liabilities' in Maunder, P. (ed.) *Case Studies in International Economics*. Heinemann Educational Books.

Lomax, R. and Mowl, R. [1978], 'Balance of Payments Flows and the Monetary Aggregates in the UK', *Government Economic Service Working Papers*, no. 5. H.M. Treasury.

Major, R. (ed.) [1979], *Britain's Trade and Exchange Rate Policy*. Heinemann Educational Books.

Midland Bank [1979], 'The dollar: an end to benign neglect?', *Midland Bank Review*, Autumn 1979, pp. 14–19.

Miller, R. and Wood, J. B. [1979], 'Exchange Control For Ever', *I.E.A. Research Monograph*. Institute of Economic Affairs.

Milner, C. R. and Greenaway, D. [1979], *An Introduction to International Economics*. Longman.

NIESR [1972], 'The effect of the devaluation of 1967 on the current balance of payments', *Economic Journal*, Vol. 82 Supplement, March 1972, pp. 442–64.

NIESR [1976], 'Forecasts with alternative assumptions', *National Institute Economic Review*, no. 78, p. 18.

Richardson, Sir Gordon, 'The prospects for an international monetary system', Henry Thorton Lecture, *Bank of England Quarterly Bulletin*, Vol. 19, no. 3, pp. 290–7.

Tew, J. H. B. [1978], 'Policies aimed at improving the balance of payments' in Blackaby, F. T. (ed.) *British Economic Policy 1960–74*. Cambridge University Press, pp. 304–59.

Thirlwall, A. P. [1978], 'The UK's economic problem: a balance of payments constraint?', *National Westminster Bank Review*, February 1978, pp. 24–32.

Triffin, R. [1961], *Gold and the Dollar Crisis*. Yale University Press.

Triffin, R. [1978], 'Gold and the Dollar Crisis: yesterday and tomorrow', *Essays in International Finance*, no. 132. Princeton University.

Tsiang, S. C. [1977], 'The monetary theoretic foundations of the modern monetary approach to the balance of payments', *Oxford Economic Papers*, Vol. 29, pp. 319–38.

Williamson, J. [1978], 'The balance of payments' in Posner, M. V. (ed.) *Demand Management*. Heinemann Educational Books, pp. 200–8.

10 International Trade

by Peter Maunder

Introduction

The concern of all British governments since the end of the Second
World War about the balance of payments is well-known. The broad
objective of at least balance on current account has long been taken
as so obvious as not to need stating. However it is not at all so easy
to find clearly stated objectives of trade policy during the last two
decades at a less aggregated level as for example in terms of the desired
composition of British exports and their geographical destination.
It is true that the three attempts to join the EEC after 1960 did reflect
concern over the sluggish growth of Britain's Commonwealth-oriented
trade. However the case for EEC membership was always held to
be much wider than to rest on trade considerations alone. The growth
in imports of semi-manufactured and finished manufactures in the
1960s clearly worried the Wilson government, but it is not easy to
trace an explicit policy objective concerning this problem. But if then
there are difficulties in stating the various aims of trade policy, it is,
strangely enough, not easy to recognise all the various policies that
have been pursued to achieve it. There are several reasons which
account for the difficulty in stating – in a succinct manner – British
international trade policies during the past decade. The first is the
diffused nature of policy-making concerning trade in the UK. A
second is the basic problem of identifying trade policies as such. It
is appropriate to explain both these points.

Firstly, there is no single Ministry that involves itself purely with
external trade matters. The present Department of Trade (DOT) is
concerned with both overseas as well as internal trade. Part of its work
is explicitly aimed at improving the UK's trade balance but this goal
is not immediately obvious in the case of some of its other responsibilities. Part of the DOT's function is to promote United Kingdom
commercial interests overseas, negotiate on trade matters and administer protective tariffs. The DOT's work in promoting British

exports by its support for overseas trade fairs and overseeing the Export Credits Guarantee Department (ECGD) is clear enough. It is the sponsoring government department for the shipping and aviation industries, the hotel and travel trades, tourism and the film industry. Government measures to boost the invisible earnings of these industries clearly reflect the external aspect of the DOT's work. But it also has responsibilities concerning the conduct of internal commerce and industry, for example competition policy, patents, trade marks and company law. These matters are of course far from being wholly domestic in character but external aspects are less evident than in those responsibilities cited earlier. The DOT is thus concerned in many ways with the promotion of the UK's commercial interests, whether goods or services. But this task is shared with other arms of government such as the Ministry of Agriculture, Fisheries and Food (MAFF) and the Department of Industry (DOI). In the case of MAFF trade matters are readily discernible whether as medium-term aims such as the import-saving role of British farmers or more pressing issues such as the state of the green pound and the deliberation of Common Market farm prices. The Department of Industry's responsibilities broadly concern the nation's industrial performance, one measure of which is its competitiveness in relation to other countries, both developed and developing, in both home and overseas markets. The DOI thus illustrates the second problem, that of specifying what are trade policies.

The much more rapid rise in the volume of imports of manufactured goods as compared with exports during the 1970s was one indication that Britain was in difficulties concerning her ability to face international competition. The response of both Labour and Conservative governments to this worrying situation was to try to take measures aimed at improving the general health of UK manufacturing industry. The extension of public ownership, the payment of job subsidies, discretionary aid to companies and the rescue of lame ducks were all attempts to help remedy the problem. So too was the Labour government's so-called 'new industrial strategy' based on tripartite sector working parties. Much of the policy has been micro in character. The range of measures specific to particular industries adds to the problem indicated at the outset of defining the boundaries of trade policy. Trade policy and industrial policy have become impossible to disentangle from each other.

Even when one recognises these problems of defining trade policy one has to recognise the restrictions on the UK to pursue an active strategy in practical terms. There are important constraints within which any British government has any freedom of manoeuvre. Some of these constraints have been self-imposed such as the obligations to uphold the membership rules of the General Agreement on Tariffs and Trade.

GATT's 'most-favoured nation' principle limits the setting of discriminatory tariffs by the UK as of any other member. GATT membership also involves some restraint on independent tariff policy because of this body's continuing efforts to co-ordinate a multilateral reduction in barriers to trade. The early part of the 1970s witnessed the final implementation of the Kennedy Round of tariff cuts as had been agreed during negotiations that had taken place between 1964 and 1967. The seventh 'Tokyo' round of GATT negotiations which began in 1973 and not completed until six years later have imposed some pressure on the UK to seek an agreed position with other countries on a further liberalisation of world trade. Moreover in this latter round of trade talks the EEC countries bargained as a group with Japan, the US and other major trading nations. Thus the UK's interests were now subsumed within those of the community as a whole during the Tokyo round whereas hitherto the UK had been a separate negotiating party in GATT discussions. Joining the Common Market has thus limited the possibility of the UK pursuing trade policies wholly independent of other members (see Chapter 11).

However whatever the true inhibiting character of upholding the rules of GATT and being an EEC member, the world state of the trading system as a whole imposes a more powerful constraint on the growth of UK trade both physical and invisible. Overseas demand for British goods is affected by the level of economic activity in the world's major industrial nations, a factor over which the UK is virtually powerless to influence. The same is true of invisible trade. The potential to boost shipping earnings will be obviously influenced by the growth rate of world trade in goods. Expenditure by tourists in the UK is affected by the growth of personal incomes in the countries from which they travel. Britain's income on overseas assets will be determined by the volume and profitability of previous foreign investment. Variations in trading conditions among overseas countries will affect the total level of this income.

The constraints on the determination of UK trade policy of course can be exaggerated. Indeed it became clear as the decade unfolded

Table 10.1 The commodity structure and geographic basis of UK visible trade, 1968–78

£m

	1968	1969	1970	1971	1972	1973	1974	1975	1976	1977	1978
Visible Exports											
Food, beverages and tobacco	418	436	505	569	637	849	1 034	1 388	1 654	2 182	2 865
Basic materials	213	224	269	279	317	420	583	556	777	956	1 006
Mineral fuels and lubricants	172	177	210	239	242	374	782	827	1 264	2 092	2 375
Semi-manufactured goods	2 256	2 563	2 783	3 008	3 118	4 231	5 823	6 048	8 331	10 614	11 415
Finished manufactured goods	3 171	3 648	4 074	4 704	4 855	5 873	7 719	9 934	12 575	15 385	16 760
Commodities and transactions not classified according to kind	203	221	280	261	281	368	597	710	810	919	1 011
Total	6 433	7 269	8 121	9 060	9 450	12 115	16 538	19 463	25 411	32 148	35 432
of which to:											
European Economic Community	1 716	2 010	2 347	2 511	2 835	3 944	5 581	6 273	9 052	11 878	13 675
Other Western Europe	968	1 170	1 392	1 519	1 604	2 055	2 755	3 086	3 996	4 848	4 542
North America	1 122	1 178	1 221	1 416	1 553	1 872	2 260	2 297	3 043	3 751	4 157
Other developed countries	806	873	975	1 077	931	1 208	1 721	1 847	1 943	2 095	2 311
Oil exporting countries	364	452	474	580	638	790	1 224	2 267	3 158	4 315	4 633
Rest of world	1 457	1 586	1 712	1 957	1 889	2 246	2 997	3 693	4 219	5 261	6 114
Visible Imports											
Food, beverages and tobacco	1 727	1 744	1 847	1 971	2 138	2 834	3 478	4 093	4 613	5 484	5 663
Basic materials	996	1 033	1 142	1 078	1 114	1 676	2 202	1 952	2 870	3 202	2 919
Mineral fuels and lubricants	669	662	681	914	943	1 326	4 213	3 964	5 266	4 925	4 536
Semi-manufactured goods	2 028	2 193	2 364	2 299	2 620	3 754	5 703	5 384	7 036	8 860	9 755
Finished manufactured goods	1 574	1 706	2 005	2 409	3 221	4 718	5 759	6 776	8 762	11 283	13 234
Commodities and transactions not classified according to kind	121	103	124	128	136	190	418	530	465	438	500
Total	7 115	7 441	8 163	8 799	10 172	14 498	21 773	22 699	29 012	33 892	36 607

of which from											
European Economic Community	1 967	2 084	2 308	2 702	3 426	5 135	7 623	8 685	11 179	13 611	15 922
Other Western Europe	998	1 066	1 217	1 404	1 645	2 338	3 113	3 157	3 998	4 623	5 078
North America	1 425	1 388	1 709	1 591	1 635	2 155	2 963	2 959	3 869	4 510	4 938
Other developed countries	761	823	828	856	1 088	1 416	1 623	1 862	1 930	2 484	2 557
Oil exporting countries	553	568	588	768	769	1 120	3 441	2 981	3 867	3 430	3 055
Rest of world	1 411	1 512	1 513	1 478	1 609	2 334	3 010	3 055	4 169	5 234	5 057
Visible balance in:											
Food, beverages and tobacco	− 1 309	− 1 308	− 1 342	− 1 492	− 1 501	− 1 985	− 2 444	− 2 705	− 2 959	− 3 302	− 2 798
Basic materials	− 783	− 809	− 873	− 799	− 797	− 1 256	− 1 619	− 1 396	− 2 093	− 2 246	− 1 913
Mineral fuels and lubricants	− 497	− 485	− 471	− 675	− 701	− 952	− 3 431	− 3 137	− 4 002	− 2 883	− 2 161
Semi-manufactured goods	+ 228	+ 370	+ 419	+ 709	+ 498	+ 477	+ 120	+ 664	+ 1 295	+ 2 054	+ 1 660
Finished manufactured goods	+ 1 597	+ 1 942	+ 2 069	+ 2 295	+ 1 634	+ 1 155	+ 1 960	+ 3 158	+ 3 813	+ 4 102	+ 3 526
Commodities and transactions not classified according to kind	+ 82	+ 118	+ 156	+ 133	+ 145	+ 178	+ 179	+ 180	+ 345	+ 481	+ 511
Total	− 682	− 172	− 42	+ 261	− 722	− 2 383	− 5 235	− 3 236	− 3 601	− 1 744	− 1 175
of which visible balance with:											
European Economic Community	− 251	− 74	+ 39	− 191	− 591	− 1 191	− 2 042	− 2 412	− 2 127	− 1 733	− 2 247
Other Western Europe	− 30	+ 104	+ 175	+ 115	− 41	− 283	− 358	− 71	− 2	+ 225	− 536
North America	− 303	− 210	− 488	− 175	− 82	− 283	− 793	− 662	− 826	− 759	− 781
Other developed countries	+ 45	+ 50	+ 147	+ 221	− 157	− 208	+ 98	− 15	+ 13	− 389	− 246
Oil exporting countries	− 189	− 116	− 114	− 188	− 131	− 330	− 2 217	− 714	− 709	+ 885	+ 1 578
Rest of world	+ 46	+ 74	+ 199	+ 479	+ 280	− 88	− 13	+ 698	+ 50	+ 27	+ 1 057

Source: Central Statistical Office, *United Kingdom Balance of Payments, 1979*, HMSO, pp. 19–20.

that covert protectionist measures were being applied not only in the UK but elsewhere in Europe and North America. 'Orderly marketing arrangements' to circumscribe the GATT rules have become much more well established than hitherto as the UK and other developed nations have become concerned about historically high and rising levels of unemployment while import penetration levels have risen (Page [1979]). These trade restraints are indicated in the next section which reviews the development of trade policy concerning physical goods.

Visible Trade

The decade began with the current account at least in surplus following the devaluation of sterling in November 1967. Indeed the change in the exchange rate seemed to have proved those who had long argued that 'the great unmentionable' should have been made much earlier. The radical improvement in visible trade after 1967 (see Table 10.1) was supported by strong deflationary measures at home, which helped check the growth in imports and externally, by a marked increase in the growth of world trade, assisted by the Kennedy round tariff cuts. One other policy measure in support of devaluation, applied by the Labour government in November 1968 – an import deposit scheme – in respect of manufactured goods was maintained by the new Heath government until the end of 1970. However the restraining effect on imports achieved by this measure – in effect a six-month interest-free loan to the government on a proportion (initially 50%) of the value of imports of manufacture is open to doubt. But this protectionist act can be seen as setting the trend for later attempts to restrict imports in ways which hardly upheld the spirit of the rules of GATT. Compared with the import surcharge imposed by the new Labour government in November 1964 and which lasted for two years, the deposit scheme was less open to the objection of distorting trade flows. But, by the same token, it could do little to deter foreign suppliers keen to sell in the UK and, like the earlier measure, did nothing to help boost exports.

Devaluation had given Britain an improvement in the price competitiveness of her exports, and as the decade opened there was little doubt amongst economists about the fundamental role of the exchange rate in determining export performance. Lord Kaldor's Presidential Address to Section F of the British Association stated the virtual consensus viewpoint.

The main autonomous factor governing both the level and the rate of growth of effective demand of an industrial country with a large share of exports in its total production and of imports in its consumption is the external demand for its exports; and the main factor governing the latter is its international competitiveness, which in turn depends on the level of its industrial costs relatively to other industrial exporters. Since the level of money wages is bound to be sticky in a downward direction, and is not greatly influenced by world prices in an upward direction, the degree of competitiveness, given the relationship of wage rates and productivity levels of different industrial countries, depends largely on the exchange rate.

(Kaldor [1971] pp. 7–8)

However later in the decade Lord Kaldor and others came to lose their faith in the efficacy of the exchange rate mechanism. They argued that depreciation of sterling could not be expected to secure a long-term improvement in trade performance because the resulting cost and price changes themselves eroded the initial effect on price competitiveness (Kaldor [1976]). Furthermore there came to be a growing doubt over the importance of price as a variable in export competitiveness. But this is to comment in retrospect. It is necessary as we start in 1970 to review the decade to say that at the time there was much less pessimism about the competitive strength of British industry in world markets than for many years previously.

The year 1971 in part confirmed this optimism for British exports because the growth of demand for British goods was similar to that in the volume of world trade in manufactured goods as a whole. As Table 10.1 shows, there was a net surplus on visible trade. Thus, for once, Britain held its hitherto declining share of this trade at about 11%. On the other hand there were disturbing signs of growing uncompetitiveness. The rate of change in the available indicators of export competitiveness such as relative export prices and unit manpower costs suggested a more worrying situation. It seemed that after mid 1970 prices of British manufactured exports were rising at about twice the rate as those of other industrial countries and within two years nearly all the relative price advantage achieved through devaluation had been dissipated.

Furthermore research by two economists at the National Economic Development Office suggested a disturbing situation concerning the product mix in the structure of UK trade. Compared with ten other major competitors the UK's export performance in the 1960s was shown to have been relatively weak in the case of internationally traded goods which had shown the most rapid rate of growth such as advanced engineering and chemical products. Because these accounted for a high proportion of UK exports the economists argued that it was important to establish why there had been this failure to compete more effectively at the industrial and at least large firm levels (Panić and Rajan [1971], p. 18). One can take this research as an indicator that trade policy is not a clearly defined issue to be solved at the macro level. Indeed a micro level approach to improving Britain's trade and industrial performance follows logically from studies such as this one by NEDO.

However what really transformed the visible trade picture was the surge in the value of imports in 1972 as a result of the boom in commodity prices, particularly oil. The simultaneous expansion of demand in most advanced nations resulted in world-wide shortages in foodstuffs and raw materials, and the terms of trade deteriorated sharply. The response by the Heath government in July 1972 to allow sterling to float is without doubt the major policy decision during the past decade of concern in this present chapter. It therefore requires due consideration.

The decision, effectively to devalue the pound again, attracted few criticisms either within or outside government at the time. It seemed the obvious solution to restore Britain's competitive position in terms of price and also permit continued growth of the domestic economy without prejudice to external balance. But the surge in commodity prices, and in particular the quadrupling in oil prices, resulted in more severe pressure on the pound than the strategy intended and obliged the Heath government to resort to their prices and incomes policy. In fact the commodity price boom so strained the credibility of price and wage controls after their re-introduction in November 1972 that within sixteen months there was a new government. In retrospect the view that 'the commodity price explosion was the largest single factor that destroyed the Tories' strategy' (*The Economist* [1974], p. 63) is surely correct, for the volume of exports increased at a faster rate than that of imports between mid 1972 and mid 1973. Suggestions made in several quarters that it was the Heath 'dash for growth' which resulted in the dramatic turnround in the current account between 1971 and 1973 therefore do not bear close inspection. It was the deterioration in the terms of trade which really transformed a visible surplus of £261m into a deficit of £2383m in 1973.

The Labour government, 1974–9

The incoming Wilson government now had to face the OPEC-induced recession in the world economy. However it did not respond by trying to stimulate the economy, but reinforced the demand-deflationary effect of higher oil prices. Despite a fall in the volume of imports the visible deficit more than doubled to £5235m (Table 10.1). Although there was no major depreciation of the pound in 1974 it was in the following year that doubts about the trade balance surfaced once more. An indication of a change of thinking was the suggestion by the chief economist at NEDO that the UK still suffered from a 'structural disequilibrium' (Panić [1975] p. 11). Panić argued that current exchange rate strategy and macroeconomic policies were not tackling the root of the country's trading problems. He pointed to weaknesses in quality, design and technical performance of UK products as being responsible for the high income elasticity of demand for imports of manufactures. The New Cambridge group of economists then called for import controls and a reduction in the PSBR to rectify the balance of payments deficit (CEPG [1975]). Inevitably there followed a keen debate amongst academic economists on the respective merits of import controls and devaluation (Corden et al. [1975]; Greenaway and Milner [1979]).

In general terms the Wilson government still set its face against this suggestion but faced a growing demand for protectionism from both the TUC and firms facing keen import competition. The Prime Minister said that 'As a big trading nation we have set ourselves very strongly against physical import controls. But we are not going to sit back and watch a remorseless increase in British unemployment. If the slump does not begin to improve quickly, we obviously reserve our rights to protect our balance of payments by various means.' (*The Economist* [1975] p. 78). His final sentence really meant – of course – protection of jobs. Despite joining with other OECD countries in making a pledge not to extend trade controls, government ministers clearly were aware of the growing pressure from back-bench MPs and the TUC for selective restraints on imports. Thus Peter Shore, Secretary of State for Trade, was quoted as saying that action would be taken if a major British industry was 'really threatened'. The TUC were asked to 'search their consciences' when considering purchase of foreign cars. In October 1976 Mr Varley, Secretary of State for Industry, declared that a situation in which overseas car manufacturers served over 40% of the British market could not be accepted.

Although car imports caused much concern the pressure for quotas also included television tubes, textiles and clothing, footwear and electrical components. Both sides of industry argued that unfair competition from cheap imports was difficult to prove under the terms of Britain's existing anti-dumping legislation. Even where action was eventually taken against dumped imports it was held that jobs have already been lost. The DOT in defence claimed its response was neither tardy nor ineffective. Action against dumped imports is technically different from emergency measures which can be taken to prevent injury to home industries as permitted by Article 19 of the GATT rules. At the time these two aspects of trade controls were not distinguished because the UK in common with other GATT members was not keen to invoke Article 19. The preferred route to achieving restraints on imports was by securing 'voluntary undertakings and assurances' from offending countries concerning their expansion of exports. Thus Mr Shore received a promise in October 1975 from Japan's car manufacturers that their shipments to the UK would remain steady until the end of the year and that thereafter exporting would be 'orderly'.

Concern about import penetration of manufactures into the British market since 1969 was the basis for another pessimistic forecast from the New Cambridge economists in February 1976. In its second Annual Economic Policy Review it envisaged an increasingly severe recession and rising unemployment unless general import controls were introduced. The CEPG rejected devaluation as an alternative to import controls to prevent further de-industrialisation because the required fall in sterling of some 30% was considered unacceptable to foreign lenders. Although in his April 1976 budget the Chancellor was broadly critical of the New Cambridge school he later conceded that 'import controls may have a valuable role to play in protecting particular industries whose survival is threatened by excessive imports which cause market disruption'. (Hansard [1976]). Within the Cabinet Tony Benn openly championed the cause. But the Government's stance on import controls was now explicitly interwoven with its industrial policy. The 'new industrial strategy' viewed Britain's trade position firmly in the context of the economy as a whole. The White Paper *An Approach to Industrial Strategy* stated baldly that 'Our manufacturing industry has not done as well as its competitors. In particular it has not responded adequately to changes in the pattern

of world trade and suffers from structural rigidities which show themselves particularly in bottlenecks both of manpower and components
in the early stages of economic upturns.' (Cmnd 6315 [1975] p. 4).
This last sentence pointed again to Britain's high propensity to import
when the economy expanded rapidly. The rapid downward float of
the pound in August brought about the adjustment in sterling's
exchange value that the CEPG had considered so difficult to effect.
However the autumn of that year witnessed a keen debate in *The
Times*, as to whether the UK could as a result now be expected to
move towards external balance. Those economists such as Lord
Kaldor who had advocated devaluation in the mid 1960s and had
previously favoured floating currency rates now argued that the long-
run effects of exchange rate changes in the UK and also the United
States, West Germany and Japan were perverse (Kaldor [1976]).
Doubts about the importance of price as the basis of international
competitiveness were then stressed in a NEDO study (Stout [1977]).
In the following year two Treasury economists suggested that devaluation was unlikely to lead to external balance without rapidly accelerating price inflation (Odling-Smee and Hartley [1978]). The rider
to this growing scepticism over the efficacy of exchange rate policy
was a growing preparedness by government to favour concealed
protectionist policies. Mr Dell now warned Japanese car manufacturers to restrain exports to Britain at a level of about 10% of the
market or face import quotas. However there was no action concerning car imports from West Germany which were at a much higher
level than those from Japan. The number of French cars imported
(which were then only just lower than those of Japanese origin) were
also not subject to official criticism. Nor were those from Italy which
were winning a more rapid market share than cars from any other
country. It was not therefore surprising that dealers in Japanese cars
felt government policy to be discriminatory: the Datsun Dealers'
Association even took the step of taking whole page advertisements
in daily newspapers and periodicals to vent their opposition to the
restraints imposed on their sales effort. They argued that curbing
Japanese car imports would have as much effect in curing British
Leyland's problems 'as an aspirin in curing pneumonia'. (*The
Economist* [1978], p. 74).

In May 1978 the Prime Minister urged industrialists attending the
annual dinner of the Confederation of British Industry to review their
purchasing policies. Mr Callaghan claimed he was not calling for a

'Buy British' campaign when posing the question 'Is it in the long-term interests of British industrial purchasers to give so much of their custom to foreign suppliers?' However, his answer was emphatic ('I am certain it is not') and his conclusion pointed 'We are giving profit and jobs to our overseas suppliers and in the longer run it will result in running down our industrial base.' (*Financial Times* [1978]). The Prime Minister's comments followed the advocacy of 'organised free trade' by his counterpart in France, Mr Raymond Barre and the response of both Premiers reflected common concern over their depressed economies. Indeed throughout Western Europe governments resorted to subsidies to prop up the ailing steel, shipbuilding and textile industries. It should be noted that in the case of the latter imports were already regulated by international agreement through the Multi-Fibre Agreement. The UK had also imposed a tariff on Commonwealth imports in 1972. All these suffered from over-capacity, a problem aggravated by keen competition from Japan and the newly industrialising developing countries. 'Crisis cartels' were actually encouraged for the steel and synthetic fibres industries by Viscount Davignon, the EEC Commissioner for Industry (see Chapter 11). In Britain the 'temporary' employment subsidy aided the textile and clothing industry until the EEC Commission in 1978 finally insisted that this aid be drastically curtailed. The political pressures from those industrial lobbies protesting against foreign goods from low-wage countries were inevitably stronger than those who protested that only a small proportion of jobs lost were actually caused by imports (Cable [1979]).

For comment on how the government viewed the retreat into protectionism the Secretary of State for Trade, Edmund Dell, has provided at least some perspective. In several speeches during 1977 he referred to the nature of world trade being 'a war of all against all'. Mr Dell candidly stated the conflicting interests of free trade and protectionism. His recent policy towards Japan's exports of cars to the UK reflected his view that the world had taken a turn towards more mercantilist principles. 'Mercantilism expresses the belief that international trade is a kind of war in which it is better to win than to lose. You win by having a surplus and lose by having a deficit.' However it should be stressed that Mr Dell opposed the application of general import controls in the UK as the logical conclusion of such thinking. He said import controls provided no escape from 'this harsh, Hobbesian world'. The main rule of international trade was that 'to survive you have to be able to compete'. (Dell [1977]). Mr Dell's analysis was open to criticism (Lal [1978] and reply by Dell [1979]), but he had at least acknowledged the dangers for the continuance of an open world trading system.

Mr Dell was not a candidate in the 1979 General Election when in its Manifesto the Labour Party asserted that in the quest for a healthy expanding economy protectionism had a part to play. It stated that what was needed was 'a programme to protect employment while the necessary changes and modernisation of our industry takes place. We will not allow our industries to be wiped out by excessive imports before they have had a chance to recover their strength. The Labour government will ensure that imports enter our market only within acceptable limits.' (Labour Party [1979] p. 11). The Conservative Party in contrast made no such clear commitment on import controls and since their return to office the new Minister of State for Trade has declared that protectionism was 'self-defeating'. He reaffirmed the Government's 'total support to the open trading system internationally and a more flexible and competitive market economy in Britain'. (Parkinson [1979], p. 108). However, this credo is likely to come under severe pressure in the mid 1980s as the benefit of North Sea oil stabilises. The new government's policy to keep the pound's exchange rate high as part of its anti-inflationary strategy is accommodating for foreign competitors. Car imports reached a record 60% share of the UK car market in November 1979 – a figure well above Mr Varley's 'unacceptable' level. Increasing import penetration in finished manufactures will certainly test the Thatcher government's nerve in holding to its exchange rate policy which is forcing industry to switch to production of more higher value-added, income elastic goods. The low value of world income elasticity of demand for British exports as found for many manufacturing industries by Thirlwall [1978] is a handicap enough. Given also that in this research Thirlwall found typically a higher income elasticity of demand for these goods when imported, then we have in a nutshell Britain's basic problem of a lack of competitiveness in home and overseas markets.

We turn next to policy towards invisible trade and a body previously mentioned, the Export Credits Guarantee Department (ECGD), provides us with a neat link between the tangible and intangible aspects of trade. As in other developed countries Britain has for many years offered special credit facilities for exporters and also provided credit insurance through the Export Credits Guarantee Department. In 1977 the ECGD introduced the foreign currency buyer credit scheme so as to reduce the public expenditure burden of re-financing fixed rate sterling export lending. However, rising market rates of interest in 1978–9 meant that there was a marked escalation in the cost to be met by government of providing interest rate subsidies in the cause of winning export orders.

The public expenditure burden of interest rate support (in 1978 over £200m) was far greater than sums disbursed on export promotion and trade co-operation which have been barely changed since the early 1970s at around £17m per year. The ECGD attracts little public attention and is one government body whose expanding range of activities in the service of British exports has as yet involved no political controversy.

Invisible Trade

The deficits in visible trade during the 1970s were generally compensated for by surpluses on invisible account in keeping with the long-run tradition of adverse physical trade balances being offset by net earnings from services, interest, profits and dividends, and transfers. Close examination of the invisible account is necessary to determine what the effect has been of government policies on these transactions, not least because of the heterogeneity of the items involved. Even so it is clear that government policy has not been explicit in terms of objectives concerning many of the relevant transactions. This is partially explained by the fact that broader macro-economic goals have been more important than those in mind for this mixture of private sector and government activities. This is well illustrated by the basic antipathy to the service sector shown by the Wilson government through the imposition of selective employment tax in 1965. The check on foreign investment through the introduction of corporation tax in 1965 provided another example. It was not surprising that institutions in the City of London in due course rose in defence of those involved in earning foreign currency and pressed for a reversal of these policies. The 1967 (Clarke) report by the Committee on Invisible Exports embodied this outlook. It strongly argued that the UK was the second most important country in the world in terms of its net invisible surplus but that this was not appreciated by government. The report, not unfairly, stated that invisibles had been invisible for too long. It said 'Virtually every sector of the service trades giving evidence to the Committee contrasted the facilities and encouragements provided for visible exporters with the lack of support (and often understanding) given to invisible exports.' (Committee on Invisible Exports [1967], p. 259). The bias against services in both the export rebate scheme and SET, together with the exclusion of the sector from the Queen's Award to Industry Scheme supported this viewpoint.

Implicit in the Committee's report was the viewpoint that the buoyancy of private invisible earnings – providing 37% of the UK's total foreign exchange in 1966 – was utterly necessary to offset the rapid rise in government overseas expenditure but the latter was really outside the committee's terms of reference. However it is necessary to point out that at this time and indeed since then that the size of the government's spending abroad exaggerates the true balance of payments effect of its activities. This is because government 'invisible' spending includes both aid to developing countries and information and trade services both of which directly aid British exports. The private–public sector distinction is further blurred when one considers expenditure on diplomatic services. That spent in the UK by overseas governments will generally accrue to the private sector but because there is a reciprocal UK presence abroad, the cost then falls within the public sector. Thus there is no unambiguous distinction between the contributions of the private and public sectors to the total invisible account. Given these caveats Table 10.2 gives a breakdown of items on invisible account of both sectors for the period 1968–78. We now discuss the component parts of the invisible accounts and indeed give them special attention because this part of Britain's current accounts is poorly documented, at least from a policy standpoint.

Services
The service transactions of government continued to be in deficit throughout the 1970s, the major debit item being military expenditure in the German Federal Republic. The additional cost of overseas defence spending effected by the downward adjustment of the pound in 1967 inevitably made the Wilson government determined to seek economies. Thus in January 1968 plans were announced to accelerate the withdrawal of forces from the Persian Gulf, Malaysia and Singapore. Appreciation of foreign currencies in terms of sterling following the freeing of exchange rates in 1972 had the effect of raising the sterling cost of maintaining troops in West Germany and elsewhere.

Table 10.2   The UK balance of payments invisibles (a) Services, 1968–78

£m

	1968	1969	1970	1971	1972	1973	1974	1975	1976	1977	1978
General government											
Credits											
European Communities' institution	—	—	—	—	—	13	19	32	44	76	91
US forces expenditure	12	20	18	19	19	19	18	21	25	43	59
Other military receipts by UK government	16	7	11	9	22	45	38	42	84	60	107
Other receipts	16	21	22	31	31	27	35	44	62	61	61
Total credits	44	48	51	59	72	104	110	139	215	240	318
Debits											
Military											
German Federal Republic	99	108	130	148	184	248	304	350	439	546	538
Other	176	174	171	167	166	176	228	245	307	284	334
Administrative, diplomatic, etc	56	56	59	59	73	89	97	114	136	141	153
Total debits	331	338	360	374	423	513	629	709	882	971	1 015
Balance of general government	−287	−290	−309	−315	−351	−409	−519	−570	−667	−731	−697
Credits											
Private sector and public corporations											
Sea transport	1 053	1 051	1 357	1 615	1 607	2 055	2 658	2 634	3 209	3 428	3 163
Civil aviation	235	287	316	354	410	480	625	780	1 051	1 203	1 448
Travel	282	359	432	500	576	726	898	1 218	1 768	2 352	2 503
Financial services^a	266	356	439	471	529	601	767	1 005	1 286	1 371	1 488
Other services	697	753	817	925	1 041	1 220	1 510	1 906	2 495	2 993	3 284
Total credits	2 577	2 854	3 412	3 924	4 235	5 186	6 568	7 682	10 024	11 587	12 204

£m

Debits											
Sea transport	1 018	1 084	1 437	1 673	1 688	2 160	2 796	2 603	3 222	3 445	3 334
Civil aviation	201	238	266	297	333	405	529	664	810	959	1 100
Travel	271	324	382	442	535	695	703	917	1 068	1 186	1 548
Other services	414	468	514	548	601	707	995	1 426	1 785	2 035	1 918
Total debits	2 235	2 452	2 959	3 334	3 580	4 480	5 622	6 319	7 767	8 596	8 915
Balance of general government and private sector	+342	+402	+453	+590	+655	+706	+946	+1 363	+2 257	+2 991	+3 289

a The figures for this item are obtained net of overseas payments and the similar earnings in the United Kingdom by overseas financial institutions are negligible. For these reasons this item appears as a credit entry only.

(b) Interest, profits and dividends

General government	Credits	31	31	54	91	156	176	237	266	253	411	766
	Debits	272	371	323	295	298	375	589	780	901	1 099	1 222
	Net	−241	−340	−269	−204	−142	−199	−352	−514	−648	−688	−456
Private sector and public corporations	Credits	1 079	1 311	1 398	1 397	1 585	2 662	3 060	2 570	3 641	3 553	4 281
	Debits	502	471	570	683	905	1 203	1 285	1 294	1 694	2 664	2 989
	Net	+577	+840	+828	+714	+680	+1 459	+1 775	+1 276	+1 947	+889	+1 292

Source: CSO, *United Kingdom Balance of Payments, 1979*, HMSO, pp. 11, 27.

It is worth noting that monthly and quarterly data on visibles and invisibles that is widely quoted on publication is subject to considerable later revision. Thus an early estimate of a zero balance on invisibles for the second quarter of 1979 was later in 1979 revised to a surplus of £107m.

Inevitably the Heath government made efforts to try and offset the growing burden. This resulted in a greater contribution from the German Federal Republic towards maintaining the British Army on the Rhine. After 1972 NATO countries contributed towards the cost of maintaining military facilities in Malta. These policies had some success because the rate of increase in military receipts exceeded that of debits. Nonetheless, as Table 10.2 shows, the balance of such expenditures rose every year after 1970 until 1977 before falling back a bit in 1978.

Non-military expenditure on services by government includes the operating costs of UK embassies, High Commission offices and consulates. Although the total sum involved has not risen dramatically during the decade – rising from £59m in 1970 to £153m in 1978 – the period witnessed considerable debate over the role of Britain's diplomatic service. This was because in 1969 the Duncan Committee on overseas representation had recommended a radical rationalisation of the Diplomatic Service in view of Britain's position as 'a major power of the second order'. (Cmnd 4107 [1969]). The Committee had noted that the concentration of foreign policy on Western Europe and North America following the 1968 decision to abandon an East of Suez military role was increasingly guided by commercial considerations. Accordingly it had proposed to strengthen overseas representation in these two 'areas of concentration' and reduce staffing in the 'outer areas'. This distinction proved unacceptable to either the then Wilson government or the later Heath administration. But the Report at least had emphasised the critical role of economic and trade matters in the future work of the overseas missions. It lamented the fact that the existing system had failed to produce an effective dialogue about export strategy between overseas posts and government departments at home.

The more wide-ranging inquiry by the Central Policy Review Staff provoked even more hostile reaction than that following the report of Sir Val Duncan's three-man team. The 'Think-Tank' was asked in 1976 to recommend on the means required both at home and overseas to promote Britain's overseas interests. This meant that the work in London of the Foreign and Commonwealth Office together with all other government departments and state-financed organisations with overseas interests required appraisal by the CPRS. The prospect of a radical assessment of the FCO, the BBC and the British Council by the so-called 'bright young things' in the 'Think-Tank' prompted much consternation in Whitehall. In its report the CPRS [1977] indeed offered a controversial analysis of how Britain should organise its overseas representation. But its proposals to merge the diplomatic service with the home civil service, reduce the overseas services of the BBC, modify the work of the British Council and prune diplomatic entertainment expenditure proved too sweeping both for the Labour government and a sub-committee of the House of Commons Expenditure Committee. Both the Foreign Secretary and this group of back-bench MPs felt unable to accept the CPRS's proposition that Britain's overseas representation should reflect her declining political and economic influence on world affairs.

Table 10.2 indicates that service transactions are dominated by those relating to businesses and individuals in the private sector. But the private–public division is not clear-cut for there are the service earnings of the nationalised industries, i.e. British Airways. Moreover, one has to recognise government involvement in the cartelisation of both shipping (the so-called conference system) and civil aviation (notably the International Air Transport Association).

Earnings from shipping provided the largest single contribution of all service credits in 1970, though the balance on shipping overall was in deficit. This was because the net surplus earnings on trade in dry cargo were more than offset by a net deficit on tanker services. But by 1978 the miscellaneous category – other services – had grown to form the largest credit item and thus result in a large net balance. The relative demise of shipping during the 1970s was in fact inevitable as many developing countries attempted to stimulate their own sea transport facilities rather than have recourse to British shipowners and operators. At the four meetings of the United Nations Conference on Trade Aid and Development (UNCTAD) since 1964 British governments have had to face demands for a larger share of shipping services from the Third World. Given that the importance of flags of convenience has increased in recent years it should not be inferred that British shipowners have not sought to expand business or that government policy to the industry has been unhelpful. But one has to recognise that the industry has a real difficulty in expanding in this price-sensitive market given existing low returns on capital employed. As for government policy it has strongly opposed flag discrimination and the *Merchant Shipping Act 1974* incorporates measures for retaliation against foreign governments when domestic interests are threatened. (Couper [1977]).

Civil aviation credits rose steadily throughout the decade in parallel with the development of tourism and in every year of the decade there was a net favourable balance. Government policies intended to enhance earnings have thus had a twofold effect on the overall invisible account.

Until 1967 Britain was in deficit on the *travel* account but since then has enjoyed a surplus, notably so in 1976 and 1977. Government policies towards tourism have contributed to this improvement but are open to the criticism that they have been introduced almost reluctantly and without enthusiasm. Indeed one can fairly say that until the late 1960s British governments had no explicit policy towards tourism at all, either in terms of its revenue-earning possibilities or in regard to its social implications. Neither of the major parties had any enthusiasm to consider the foreign exchange potential. As one travel expert put it: 'The Tories were hampered by the seaside land-lady vote and ultra-preservationism in resort areas, and the Labour Party trapped in its own houses-before-hotels syndrome.' (Sandles [1974], p. 41). The fact that explicit policies towards tourism emerged at all thus deserves particular attention.

It seems clear from survey data that expenditure on travel is highly price (and income) elastic. The recent improvement in Britain's competitiveness in providing tourist services must thus be principally ascribed to the decline in the external value of sterling. The devaluation of the pound in 1967 made foreign travel more expensive for British holidaymakers and at the same time increased the attraction to foreigners to take a holiday somewhere in the UK. The beneficial effect of the lower value of sterling on tourist earnings was supplemented by exchange control restrictions (the £50 travel allowance imposed from 1966 to 1970) and also tight monetary policies which reduced the number of holidaymakers going abroad. But whether the UK was really prepared in the late 1960s to receive the rapid rise in visitors from overseas arising from these policies was open to doubt. When ranked by tourist receipts Britain was fourth in 1959 behind Italy, West Germany and France but had dropped by 1965 behind Austria and Spain. The growth rate of earnings during this period was lower than in any other country in Western Europe. Hoteliers complained that they did not receive the same tax treatment as manufacturing industries, were adversely affected by selective employment tax and said that there should be tourist development areas which had financial incentives similar to industrial development areas. The industry resented the abolition of investment allowances on plant and equipment in January 1966 because hotels were not eligible for the investment grants which replaced them. On the other hand the industry itself was open to criticism for being backward as indicated by the lack of any grading scheme for hotels, inflexible menus and dining hours and parochial attitudes as manifested by notices displayed merely in English. What is certain is that Britain did not assist the tourist trade as did other European countries which also tended to have a minister for tourism.

The *Development of Tourism Act 1969* represented the beginnings of a tourism policy. It established four statutory bodies – the British Tourist Authority (BTA) and separate tourist boards for England, Scotland and Wales to promote and encourage the provision and improvement of tourist amenities. The BTA's responsibilities included the promotion of overseas tourism to Britain and in common with the other new tourist boards was set up with government finance and no direct contributions from the industry. The Act also provided for government grants for the building and extension of hotels under the Hotel Development Incentive Scheme. Some £50m was in fact claimed in grants during the period 1969–74. The Labour government had thus finally accepted the case that tourism was one of the world's fastest growing industries and taken steps to ensure that the UK was not left unable, because of a shortage of tourist beds, to increase this source of foreign exchange earnings. The Hotel Incentive Scheme was not without criticism: it arguably resulted in excessive provision of high priced accommodation in London while development of capacity for tourists on more limited budgets was inadequate. But at least the industry could no longer claim to be totally neglected by government. It is true that financial assistance from the three national Tourist Boards for projects has been rather limited. The industry could also point to the absence of any financial provision by government to meet the costs imposed by the *Fire Precautions Act 1971*. But the industry's political strength has never been great because it comprises many geographically widespread operators who receive the doubtful benefit of both minimal pressure from organised labour and antipathy from local residents. To take the latter point enthusiasm for overseas tourists has worn rather thin in recent years in places such as Oxford, Stratford-on-Avon and Edinburgh. The Greater London Council's suggestion of a tourist tax in 1973 was an indication of the ambivalent attitude of Londoners to the benefits of a boom in overseas visitors.

Not surprisingly the BTA and the Tourist Boards have pointed to the rather hidden contribution by tourists to the national exchequer through the payment of VAT, petrol, tobacco and alcohol taxes quite apart from maintaining the viability of hotels, shops, restaurants and theatres in the capital.

In 1974 the BTA was directed by the Government to publicise tourism in areas of high unemployment, but this change in policy proved short-lived. Nonetheless London's share of overseas travel business has been in decline. The BTA has developed a tourist 'growth points' strategy to maximise the potential of those areas which can absorb more visitors. Certain development areas such as Cornwall and the Lake District hardly justified more facilities in view of pressures from the existing seasonal influx of tourists.

In general government policy has been arguably somewhat half-hearted (see Table 6.2) but the extension in April 1978 to hotels of the tax allowances available on new industrial buildings indicated the growing official recognition of tourism's role in the economy. The rise in VAT to 15% in 1979 prompted hotel and theatre companies to press for continuance of the former 8% on foreign tourists' accounts. However, quite apart from the administrative problems that would be involved in a concessionary rate, the government was never likely to concede the lower rate despite the decline in the number of foreign tourists visiting Britain in 1979 – what with a poor summer, rapidly rising hotel prices, a rising exchange rate and a weak dollar to deter American visitors.

In contrast to tourism the miscellaneous category *other services* warrants little comment simply because the diversity of the transactions involved does not highlight the relevance of government policies. This category includes for example the fees of architects and consulting engineers on construction work overseas and also royalties on printed matter, cinematograph and television films. But whereas it is difficult to identify explicit policies to boost the construction industry's overseas earnings, British governments have had special policies since the war to assist the cinematograph industry. In the case of telecommunication and postal services the British government is a party to various inter-governmental agreements.

Overseas earnings of financial institutions
The overseas earnings of UK financial institutions comprise both receipts for work done in the way of services and investment income

defined as interest, profits and dividends. Although these two types of income are traditionally allocated to different accounts in the Pink Book it is also convenient to aggregate them to establish the net earnings of those financial institutions generally recognised as the 'City of London'. Thus defined the City's total net earnings from banking, brokerage, merchanting, underwriting and insurance have risen each year with the single exception of 1977. This definition of course highlights the private sector contribution to overall invisible earnings. Given the absence of financial service earnings of government it is necessary to turn to the public–private sector split of income from interest, profits and dividends to indicate the consistent deficit balance of government on this item. The highly variable size of the net income accruing to the government (see Table 10.2) is essentially explained by policy decisions concerning the borrowing and repayment of overseas debt. Thus a reduction in official overseas debt results in a fall in subsequent interest payments: this helps explain the reduction in the public sector deficit on interest, profits and dividends between 1969 and 1972. Exchange rate policy of course has crucial effects on the size of foreign earnings. Thus the depreciation of the pound in 1972 resulted in a large increase in the sterling value of private sector investment income in the following year. In contrast in 1977 the level of this income was less than half that of the previous year. The year 1977 witnessed an appreciation in the sterling exchange rate.

Given that by far the greater part of the transactions concerning income from interest, profits and dividends relate to the private sector, one should not be surprised to find that the City has expressed its concern about the effect of government policies. Throughout the decade the City has criticised the exchange controls which limited the use of official exchange for overseas investment. It disliked the 25% surrender requirement because it discouraged active management of portfolio investment abroad. Emphasis was laid on the physical exports and invisible services generated by UK direct investment. But in the case of the banks there was much less concern about government policy affecting their external operations. The explanation is not hard to find: the banks have faced very little interference. Paradoxically it was the imposition in 1957 of restrictions on the use of sterling to finance trade between non-sterling countries that created the opportunity for a new market to develop unhampered by exchange controls. The demand for dollars to finance world trade provided the basis for London to rapidly develop the Eurodollar market. The

Table 10.3   The UK Balance of Payments Invisibles: Net Overseas earnings of United Kingdom financial institutions ('the City'), 1970–8

£m

	1970	1971	1972	1973	1974	1975	1976	1977	1978
UK insurance institutions	294	345	370	347	375	437	790	893	970
UK banking institutions	90	71	122	159	181	202	382	318	652
Commodity trading, etc.									
Commodity trading	60	70	90	110	140	209	201	110	163
Merchanting of other goods	27	30	35	55	69	77	108	120	132
Total	87	100	125	165	209	286	309	230	295
Investment trusts	31	31	31	33	40	41	47	51	58
Unit trusts	3	3	5	6	8	9	11	12	17
Pension funds	3	4	6	9	10	16	14	17	23
Solicitors	9	11	12	13	15	19	29	36	44
Brokerage, etc. earnings									
Baltic Exchange	47	25	35	53	103	146	147	155	154
Stock Exchange	9	10	15	18	19	18	16	20	21
Lloyd's Register of Shipping	4	4	6	7	10	18	17	21	23
Other brokerage	25	18	18	21	28	29	35	37	50
Total	85	57	74	99	160	211	215	233	248
Total net earnings of above institutions	602	622	745	831	998	1221	1797	1790	2307

Source: CSO, United Kingdom Balance of Payments, 1979, HMSO, p. 43.

Bank's informal regulatory style appears to have provided both domestic and foreign banks with much freedom of manoeuvre. It is evident that the Bank has not favoured major official supervision of the Eurocurrency market: indeed it has encouraged its existence to enhance London's position as an international financial centre and thus augment invisible earnings.

Transfers

The outstanding aspect of the UK's invisible transactions left un-discussed are transfers (Table 10.4). At the beginning of the decade few of the constituent items, let alone their magnitude, involved much public attention. The only exception that one would make would be the largest single government item – *economic grants to developing countries*. But after 1973 a new entry in the transfers account – our *contributions to the institutions of the EEC* immediately dwarfed all others and by 1978 had risen eightfold. Only in 1975 was the large debit item cancelled out by receipts arising from the payment of monetary compensatory amounts (MCAs) on food imports from the other EEC countries. It is clearly necessary to explain the nature of Britain's payments to the EEC, but we turn our attention first to aid flows to LDCs because these payments continued throughout the decade.

At a first glance at Table 10.4 it appears that during the 1970s Britain was not unwilling to increase technical assistance and cash grants offered to the Third World on a bilateral basis. However, the very clear uncertain lack of a similar upward trend in the figures as disbursed indirectly through international organisations is a more accurate indicator of Britain's lack of enthusiasm to make increasing donations in real terms for the cause of world economic development. Further evidence lies in Britain's failure to meet the United Nations' target that net official aid (defined as the gross sum less interest and capital repayments) should be not less than 0.7% of GNP.[1] In 1976 the actual figure was 0.38%. This was despite the fact that the Labour government had in 1974 formally accepted the 0.7% goal. However, because the Government did not commit itself as to when it would achieve that goal one has a pretty meaningless comparison between formal principle and actual practice. This very half-hearted willing-ness to do more but not to do so within a particular time horizon of the UN's second development decade sums up Britain's role as an aid donor in the 1970s.

Table 10.4   UK Balance of Payments, Invisibles Transfers, 1968–78

£m

	1968	1969	1970	1971	1972	1973	1974	1975	1976	1977	1978
General government											
Credits											
European Communities' institutions	—	—	—	—	—	63	130	363	251	292	454
Debits											
Economic grants (aid to LDCs)	88	87	85	103	100	106	118	166	276	290	421
Contributions and subscriptions to international organisations											
European Communities' institutions	—	—	—	—	—	187	186	350	474	750	1367
Multilateral economic assistance	8	11	11	24	16	25	19	47	53	105	78
Other transfers	83	79	81	78	94	104	127	167	232	258	288
Total government debits	179	177	177	205	210	422	450	730	1035	1403	2154
Balance	−179	−177	−177	−205	−210	−359	−320	−367	−784	−1111	−1700
Private transfers											
Balance	−59	−44	−17	−6	−53	−99	−121	−143	−13	−44	−218

Source: CSO, *United Kingdom Balance of Payments, 1979*, HMSO, p. 45.
This table excludes repayment of loans by LDCs and the UK subscriptions to the International Development Association and other international lending bodies. These are capital transactions. Table 12.3 of the 1979 Pink Book shows that the toal sums lent to LDCs in 1970 was £88om. In 1978 it had risen to £127om. Of the eight countries for which data is available only India had borrowed substantially more over this period: in 1979 she owed £521m to the UK.

Overseas aid flows have in fact not been protected from the cuts in public expenditure programmes affecting residents in the UK. Successive governments have claimed that Britain's poor balance of payments situation has meant that we could not afford to be more generous in offering aid to foreigners, however poor their plight. But in truth this excuse hides the real fact that governments have lacked the will to develop a clear and consistent policy on aid. Electoral considerations count for nothing because foreigners do not vote, and in any case it appears that many believe that aid lines the pockets of ungrateful nationalist politicians in our former colonies. However, moral and humanitarian considerations are far from being the total basis for offering money to poor countries. Self-interest is clear when one considers the importance of aid offered on condition that it be spent only on British goods and services. More than half of bilateral aid in 1975 was aid of this sort, i.e. tied aid. Further it has been calculated that even in the case of untied aid Britain gets back a large proportion of what she first donates. In 1969 it was estimated that overall, roughly 67 out of every £100 of aid was returned in spending on British products and services. In a brief review of Britain's aid policy it is important to note that in a postwar context overseas assistance has become the subject of new formal administrative mechanisms. It was not until October 1964 that a Ministry of Overseas Development (MOD) was created to bring existing aid programmes under one body. The MOD was one of the first acts of the new Wilson government and as part of its creation two expert development economists, Dudley Seers and Paul Streeten, were appointed to head a strong planning staff of economists and statisticians. As these two were later to comment, until this time the Commonwealth Relations Office 'had been lending or granting more than £100m a year, allegedly for purposes of economic development, without the help of a single economist'. (Seers and Streeten [1972], p. 123). However, the intended development of a clearly defined aid policy was checked both by the cuts in public spending of July 1966 and the failure of successive Ministers to win support in Whitehall for 'a more international, development orientated strategy' (Seers and Streeten [1972], p. 150). In January 1967 the Minister had been dropped from the Cabinet, an indication of how poorly the aid programme had come to rate in political terms.

In the first year of the Heath government the Ministry was dissolved and the Secretary of State for Foreign and Commonwealth Affairs assumed the functions of the former Minister. Within the Foreign and Commonwealth Office (FCO) development matters were handled by the Overseas Development Administration (ODA). But this was not the end of change in the administration of aid policy. Soon after its return to power the Wilson government re-instituted the ODA as a separate Ministry with its own Minister. Then in June 1975 the Secretary of State assumed overall responsibility as Minister of Overseas Development while having a Minister of State in the FCO. However the Ministry of Overseas Development remained in existence under this latter change being referred to not as 'MOD' but as 'ODM' to avoid confusion with the Ministry of Defence! Then in November 1979 full responsibility for aid was once more assumed by the Secretary of State for Foreign and Commonwealth Affairs, his title also including Minister of Overseas Development. The former Ministry of Overseas Development became again an Overseas Development Administration within the FCO. The reader may be forgiven for feeling confused by all these changes. If we also add that Mrs Judith Hart was alone three times a Minister of Overseas Development in two Labour administrations and since 1964 there have been ten changes in the holders of this office it can be appreciated that continuity has not characterised Britain's administration of her aid programme.

The notable jump in aid flows in 1978 also illustrates the vacillation in aid policy. Having reduced the aid programme by £50m in the December 1976 public expenditure 'cuts' the Callaghan government a year later committed itself to a rise in real terms of 6% per year until 1982.

In terms of the direction of aid policy the decade witnessed little major change. It is true that in 1975 a White Paper subtitled *More Help for the Poorest* argued that British aid flows should be directed in future to the poorest countries and the poorest people within those countries. But the case that more emphasis was needed on 'integrated rural development' was hardly revolutionary (Ministry of Overseas Development [1975], p. 16). The World Bank, to name but one obvious interested party, had already recognised doubts aired by development economists that existing aid programmes had not effectively improved the distribution of incomes in most LDCs. Moreover the escalating problem of urban unemployment in many developing countries was bound to trigger a global re-think about the role of agriculture in the development process. Thus the White Paper has to be seen as but part of an international recognition of the need for a new philosophy of aid. But yet it is not easy to perceive its effect. Indeed the House of Commons Select Committee on Overseas Development complained in 1977 that it lacked adequate information by which to determine whether policies towards LDCs were being properly formulated. In particular it severely criticised Whitehall for failing to appreciate the interdependence of aid, trade and foreign investment (HCP 125 [1977], p. x).

The furore over Britain's growing burden of net payments to the EEC as the decade ended makes it crucial to understand the details of the debit–credit relationship. Britain made large payments to the EEC budget at the end of the transitional period of membership essentially because she paid in 90% of her proceeds from both the common external tariff and the levies on food imports. (She also paid over an amount equivalent to a 1% rate of her VAT receipts). Now these proportions (leaving 10% in each case to meet the costs of collection) were the same for all EEC members, and furthermore in the transitional period between 1973–7 Britain's contribution to the community budget only rose gradually. What came to concern the Wilson, Callaghan and Thatcher administrations was firstly the effect that these uniform methods of finance had on Britain because of her pattern of trade and, secondly, our failure to derive significant benefit on the expenditure side so as to recoup much of our payments. What finally caused consternation was a Treasury forecast made in 1977 that Britain's net payment in 1980 would be £830m, a sum well above that paid by any other EEC member. When a year later the EEC's own economic policy committee itself forecast a figure of £770m it is clear that Britain's anxiety was based on incontrovertible evidence. In 1979 it was forecast that Britain's net contribution to the EEC budget would be nearly £1200m in 1980. Table 10.5 identifies the elements in the EEC transfers account and shows the dramatic rise in the sums crossing the exchanges arising from EEC membership.

As part of the renegotiation of the Heath government's terms of entry the Labour government had secured at the 1975 Dublin EEC summit a 'corrective mechanism' to provide refunds to member countries paying in more than their fair share of the budget. However since this mechanism applied to a country's gross contributions, not its net position, and a refund was limited to 250m units of account per annum it turned out to have been totally ineffective, at least as far as Britain was concerned, in checking the growing burden of her budgetary contribution. Britain's problem has been that her imports

*Table 10.5   General government transactions with the institutions of the
European Communities: services and transfers   £m*

	1973	1974	1975	1976	1977	1978
Credits						
Services	13	19	32	44	76	91
Transfers						
European Economic Community:						
Agricultural Guidance and Guarantee Fund	63	112	341	207	181	347
Social Fund	—	16	19	11	48	63
Regional Development Fund	—	—	—	29	60	35
Other	—	—	—	—	—	2
European Coal and Steel Community	—	2	2	4	4	7
Total transfers[a]	63	130	363	251	292	454
Services and transfers[a]	76	149	395	296	369	545
Debits						
Transfers						
Contributions to budget of European						
Communities	181	179	342	463	737	1348
Other payments	6	7	9	12	13	19
Total transfers[a]	187	186	350	474	750	1367

Source: CSO, *United Kingdom Balance of Payments, 1979*, HMSO, p. 91.
[a]Components do not always add to totals in this table as all figures have been rounded independently.

from outside the EEC were significantly higher than in most other
member countries and she thus contributed a disproportionately high
proportion (above one-quarter) of total EEC customs duties in 1979.
Furthermore large food imports from third countries, particularly
Commonwealth suppliers, have meant that Britain was the third
largest contributor of agricultural levies. In return Britain has gained
little benefit from the Common Agricultural Policy which has accounted for more than two-thirds of EEC spending. In retrospect it
now seems so obvious that Britain, as a major food importer, would be
paying subsidies to the more self-sufficient members such as France and
Germany, and, secondly, that our pattern of trade could not be
expected to adjust rapidly enough to minimise the budgetary penalties
incurred. But equally it was naive to expect this major issue to be
solved quickly, as Mrs Thatcher seems to have hoped, in one meeting at the December 1979 EEC summit. Mrs Thatcher found the other
member states unwilling to concede to the UK a sum of £350m to
modify the existing 'corrective mechanism'. She rejected this sum
offered as a full and final settlement of Britain's claim, on the grounds
that it did not deal with the problem that Britain's receipts per head
from Community expenditure were less than half the average for the

whole Community. This problem will no doubt be solved during 1980 as part of a package deal (see Chapter 11).

Conclusion

At the outset of the decade Britain's trade prospects seemed good. However at the time of writing (December 1979), the decade seems likely to end with a current account deficit of over £2bn. Prospects for non-oil exports in 1980 look poor. The invisible surplus has fallen sharply. Import penetration levels continue to rise. The decade had opened with exchange rate policy seemingly at long last resolved. It ended with economists as divided as ever as to the best strategy for sterling in the 1980s. Furthermore the Cambridge economists in favour of import controls seem to be gaining further support (Beckerman [1979]). At the very least one suspects that few economists would be likely to agree with the proposition that Britain will *not* take measures which add to protectionist tendencies in the world's trading system in the 1980s.

Note

1. Strictly speaking the UN aid target is defined as official development assistance and includes certain flows that are outside the public expenditure category of overseas aid which is the usual UK definition of aid. The UK 'national' definition includes both aid funds authorised by Parliament under the Annual Supply Estimates less repayments of past loans and net investment by the Commonwealth Development Corporation.

References

Beckerman, W. [1979], 'A plan to rescue the economy', *New Statesman*, 2 February 1979, pp. 146–7.

Cable, V. [1979], 'Britain, the "new protectionism" and trade with the newly industrialising countries', *International Affairs*, Vol. 55, no. 1, pp. 1–17.

Cambridge Economic Policy Group [1975], *Economic Policy Review*, no. 1, Department of Applied Economics, Cambridge University.

Central Policy Review Staff [1977], *Review of Overseas Representation*, London: HMSO.

Cmnd 6315 [1975], *An Approach to Industrial Strategy*. London: HMSO.

Committee on Invisible Exports [1967], *Britain's Invisible Earnings*, London: British National Export Council.

Corden, M., Little, I. M. D. and Scott, M. F. [1975], *Import Controls Versus Devaluation and Britain's Economic Prospects*. London: Trade Policy Research Centre.

Couper, A. D. [1977], 'Shipping policies of the EEC', *Maritime Policy and Management*, Vol. 4, pp. 129–39.

Dell, E. [1977], 'The Politics of Economic Interdependence', Rita Hinden Memorial Lecture, London, 13 February in *Socialist Commentary*, April 1977, pp. i–xii.

Dell, E. [1979], 'The Wistful liberalism of Deepak Lal', *World Economy*, Vol. 2, no. 2, pp. 189–98.

Duncan, Sir V. [1969], *The Report of the Review Committee on Overseas Representation, 1968–69*. Miscellaneous no. 24, Cmnd 4107. London: HMSO.

Financial Times [1978], 'Buy British goods, Premier tells CBI', 17 May 1978.

Hansard [1976], *House of Commons Parliamentary Debates*, 6 April 1976, Vol. 909, col. 244.

Greenaway, D. and Milner, C. R. [1979], *Protectionism Again . . .? Causes and Consequences of a Retreat from Free Trade to Economic Nationalism*. Hobart Paper. Institute of Economic Affairs.

HCP 125 [1977], Select Committee of the House of Commons on Overseas Development. First Report – Trade and Aid, Vol. 1.

Kaldor, Lord N. [1971], 'Conflicts in national economic objectives', *Economic Journal*, Vol. LXXXI, pp. 1–16.

Kaldor, Lord N. [1976], Letter to *The Times*, 12 October 1976.

Lal, D. [1978], 'The Wistful mercantilism of Mr Dell', *World Economy*, Vol. 1, no. 3, pp. 263–77.

Labour Party [1979], The Labour way is the better way. The Labour Party Manifesto 1979.

Ministry of Overseas Development [1975], *Overseas Development: The Changing Emphasis in British Aid Policies – More Help for the Poorest*, Cmnd 6270. London: HMSO.

Odling-Smee, J. and Hartley, N. [1978], Some effects of exchange rate changes, *HM Treasury Working Paper no. 2*, London.

Page, S. A. B. [1979], 'Management of International Trade', in Major, R. (ed.), *Britain's Trade and Exchange Rate Policy*. London: Heinemann Educational Books, pp. 164–99.

Panić, M. [1975], 'Why the UK's propensity to import is high', *Lloyds Bank Review*, January 1975, pp. 1–12.

Panić, M. and Rajan, A. H. [1971], *Product Changes in Industrial Countries' trade: 1955–68*, NEDO.

Parkinson, C. [1979], 'Protectionism no answer', *British Business*, 19 October 1979, p. 108.

Sandles, A. [1974], 'Common dilemma for tourism', Survey on Invisible Exports in *Financial Times*, 9 December 1974.

Seets, D. and Streeten, P. [1972], 'Overseas development policies', Chapter 3, in Beckerman, W. (ed.), *The Labour Government's Economic Record: 1964–70*. London: Duckworth, pp. 118–56.

Stout, D. K. [1977], *International Price Competitiveness, Non-Price Factors and Export Performance*. London: NEDO.

The Economist [1974], 'Learning from Ted's mistakes', 28 September 1974, pp. 62–3.

The Economist [1975], 'Import controls: absolutely not, but . . .', 2 August 1975, pp. 78–81.

The Economist [1978], 'Time to put the record straight', 11 March, 1978, pp. 74–5.

Thirlwall, A. P. [1978], 'The UK's economic problem: a balance of payments constraint?', *National Westminster Bank Quarterly Review*, February 1978, pp. 24–32.

11 The European Community Dimension

by Dennis Swann

Introduction

The preceding chapters have all dealt with the aims of various economic policies and with the specific instruments evolved by successive UK governments in order to achieve them. It is however undeniable that in the postwar period international obligations and relationships have exerted a powerful influence on the process of policy formulation in nation states, and in the case of the UK this became even more apparent when she finally became a full member of the three European Communities, i.e. the European Economic Community (EEC), the European Coal and Steel Community (ECSC) and the European Atomic Energy Community (Euratom). The purpose of this chapter is to seek to expose the influence of this membership on UK domestic economic objectives and conduct.

The focus of the book is the decade of the 1970s and in that context we should note that the UK did not become a full member until 1 January 1973. It is true that the prospect of full membership was apparent as early as 1969. The reader may recollect that at the Hague (EEC) Summit meeting in December 1969 the Heads of State and of Government agreed to open negotiations with applicant countries. Moreover the UK actively participated in Community policy formulation prior to entry – for example, the applicants played a full part in the Paris Summit of October 1972. Nevertheless it is quite clear that Community membership only began to bite in earnest from 1973 on. But even then the process of adaptation was attenuated by several factors. Firstly, the UK enjoyed a four year transition period. Secondly, she was able to obtain derogations from the originally agreed timetables. Thirdly, the process of coming into line was impeded by the decision of the Labour Party, when in Opposition, to seek renegotiation of the terms of entry – it will be recollected that the original terms were secured by the previous Heath government. The renegotiation by the new Labour government began in April 1974 and was not finally laid to rest until the referendum of June 1975. We must also allow for the fact that in some areas of policy all the Member States and not just the British have dragged their feet when complying with Community undertakings. The Community machinery is also time consuming. It may take years for a particular national policy to be vetted. Even if at the end of that process the Commission declares against it, the Member State can always have recourse to the further delaying tactic of an appeal to the Court of Justice. The latter may support the Commission, but the Member State may seek ways of delaying its final conformity.

It will also become apparent that the influence of the Community has been very variable. In respect of some of the topics discussed in the previous chapters there may be little to identify in the way of tangible influence. On the other hand there are areas of policy, such as agriculture, where the effect of the Community has been, if not total, then at least overwhelming.

Macroeconomic Policy

Reflecting the nature of the Community approach, the following account will cover not only domestic monetary, budgetary and incomes policies but will also take in external matters such as the balance of payments, exchange rates and capital movements.

In its original conception the EEC did not envisage a centralised control over macroeconomic management. In broad terms the basic responsibility for the conduct of such affairs was left in the hands of Member States. However, recognising the growing economic interdependence flowing from increasing economic integration, the Rome Treaty does emphasise the importance of collaboration and coordination. This is the essential message of Articles 3(g) and 103–9.

Article 104 places the responsibility for ensuring a high level of employment, stability of prices, equilibrium in the balance of payments and continued confidence in the foreign exchange value of the currency firmly in the hands of each Member State. However Article 103 stresses that macroeconomic management is nevertheless a matter of common interest, and Article 105 lays upon the Community partners a duty to co-ordinate policy. Although as we have seen the initiative for dealing with balance of payments problems lies with the Member States, this does not preclude the possibility of Community advice and assistance (Article 108). Moreover, if necessary, the Community could call for the termination of protective measures (Article 109). Exchange rates are declared to be a matter of common concern, but the wording of Article 107 makes it clear that ultimately countries are free to change them. In practice in the early days the Community operated what has been called a diluted *de facto* monetary union (Dennis [1980a]): the stability of exchange rates was indeed a presumption upon which the Common Agricultural Policy was to be founded.

However at the same time as full UK membership became a real possibility the state of affairs outlined above began to change in that the 1969 Hague Summit also embraced the notion of a move forward to an economic and monetary union (EMU). There was a good measure of agreement about the final objective. This consisted of an irrevocable locking of exchange rates. Moreover because one currency could always exchange into another at a given rate it was possible to envisage the further step of sweeping the separate currencies away and substituting one Community currency. Assuming the latter to exist the scenario also included a Community management of its supply as well as Community control of its external value. But differences did exist about how to reach the final goal and in particular about the nature of the first stage in that evolution. The 'economists' represented by Germany, the Netherlands and at a later stage the UK, emphasised the importance of the co-ordination of economic policies before exchange rates were irrevocably fixed. The 'monetarists' represented by France, Belgium, Luxembourg and the Commission opted for an immediate locking of exchange rates and looked to this to provide the discipline which would force countries to co-ordinate their policies. The Werner Report, which provided the basis of the Community's plan to achieve EMU by 1980, embodied a compromise between these views. Only the first stage, which covered the period from 1971 to 1973, was settled in detail. In line with monetarist thinking a narrowing of exchange rate fluctuations was agreed – the fluctuation around the central parities in respect of exchanges between Community currencies was to be smaller than the fluctuation allowed in respect of exchanges with the US Dollar. This was the famous 'snake in the tunnel'. As a concession to the economist viewpoint there was to be a system of economic policy harmonisation. The first stage also envisaged the creation of a medium-term aid arrangement which would eventually be monitored by a formal reserve fund – short-term aid arrangements had been agreed early in 1970. In the later stages there was to be a fully unified capital market, a pooling of foreign exchange reserves and the creation of both a Community central bank and a centralised budgetary authority. Finally exchange rates would be irrevocably locked.

It was a Community set on this course into which the UK negotiated entry. Had the objectives of EMU been achieved the effect on UK policy would have been enormous. Economic sovereignty would have progressively been yielded as the Community came to exercise more and more control over domestic monetary and budgetary policy and the power to devalue or revalue would ultimately have had to be surrendered.

In practice the subsequent course of events was quite different. The snake in the tunnel finally emerged in April 1972 and the UK participated prior to full membership. However the pound came under heavy speculative attack in June. The Bank of England intervened in order to keep the currency within the snake but finally, because of the heavy losses of reserves it was decided to float. The UK in fact went back on its obligation to keep the pound not only within the snake but also within the tunnel. The basic cause of the speculation seems to have been growing concern about the over-valuation of sterling as determined by the Smithsonian Agreement in 1971, industrial unrest and receding hopes about containing inflation (Tsoukalis [1977], p. 122). The grand exchange rate design itself did not survive. It was indeed overtaken by events in the sense that the tide of opinion moved against fixed exchange rates. Instead a significantly different system emerged. The IMF tunnel disappeared and the snake took the form of a joint float in which there were frequent parity changes and a regularly changing and ultimately greatly diminished membership. As for the co-ordination of economic policies the conclusion is that this never got off the ground. The consequent divergence of economic performance was one, but only one, of the factors which undermined the Werner Plan. When the UK made opposition to EMU one of the planks of its renegotiation platform it quickly found that its grounds for concern were ill-founded – indeed at the Paris Summit in December 1974 EMU was to all intents and purposes shelved.

The idea of monetary union was revived in 1978 at the Bremen Summit and subsequently took shape in the form of the European

Monetary System (EMS) which began to function in March 1979. This arrangement, although it represents a swing back towards the idea of fixed exchange rates, is a much more accommodating arrangement than its predecessor. The EMS emphasises the idea of a zone of monetary stability as opposed to the ultimate fixity of EMU. Significant exchange rate fluctuations are provided for around the rates contained in the parity grid, particularly in the case of non-snake countries, and provision is expressly made for changes in those parities (i.e. devaluations and revaluations) as well as for a period of absence from the scheme. There is a noticeable absence of explicit emphasis on the need to surrender control over domestic macroeconomic policy. Despite all this the UK has chosen to stay outside the exchange rate arrangement.

Does this then mean that UK macroeconomic management has been totally unconstrained by Community membership? The answer is no – for several reasons. Firstly, there can be no doubt that the increasing exposure of UK industry to competition from the Community and the realisation that the reimposition of tariff protection is not a realistic option have added urgency to the need to keep inflation in check. Secondly, there is always the possibility that the policy instruments may themselves have been influenced. One possible area of influence is fiscal policy.

The adoption of the VAT is an obvious candidate for consideration. However, the decision to introduce it pre-dated our membership although it could be that the prospect of membership might have inclined the UK to espouse a system that had already found favour with the Community. In fact the Conservative government indicated that it favoured the VAT because it wished to broaden the basis of indirect taxation. The selective employment tax and purchase tax discriminated arbitrarily and unfairly among forms of productive activity. It was also pointed out that the introduction of the VAT would enable the burden of indirect taxation to be removed from exports but applied to imports. However Chancellor Barber did observe that if the UK succeeded in its membership bid it would have to introduce the VAT. This was an argument in favour but it was not the main one – the main reason was that on its merits VAT was superior to the then existing system (Hansard, 30 March 1971).

The VAT having been adopted, a further influence could have proceeded from the harmonisation of rates but this has not occurred and does not seem likely in the foreseeable future. In fact the

Community-wide adoption of the VAT enables unintentional or intentional distortions of competition, arising in connection with export restitutions, to be easily identified and the destination system eliminates distortions arising from differences in national rates. In short the present system is a very effective halfway house wherein the Community may find it convenient to lodge for a long time to come.

In the field of direct taxes there is clear evidence of a Community impact. Whilst the EEC is not concerned to harmonise the income tax, it does have plans for the corporation tax. In 1971, when the British entry negotiations were in full swing, the then Conservative government indicated its intention to shift away from the classical corporation tax system. The objective was to achieve neutrality in tax treatment between distributed and retained profits. A number of alternatives were canvassed including a dual rate system and the imputation system (Cmnd 4630 [1971]). The Government initially preferred the former but was persuaded by the Select Committee on Corporation Tax to adopt the latter (HCP 622 [1971]). The Government had asked the Committee amongst other things to consider developments in EEC company taxation. In fact the Committee in coming out in favour of the imputation system was influenced by the fact that France and Belgium were then operating such an arrangement and that West Germany was just about to move over to it. The Select Committee concluded that if the UK did not opt for the imputation system it would be swimming against the tide, whilst if it adopted it the process of harmonisation would be facilitated. The Committee was in fact aware that in his report to the Commission Dr A. J. van den Tempel had advocated the classical (i.e. the then existing British) system as the basis for harmonisation, but the Committee obviously throught that the national practice of France, Germany and Belgium would be more likely to prevail at Community level. In this it was correct because the Commission subsequently proposed that all the Member States should adopt a common imputation system together with a common system of withholding tax on dividends. The proposal envisaged similar but not identical rates of corporation tax and tax credit and an identical rate of withholding tax. However this proposal has not yet been adopted and agreement seems a long way off.

In the area of controls on capital movements Community membership has left its mark. Although a unified capital market was a feature of EMU, the liberalisation which the Community has insisted on has been prompted by Articles 67–73. These relate to the Rome Treaty objective of freedom of movement for factors of production – this is of course a characteristic feature of a common market as opposed to a customs union. Although the UK gave undertakings to liberalise within the transition period it actually sought and obtained post-ponements of this obligation. However at the end of 1977 the Commission finally put its foot down and forced a series of concessions. Capital controls were gradually dismantled during 1978 and 1979, and finally abolished in October 1979. (This dismantling process was described earlier in Chapter 9).

Industrial Policy

The Rome (EEC) Treaty does not contain any separate title on the elusive subject of industrial policy. This in itself has not deterred the Community from developing one but internal differences have.[1] Nevertheless it is possible to identify a number of policy areas which can be regarded as industrial and in respect of which the Community organs enjoy certain powers. It will however be apparent that these may be negative rather than positive. For example, where an industry is in decline the Community enjoys no formal power to close firms down and in any case any attempt would almost certainly be regarded as an unwarranted curtailment of national sovereignty. However if firms survive by virtue of national aids then the Commission could attack those aids and thus force a contraction or readaptation and of course it would be possible to devise Community financial aid schemes to restructure industries or tide firms over.

The maintenance of competition can be regarded as an aspect of industrial policy. In practice domestic competition policy has not been significantly affected by the EEC antitrust rules. The reason for this is that Articles 85–90 of the Rome Treaty are not designed to root out all the restrictions of competition which may exist within the Community. They are only designed to deal with those antitrust phenomena which constitute non-tariff barriers. For the EEC antitrust rules to be invoked an effect on inter-state trade must exist or be threatened. Because in many situations this potentiality does not arise, or is miniscule, it follows that domestic antitrust policy is still left with an important role to play. It also follows that there has in the main been no need to modify domestic laws.

Four points however need to be made. Firstly, although UK law has remained largely untouched the business community in the UK has been significantly affected. It is now subject to two jurisdictions. Thus whereas under UK law export agreements escaped from the condemnatory regime originally established under the *Restrictive Trade Practices Act 1956* – they merely had to be notified in confidence and might be investigated by the Monopolies and Mergers Commission – those which affect trade among the Member States now have to be notified to the European Communities (EC) Commission and may be prohibited under Article 85. Second, some agreements may be such as to fall due for consideration under both national and Community jurisdictions. The situation is complicated here but the EC Court of Justice has made it clear that in such cases of conflict the matter must be resolved by applying the principle that Community law takes precedence. Third, although the possibility of such conflicts is relatively small some thought has been given to bringing UK restrictive practices law more into line with Article 85 (Cmnd 7512 [1979]). Fourth, under the terms of the Paris Treaty *all* agreements, abuses of dominant positions and mergers in the steel and coal industries are controlled under ECSC antitrust rules – there is no inter-state trade clause limiting Community jurisdiction.

At the 1972 Paris Summit the idea of creating a European industrial base was emphasised. This was not really new because it obviously implied the sweeping away of non-tariff barriers and this point had been a cardinal feature of policy from the very beginning. It has of course had a practical effect on the UK. Under the provisions of Articles 100–102 laws governing the labelling, design and composition of products – largely designed to protect users from physical injury and deception – have in a significant number of cases had to be brought into line with Community standards (Dennis [1980*b*]). The UK has been critical of this policy although *some* of that criticism has been misplaced (Swann [1979], p. 238). Directives have also been adopted which are designed to open up public procurement to Community-wide competition. As a result certain forms of public works and public supply contracting must be conducted in ways which eliminate discrimination against bids from other Community states (Swann [1978], pp. 138–40).

Industrial policy quite clearly covers the actions of the state in attempting both the stimulation of growth sectors and resolving the problem of industries in decline. Both may involve state financial aid.

Article 92 prohibits state aids that distort competition and affect inter-state trade. However it expressly exempts some aids and, more importantly in this context, provides for possible exemption in other cases. The latter includes sectoral aids, i.e. aids to particular firms or industries. Quite early on the Commission laid down broad rules for such aid giving. Aids should be selective and only given to firms or sectors which had a reasonable prospect of becoming viable in the longer term. Aids should be well adapted to the object in view and have as little effect on inter-state trade as possible. They should be temporary or degressive. They should be transparent, i.e. their scale should be capable of assessment (EEC [1972], pp. 129–33).

The Commission discharges a supervisory role and not surprisingly aids arising under the 1972 and 1977 Industry Acts came in for some attention. UK experience has however not been characterised by references to the Court of Justice. Rather the government has fulfilled its obligations by notifying aids to the Commission and in the main differences have been dealt with by consultation. Two examples may suffice. In 1975 the UK proposed a substantial programme of aid to the textile industry in order to deal with its structural weaknesses. The scheme involved a 20% grant for the purchase of new plant and machinery, a 50% grant for the use of consultants and the establishment of a productivity centre for the industry. The latter two were quite acceptable but the Commission objected to the 20% grant on the grounds that the firms were not required to restructure their plants or to give undertakings that they would not add to capacity – the industry was in fact suffering from an excess of the latter. The programme had to be resubmitted in the light of the Commission's criticism and aid was made conditional on programmes of rationalisation proposed by the firms (EEC [1976], pp. 79–80). In 1978 the UK proposed to grant aid to its relatively unconcentrated micro-electronics industry – in this case assistance was being given to assist the growth of a new industry. The scheme was as follows: in the case of research, grants of up to 50% recoverable by a levy on subsequent sales; in the case of development, grants of up to 25% (or exceptionally of 50% with a levy on subsequent sales) – in the case of joint development ventures the maximum grant could be 50%; in respect of investment in plant, machinery and buildings, grants of up to 25%. The scheme was to run for five years and would cost £80m. The Commission approved the motive but was concerned by the duration and scale of the scheme and feared that it might seriously distort competition among Member States. Its authorisation was therefore limited to two years and a proportionally reduced budget (EEC [1979], pp. 145–6).

In, however, the case of the Offshore Supplies Interest Relief Grant Scheme the Commission initiated a procedure under Article 93, para 2 against the UK. The UK had refused to modify its arrangement and the Commission indicated its intention to ban the scheme. Thus it ultimately did and continuance of the arrangement by the British government would have led to a reference to the Court of Justice. The Commission had originally countenanced a system whereby the UK had offered interest rebates of 3% in order to assist in the finance of equipment purchased for use on the UK portion of the Continental Shelf. The key element in the aid was that it was only available in respect of purchases of equipment manufactured in the UK. The Commission viewed this as an aid to a British infant industry. Later, when the industry had developed, it was still prepared to allow the aid to continue – this time as a stimulus to the development of new sources of indigenous energy – but it required that the rebate be allowed in respect of all purchases, thus eliminating the discrimination against other Community suppliers (EEC [1977], pp. 112–14).

The severity of Community surveillance should not, however, be exaggerated. The aids to rescue both British Leyland and Chrysler were allowed. In the case of the latter the Commissioner then responsible for the competition policy, the late Albert Borschette, is reported to have been opposed but the Commission as a whole appears to have felt it imprudent to intervene (*The Economist* [1977]). In so doing it could no doubt save face by referring to Article 92 (3b) which allows aids which will remedy a serious disturbance in a Member State (this is one of the possible grounds for exemption to which we referred earlier).

The Commission has also been concerned about the activities of the NEB. The obvious fear here was that because the Board obtained its finance from the state, any artificial advantage which it might so enjoy could in turn be passed on when the NEB intervened in industry. The Commission was aware that the Board could reflect in its lendings the advantage of favourable interest rates derived from the operations of the National Loans Fund (NLF) whilst competitors might have to pay higher commercial rates. More important might be the fact that the NEB was in part to be financed on a Public Dividend Capital (PDC) basis. Here there was no fixed interest commitment on the part of the borrower and the dividend which the state might be willing to accept might involve a competitive distortion. There might also be grounds for concern over the NEB's capital structure, i.e. the relative proportions of its NLF and PDC funding (Dashwood and Sharpe [1978], pp. 9–34).

In discussions as to the role of the NEB the British government emphasised to the Commission the independence of the Board and its requirement to operate on a commercial basis. In the light of this the Commission formulated its system of surveillance. As regards the routine operations of the NEB, where it operated on its own initiative, it would be sufficient if the UK government rendered an annual report on the Board's operations. But when the NEB was required by the Secretary of State for Industry to intervene, and where therefore the government might be tempted to use its powers to adjust the NEB's financial duties, it would be necessary for the specific intervention to be notified in advance (EEC [1978], pp. 162–5). The fact that the Thatcher government intends to curtail the activities of the NEB – see the *Industry Bill 1979* – suggests that in future the Commission will have less to fear from the Board's activities.

The above cases relate to situations where the Community rules have been applied specifically to UK sectoral aid behaviour. However in a number of cases the UK has been affected by policy actions relating to problems which have afflicted the Community as a whole. In other words particular industries throughout the Community have been undergoing structural problems. A notable example is shipbuilding. The regulation of aid giving in terms of subsidies on the selling price of ships goes back to 1969 whilst export credit aid in relation to their sale was regulated as from 1971. The former particularly was a recognition of the fact that Community shipbuilders were at a competitive disadvantage because of aid giving outside the Community. More recently the problem has become not only one of a need to offset competitive distortions but also of how to deal with the effects of chronic world-wide over-capacity. The fourth Council directive on aid to shipbuilding of 1978 (*Official Journal of the European Communities* [1978]) forbids Member States to grant sectoral aid for the creation of new shipyards or to give aid to existing shipyards which would have the effect of adding to capacity. The Commission is also empowered to vet regional or general aid schemes which might incidentally have this effect. Crisis aid is allowed but under Community supervision. Naturally the UK industry has been subject to these controls. Under the third aid directive of 1975 British assistance was due to terminate in 1975 but instead the UK chose to introduce a scheme for insuring against cost escalation which breached the deadline. Fortunately the Commission was able to persuade the Council to retrospectively amend the directive to allow the aid, although only after modification (EEC [1977], pp. 111–12). In 1977 the UK introduced an intervention fund providing grants of up to 30% of contract prices. The operation of that fund has been supervised by the Commission – in the case of the supply of six bulk carriers to Poland the Commission attacked a proposal to pitch the assistance far in excess of 30% and the UK government was forced to back down (EEC [1979], pp. 132–3). More recently the Commission has proposed the introduction of a scrap and build plan at Community level.

Other industries where Community wide problems exist are textiles, man-made fibres and steel. In the case of textiles Community rules governing aids were laid down as early as 1971 (EEC [1972], pp. 135–6; [1977], pp. 114–15; [1978], p. 146). In 1977 the Commission requested Member States to discontinue for two years aids of a sectoral, regional or general (see below) character which might add to capacity in the man-made fibre industry. Relevant aids had to be notified in advance. In 1979 this was renewed for a further two years (EEC [1979*b*], pp. 40–1). The industry also produced a cartel agreement which was designed to eliminate excess capacity. Some British producers participated in drawing up the plan. Unfortunately for the firms concerned, although the proposal was supported by the industrial Commissioner Viscount Davignon, it was rejected by the Commission as a whole as being incompatible with Article 85 (EEC [1979], pp. 49–50). In the case of steel the influence of the Community is very considerable. Not only does the Commission exercise antitrust control but it also operates a form of indicative planning in respect of the investment intentions of bodies such as the British Steel Corporation (BSC) and it supervises pricing rules (McLachlan and Swann [1967], pp. 256–97) which lay down in detail how the BSC etc. can make offers in the market place. The Paris Treaty is a relatively *dirigiste* document. Particularly important in the pricing rules are the powers conferred on Community organs when there is a manifest crisis in the industry. Because of the excess capacity in the Community steel industry the Commission had introduced the Simonet Plan in 1976. This involved voluntary co-operation between the Commission and producers whereby delivery programmes were suggested which were intended to prevent the market from being swamped. Then in 1977, under Viscount Davignon, direct intervention in the market was introduced as provided for in the Paris Treaty. In various sectors minimum prices have been stipulated by the Commission and base prices have been applied to imports into the Community (EEC [1979c], pp. 94–5).

Whilst dealing with the subject of aids it is convenient to say something about the Community's attitude towards general aid schemes and economic recovery measures. The former are, as their title suggests, available across the economy and in principle are a semi-permanent feature of policy whilst the latter are short-term devices designed to last as long as a crisis lasts. The Commission has always been opposed to general aids – it has argued that they should be transmuted into regional or sectoral assistance. However its ability to control them was severely weakened by the onset of the world depression in 1974: it has had to soft-peddle this aspect of policy (although it insists on prior notification of such assistance) and equally it has had to accept the need for economic recovery measures. The latter has not however meant that anything could get by. For example, although the UK scheme for employment subsidies for young workers, introduced in 1975, was acceptable to the Commission, the Temporary Employment Scheme of the same date met a much different fate. The continued prolongation of the scheme gave rise to protests from other Member States, not least because the bulk of the assistance was concentrated in the textile, clothing and footwear industries. When in January 1978 the UK proposed to continue to operate the scheme in the fiscal year 1978/9 the Commission intervened and compelled the British government to drastically curtail the total budget and the degree to which firms and certain industries could benefit (EEC [1979a], pp. 161–3).

Earlier, during a discussion of the NEB, the question of the effect of Community membership on the relationship of the state to public enterprises, and on the conduct of the latter, was touched upon. The impression which emerges is that thus far the Community has not had a significant influence in this area. It should be emphasised that the Rome Treaty does not preclude nationalisation or the creation of bodies vested with powers of industrial intervention. Article 222 declares 'The Treaty shall in no way prejudice the rules in Member States pertaining to forms or type of ownership.' Article 90 does however charge public undertakings with the duty of behaving in ways which are in conformity with Article 7 (avoidance of discrimination on grounds of nationality), with Articles 85 and 86 (maintenance of competition) and with Articles 91–4 (dumping and state aids). More recently the Commission has indicated that it wishes to probe more deeply into the financial relationships between the state and public undertakings and a draft directive is being prepared (EEC [1979a], pp. 173–4).

Industrial policy may be defined to include policy on science and technology. Detecting the effect of Community policy is however virtually impossible both because no positive and concerted policy exists in the UK and also because within the Community science and technology policy has been slow to develop and is indeed still in its incipiency. In the early 1970s UK policy appeared to be one of *laisser innover* in the private sector although of course the government was a major spender on science and high technology. It is true that from 1974 on a number of proposals were made involving the NEB, Planning Agreements, the Industrial Strategy and the Sector Working Parties from which might have emerged a concerted policy for stimulating private research and development activity and redirecting government funding towards private industry and more market oriented objectives. In practice the new policy was slow to get off the ground – indeed in some instances it never got beyond the discussion stage. The return of a Conservative government in 1979 clearly signalled the end of this phase of policy. As for the Community 1974 was also an important date since during that year a series of resolutions were passed calling for, amongst other things, the co-ordination of national science and technology policies, the elaboration of joint scientific and technological projects of interest to the Community, the setting up of a European Science Foundation (ESF) and for work to begin on scientific forecasting. In practice the emphasis has been on joint projects – the most notable being the funding of the JET nuclear fusion project located at Culham. In respect of co-ordination, and it would be here that a domestic effect would be most obvious, the Community seems none too clear as to how it can be achieved. The ESF now exists and a pilot programme on scientific forecasting has been launched.

The Rome Treaty provides for individuals and companies to establish themselves in other Member States (Articles 52–8). To enable this to happen a harmonisation of national company laws is called for and further legal adjustments are envisaged in Article 220 which also requires the Community to facilitate cross-frontier mergers. It is clear that the latter requires not only adjustments to national company laws but also the elimination of fiscal factors which discriminate against such amalgamations.

In practice not a great deal has been achieved. Four directives have been adopted on the harmonisation of national company laws – none of these constitute major changes in UK domestic law. A great deal of effort has been put into creating a system of Community company law alongside national laws. A European Company Statute has been drafted but not yet adopted. Draft directives on the fiscal inhibition of cross-frontier mergers are still on the table.

During the 1970s the Community became increasingly interested in consumer protection. As yet however, with the exception of the harmonisation measures concerned with labelling, design and composition discussed earlier, little has been achieved. A number of directives have been proposed on topics such as doorstep selling, unit pricing, misleading advertising and strict product liability, but as yet they remain unadopted. During the 1970s it is undoubtedly true to say that that legal protection accorded to British consumers was overwhelmingly national in origin.

Regional and Transport Policy

The potential of Community regional policy to influence both the economy and economic policy of the UK has rested on a dual foundation. Firstly, although Article 92, to which we referred earlier, forbids state aids that impede the process of economic integration; it also recognises the need to tackle the problem of regional backwardness as being a possible ground for exemption. Given the emphasis in the Rome Treaty preamble and elsewhere on the desirability of reducing differences among regions, it would have been inconsistent to adopt any other posture. Inevitably therefore the Commission has been required to supervise such regional aid giving in the same way as it has had to maintain a surveillance over the sectoral variety. From what follows it will be apparent that this system of supervision has the potential to restrict both the *choice* of policy instruments and the *size* of the financial inducements offered. The second channel of influence has taken the form of financial assistance from Community institutions which were either explicitly established to help with the regional problem or which, whilst not having that as their sole object, might nevertheless by their actions contribute to the solution of it.

In the early 1970s the Commission became increasingly concerned about the competition among Member States which was leading to an escalation of regional aids. In 1971 it therefore submitted a Communication to the Council of Ministers laying down the principles which should govern such aid giving (EEC [1971], pp. 37–49). This was accepted by Council. The Communication had a twofold aspect. It laid down certain general requirements and it prescribed specific aid ceilings. Aids should be transparent. Opaque aids should be progressively rendered transparent or, if that was not possible, they should be dropped. Aids should be regionally specific. They should not normally cover whole national territories but should apply to the problem regions therein and their intensity should be adjusted to the seriousness of the specific problem. In the Community's 'central' regions the ceiling was to be 20% of the investment in net grant equivalence, i.e. the net grant equivalent remaining to the beneficiary after deduction of profits tax. The peripheral regions were not regulated in terms of a ceiling. When the UK became a member its aid giving in its 'central' regions was subjected to the 20% rule. Almost immediately this provoked a clash because the Commission proposed to classify some of the Development Areas and Special Development Areas as central! For a while this led to those two types of areas being left unclassified. In 1975 a new ceiling system was introduced which also took in the peripheral regions. In the case of Greenland, Iceland, the Mezzogiorno and Northern Ireland the ceiling was fixed at 35%: there were, however, certain additional conditions and qualifications. In the French regions eligible for industrial development grants, in certain areas in Italy (other than the Mezzogiorno) and in the assisted areas in Great Britain (but not the Intermediate Areas) the aid ceiling was to be 30%. The reader will note that the Community had quietly accepted the British position. In West Berlin, in the areas bordering East Germany and in certain assisted areas in Denmark an aid limit of 25% was prescribed. In all other regions the ceiling was to be 20%, but it was desirable that this should be reduced as quickly as possible. In the case of the UK this latter category included all areas outside the British assisted areas and Northern Ireland. Intermediate areas were of course in the 20% category.

As noted earlier Community policy also bears on the type of aid. From the beginning the Commission did not like the REP (Mac-Lennan [1979], pp. 245–71). It was never specifically banned and this may be because initially it was only planned to run for a seven-year experimental period – it was due to expire in September 1974. Moreover the Conservatives indicated that they would get rid of it. The Commission thus had reason to hope that the problem would go away. In practice it ultimately did although not as quickly as might have been expected. It was indeed prolonged until 1977 although retained in Northern Ireland. Action against the REP was also inhibited by renegotiation – the need to retain effective control of regional policy was one of the main planks of the UK position.

The REP was unacceptable to the Commission because it broke all the rules. It was not measurable according to the Commission's formula. In essence the latter transmutes aids into a proportion of the investment involved but the REP would give different results as capital: labour intensities varied. The formula assumes an act of investment: the REP required none. The Commission is opposed to continuing subsidies, particularly of an indiscriminate kind: it envisages an initial act of assistance after which the project should be able to survive. The decision to drop REP may owe something to Community pressure although the ostensible reason according to Chancellor Healey was that there were doubts as to whether REP was any longer fulfilling its task of attracting employment to the regions and that a more selective approach was preferred.

In 1978 the Commission adopted new aid rules (*Official Journal of the European Communities*, 1979). Bowing to Italian and UK pressure to the effect that the old system was biased in favour of capital intensive projects, the new rules added an alternative criterion of units of account per job created per new investment. This allowed a wider range of aids to be measured. However, it did not save the REP type because the Commission continued to insist that the concept of *new* investment be retained. It should also be noted that the other main UK aid, the Regional Development Grant (RDG), is also not in conformity with Community rules and the Commission has reserved its position on the subject. The point here is that RDGs have been available not only in respect of original investments but also for subsequent replacements. The Commission takes the view that initial aid having been given, the replacement of capital should be regarded as a normal commercial obligation: moreover if aid is given for replacement, then the aid initially given understates the true level of assistance.

The other main influence on domestic policy has come from the funds made available by the Community. The Regional Development

Fund (RDF) was originally conceived as a necessary feature of EMU. Its aid would help to compensate for the absence of the power to change exchange rates. However, the RDF was not actually set up until 1975, by which time EMU had run into the ground. The creation of the RDF was supported by the UK with an eye to the likelihood that she would be a substantial beneficiary and this would help to compensate for the financial burden of the CAP. Originally the Commission proposed a series of criteria which would determine which regions should benefit. However the system finally introduced in 1975 dropped this idea and instead it was decided that the areas eligible for national assistance should also be entitled to Fund assistance. This involved an element of inconsistency because states differ in degree of generosity in aid giving (Armstrong [1978], pp. 511–28). The overall sum voted for the Fund is apportioned in advance. This sounds a little crude although the national quotas do in a rough way reflect the relatively seriousness of the problem; thus Italy got 40% and the UK 28% whilst West Germany received just over 6%. It should be added that in 1978 the confinement of Fund aid to national aid areas was modified by the creation of a small non-quota allocation freed from this limitation. The Fund rules also require that the principle of additionality be practised by Member States, i.e. that the Fund aid should add rather than be a substitute for national efforts. In 1975 it was widely reported that the UK government was unsympathetic to additionality (Stewart and Begg [1976], pp. 34–44). However, in the event the official position adopted did not oppose the idea. It is of course difficult for the Commission to be sure that additionality is being practised and it has expressed some lack of satisfaction on the issue.

The effect of RDF on UK policy should not be overestimated. Between 1975 and 1978 the UK received £268m in grants from the Fund. But the RDF assistance is small in relation to national efforts: in 1976/7 it represented about 10% of UK regional expenditure. The problem is that the RDF has represented only a small proportion – about 5% – of Community Budget commitments. The bulk of Budget finance has been devoted to the CAP.

There are however other sources of aid. One is the European Investment Bank (EIB). Its assistance takes the form of loans and thus it is not an aid giver in the RDF sense. Nevertheless its interest rates are highly competitive. Moreover about three-quarters of its operations within the Community have been devoted to regional development and as a reflection of this countries such as Italy and the UK have been major beneficiaries. Between 1973 and 1978 the UK received £1169m in EIB loans. Other institutions whose assistance may be relevant are the European Social Fund (ESF). It helps with training, retraining and resettlement of labour: between 1973 and 1978 the UK received ESF grants totalling £283m. Relevant also are the loans, which may be on preferential terms, and the grants of the ECSC. Loans are available for conversion of enterprises and grants are intended for retraining and resettlement. In 1973 and 1978 the UK share amounted to £930m and £17m respectively. Finally the guidance section of the Agricultural Guidance and Guarantee Fund devotes funds for farm improvements, some of which have been located in the assisted areas.

The effect of the Common Transport Policy (CTP) (Button [1979], pp. 52–73; Bayliss [1979], pp. 28–43) on UK domestic transport arrangements has not been very great. Although the Rome Treaty says little about the nature of the CTP this did not prevent the Commission in the early 1960s from putting forward some very ambitious plans which, had they been realised, would have constituted a very significant influence. In fact in 1973 the Commission was forced to admit that little had been achieved. After a stock-taking it produced a new and less ambitious blueprint and it is arguable that in broad terms the 1973 initiative moved the philosophy of the CTP closer to British practice.

The original proposals envisaged the general application of forked tariffs (an obligatory ceiling and floor to fluctuations in the rate). However, it was not until 1968 that the system was introduced and then only for international road (freight) transport. The 1973 initiative indicated an ultimate intention to shift away from control of prices towards a free market where rates were determined on the basis of inter-undertaking and inter-modal competition. Some care is needed in arguing that this represented a step in the British direction. During the early 1970s British enthusiasm for the market mechanism approach waned a little but nevertheless it is also undoubtedly true to say that the UK never embraced the idea of direct regulation of haulage rates.

Having observed a change in tack on the part of the Commission we should note that on a subsequent proposal it envisaged an extension of the forked tariff system to international rail and inland waterway transport. However, the Council rejected this and under Regulation

2831/77 confined the fork system to international road transport. In fact there was some weakening since the regulation allowed Member States a choice between obligatory forks and a reference rate system. The system is designed to run, as an experiment, until the end of 1982.

The original Commission philosophy embraced a continuance of quantitative control over capacity, notably in road haulage, through the licensing system. In this it was reflecting then existing national practice. However no regulation has ever been adopted imposing this on all Member States and following the rethinking of 1973 it seems less likely now. Incidentally although the *Transport Act 1968* accepted the principle of quantity licensing, the idea was never put into practice. The Thatcher government has indeed indicated a positive preference for free competition.

The international road haulage industry has been dominated by bilateral quota arrangements in which pairs of states have agreed on the number of vehicles that each could have on the other's territory at any moment of time. The original CTP blueprint envisaged the elimination of such bilateral licences and their replacement by a Community Quota (CQ) of licences. These would be rapidly expanded to meet the needs of trade and licencees would be able to operate anywhere in the Community without restriction. The CQ system was introduced in 1968 and upon entry the UK was allocated a number of licences. However, the CQ system is much less ambitious than originally envisaged. Although licence holders are free to operate between and through Community countries, cabotage (the carriage of goods between points in another Member State) is forbidden. Moreover instead of phasing the bilateral licences out the CQ has been added on top and has been expanded at a very slow rate. As a result 95% of Community trade is still carried under bilateral agreements. In short the arrangements operated by the UK prior to membership still hold sway.

This still leaves us with the topic of qualitative licensing. This existed in the UK prior to membership – under the *Transport Act 1968* road hauliers had to hold an 'O' licence which could be revoked in cases of poor management or weak financial standing. EEC Directive 571 of 1974 did however introduce a change. While British practice did not distinguish between own account and hire and reward activities the EEC directive did. Consequently British law had to be modified in the Goods Vehicle Operators (Qualification) Regulation of 1977 to meet the EEC directive with own account operators needing to have a less restrictive proof of their professional competence.

One of the permanent features of the CTP has been the need to create equal conditions among Member States – in other words there was a need for technical, social, etc. harmonisation. The EEC has in fact adopted no directive or regulation on vehicle size. It is true that prior to enlargement the Six had come to an agreement. But this met with considerable opposition from the UK and the matter remains unresolved. On the question of social harmonisation a packet of measures was agreed in 1969. These related to working hours, rest periods and maximum driving distances. In 1970 a regulation was also adopted requiring the introduction of tachographs. However both the Six and the new members dragged their feet on implementation and in due course the Commission was forced to resort to threats of legal action. On issues such as the length of the working day the UK encountered some difficulties in coming into line. The EEC rules limit drivers' hours to eight (between eleven-hour rest periods) whereas the *Transport Act 1968* stipulated ten hours. There was of course resistance from the industry. However, the UK was finally induced to conform – having been given a three-year extension. The *Road Traffic (Drivers' Ages and Hours of Work) Act 1976 (Commencement No. 2) Order 1978* and the *Community Drivers' Hours Rules (Temporary Modifications) Regulations 1978* provide for EEC requirements to be introduced progressively by January 1981. The UK did not however conform on the issue of tachographs. Only after the Court of Justice ruled in favour of the Commission in 1979 did the UK signify its willingness to fall into line.

The Council of Ministers has also adopted a number of regulations and decisions of significance to British Rail. These indicate that the long-term plan is that railways should enjoy a substantial measure of autonomy – they should be managed on normal business principles independent of financial support. However, in the short run financial assistance is acceptable and common rules have been set in relation thereto. The Community has emphasised the importance of compensating railways for the public and social obligations which they may be forced to bear.

Although the EEC has indicated its desire to see infrastructure costs reflected in transport rates, and work has long been in hand on the subject, an acceptable taxation system based on marginal social cost pricing has not yet been devised.

Social Policy

Within the Community social policy covers a wide range of issues: conditions of employment, industrial relations and social security

Community membership has had a minimal effect on policy relating to conditions of employment. It is true that Article 119 of the Rome Treaty requires the application of the equal pay for equal work principle but the legislative steps to bring that about were introduced in the UK prior to membership (in 1970). It is, however, possible to point to a few modest steps. The Council of Ministers has adopted directives on equality of treatment between male and female workers (access to employment, vocational training, promotion, etc.), on the handling of mass dismissals and on the rights of workers in the event of mergers and takeovers. It has issued a recommendation on a standard forty hour week and four weeks' annual holiday. Various institutions have been established including a European Centre for Vocational Training and a European Foundation for the Improvement of Living and Working Conditions. The fact that the ESF has made grants to the UK has already been noted.

For the rest – i.e. industrial relations and social security – there is little to report. The problem is that the relevant Articles (117 and 118) are cast in terms of statements of what is desirable and of indirect effect. Better conditions of living, work and employment are desirable. These will proceed from the creation of the common market which will favour harmonisation of social systems – this presumably refers to social security. Consultation among Member States will be facilitated on matters such as the law of trade unions, collective bargaining, etc. There is, however, no real compulsion to act. Not surprisingly Community influence is small and difficult to pin down – to the extent that it exists it is indirect and emulative.

Energy Policy

Energy policy has made only slow progress at Community level. An explanation for this is at least in part to be found in the twin facts that none of the founding treaties explicitly calls for a Common Energy Policy (CEP) and responsibility for energy is divided among the three treaties – the Paris Treaty deals with coal, the Rome (Euratom) Treaty obviously relates to the generation of atomic energy and all the other sources fall under the Rome (EEC) Treaty. Lack of progress was almost certainly also due to the relatively easy energy position during the period up to about 1973. There were problems, such as the decline of coal, and there was the fact of increasing import dependence, but neither constituted the necessary powerful compulsion to act. However, in 1973, the position changed fundamentally. Oil became expensive and it came to be accepted that the long-term energy outlook was bleak. The Commission has been pressing the Member States to approach the problem of high prices, vulnerability of supplies and looming shortages on a common basis.

In 1974 the Commission set the ball rolling by emphasising the importance of reducing the Community's dependence on oil. It proposed that the imported component of energy consumption should be reduced from 60 to 40% by 1985. The Council of Ministers in fact adopted a Resolution embodying the somewhat more conservative target of below 50% and if possible 40%. At the end of 1978 the European Council at Bremen put the figure at 50%. Additionally the Community has undertaken to keep oil imports in 1985 at the 1978 level.

The achievement of such reduced dependence clearly called for the development of indigenous sources of supply. To a large extent this responsibility has fallen upon the Member States and not the Community. It is the Member States who have to develop their coal industries, speed up atomic energy programmes and press ahead with oil and gas exploration and extraction. At one stage the Community did appear to be willing to make a contribution by fixing a floor price should oil prices fall to such a degree that British production costs would be unacceptably high. This was envisaged as an encouragement to rapid exploration but in the event no action was taken. On the other hand the JET project (with substantial Community funding) could if successful constitute a revolutionary influence in the longer term. Mention might also be made of other financial assistance from the Community. For example, the NCB has received loans under the provisions of the Paris Treaty: nevertheless if the UK coal industry is to expand the main financial burden will fall on the UK.

Reduced import dependence could also proceed from energy saving. Again this is essentially a national responsibility although the Council has issued a series of Recommendations on the subject.

The Community has been concerned to devise procedures which could reduce its vulnerability in times of energy crisis. Member States are required to hold stocks of oil equal to ninety days' consumption.

Also they are obliged to maintain certain minimum stocks of fossil fuels at thermal power stations. The Community has also devised a series of oil supply crisis measures. These are designed to share scarce supplies and to reduce oil usage during an emergency. However, the Community's initiative followed on discussions within the International Energy Agency on these matters in concert with the US and other developed countries.

Britain's partners in the EEC have been trying to persuade her to allow North Sea oil to be treated as a Community resource. This would presumably imply preferential access and prices. The UK has until now resisted. It is possible that it might in due course modify its posture on this and other matters (such as fisheries policy) in return for concessions in respect of the Community Budget.

Trade Policy

Readjustments arising in connection with trade policy have not surprisingly been considerable. Under the Treaty of Accession the UK was required to phase out its tariff protection against the rest of the Community by the end of 1977. Having done so she is required to refrain from restoring protection (see Article 12 of the Rome Treaty). Having said that, it should be remembered that under the provisions of Rome Treaty Article 109 a crisis in the balance of payments can be invoked as grounds for restoration of protection. Of course the Council of Ministers may require such protection to be modified or terminated. Whereas prior to membership the UK had the right to take action against dumping emanating from the Six, and was able to continue to do so during the transition period, from the end of 1977 it lost that power. Under international rules the concept of dumping does not apply to trade flows within a unified market such as the EEC any more than it applies within the territory of a single Member State.

The UK was also required to adopt the Common External Tariff (CET) over the same transition period. She was of course an ex-member of the European Free Trade Association (EFTA) but Community membership did not oblige her to adopt tariff protection against her old partners because EFTA had negotiated an industrial free trade agreement with the Community. The UK was inevitably forced to apply the CET against the rest of the world (but see below) whereas under the EFTA arrangement she had been free to determine her own external tariff and had thus been able to nurture reciprocal trade arrangements with countries in the Commonwealth etc. Membership of the Community also required the UK to accommodate itself to the various trade etc. agreements that the Six had already entered.

The Rome Treaty calls for a common commercial policy. In other words trade relationships with the rest of the world must be determined on a common basis. The foundations for such a policy were laid in 1968 and 1969. The policy laid down common rules for trade with state trading (Communist) countries and required that trade agreements among Member States and all the others should gradually be brought into line and then become a Community responsibility. In the case of the UK these requirements came into force in 1973. As far as the UK is concerned she must take the CET as given. If it is to be changed in respect of a group of countries, or more generally in the context of GATT, it will be done at the behest of the Community as a whole, the instrument of negotiation being the Commission.

Two other changes are worthy of remark. The UK is no longer empowered to take action against dumping emanating from third countries. That role is discharged by the Commission. The criteria are also different. The dumping must *normally* cause or threaten to cause material injury to a *Community* industry and not just the UK section thereof. Anti-dumping action (e.g. the application of countervailing duties) must also be in the Community interest (Department of Trade [1979]). The other change relates to the subsidisation of Export Credits Guarantee funds in connection with exports to the rest of the Community. In 1977 the Commission signalled its concern about such aid and in 1978 the UK was forced to come into line (EEC [1979a], pp. 153–4).

Agriculture and Fishing

As we noted at the outset agriculture is the case *par excellence* of massive Community influence. One of the greatest attractions of the EFTA arrangement as far as the British were concerned was that it excluded agriculture. This in effect meant that the traditional UK approach to the industry could continue more or less undisturbed. That policy was based on a deficiency payments system. At the risk of some oversimplification it could be characterised as follows. Food was allowed into the UK at low world prices. The Ministry of Agriculture negotiated guaranteed prices with the farmers' unions. The UK government paid deficiency payments (financed from the Exchequer) which were designed to bridge the gap between guaranteed prices and import prices.

By contrast the EEC had adopted an entirely different approach which can be simplified as follows. The price which is manipulated in the market provides the farmer with his remuneration directly: there is no division between price and income determination as in the UK system (but see below). Internal prices are raised to the necessary level by applying such devices as variable import levies at the common frontier. If at the common price there is an excess of Community supply over Community demand support purchasing is introduced. These purchases are dealt with in a variety of ways, of which the most important are stockpiling and disposal on the world market. Because generally speaking world prices are well below Community levels such disposals are costly. In order to finance the policy an Agricultural Guidance and Guarantee Fund (AGGF) was established fed by revenues from the Community Budget. Most of its expenditure has been on guarantee (market support) purchases: guidance expenditure (improvement of farm structure and efficiency) has been of secondary importance.

When the UK joined the Community it had to adopt the new support system. The implication being that the UK government was no longer in sole control of farm prices: these are determined annually by the Council of Ministers on the basis of proposals made by the Commission. The Treaty of Accession required that British farm prices should be increased to full CAP levels by six equal steps over the five-year transition period. Whilst UK prices were lower than CAP prices a temporary system of levies and subsidies was applied to UK exports and imports to and from the Six. Inevitably the ultimate effect of the CAP was that the British consumer was forced to pay higher prices, although some of the increase was mitigated by the complex system of 'green' exchange rates for farm products and subsidies (monetary compensating amounts) paid by the Community to agricultural exporters to the UK. By the middle of 1979 it was estimated that the CAP had raised food prices in the UK by about 13% since entry – about 2% a year. The resource cost of the CAP was estimated at £800m in 1978 (Rollo and Warwick [1979]).

Although the Council of Ministers determines the common prices, which are then translated into national currency values through the system of green rates, it is not strictly true to say that farmers in the

UK rely solely on those prices for their cash flows. In addition there are various forms of improvement grants made available by the UK government. In recent years for the Community as a whole these have been reported as constituting 60 to 70% of the total expenditure on agriculture.

The effect of Community membership on the economic welfare and balance of payments of the UK cannot be measured by considering the effect of the CAP alone. Nevertheless in focusing on the effect of Community membership much of the attention has been directed at the Community Budget and in that context the CAP bulks large. In order to provide the wherewithal to finance the activities of the Community it was decided that it should possess its own resources. These were designated as the proceeds of the CET (less 10% for collection), the proceeds of agricultural levies etc. (again less 10%) and the proceeds of up to a one percentage point of the VAT. These were to be fed into the Community Budget and would in turn be used to finance the activities of the RDF, ESF, AGGF, etc.

Unfortunately for the UK the operations of the Community Budget have proved disadvantageous to her and she finds herself as the third poorest country of the Nine facing the prospect in 1980 of making a net contribution of £1.18bn – higher even than that of West Germany and higher than any other Member State in *per capita* terms. It should be added that there is some dispute as to whether the net contribution will be £1bn or £1.18bn – this depends on how food trade subsidies are judged, i.e. whether they are a benefit to the UK or to the exporting Member States. Such a burden falls on the UK because of her large imports of food (and other goods). On the other hand she benefits relatively little in terms of receipts because the major expenditure under the Budget is on the CAP and here her receipts are small compared with those of some Member States. If the distribution of expenditure was shifted from the AGGF to the RDF, for example, she would make a smaller net contribution and indeed might even be a net beneficiary.

Fishing, innocuous though it may sound, has inflamed strong passions in the Council of Ministers and the UK has seen itself as being disadvantaged by the kind of common fisheries policy that the Community has sought to introduce. The UK has had some grounds for grievance in that the Six achieved a common position and introduced regulations in connection with fisheries at a time when applicants with substantial fishing interests were negotiating for entry!

The regulations were based on the principle of free and equal access for EEC fishermen to Community fishing waters and on a common market for fish coupled with a guidance and guarantee system similar to that for agriculture. (Incidentally the fact that something of a *fait accompli* seemed to exist was one reason why Norway finally decided not to join). The Six did allow the new members limited and temporary exclusive fishing zones but after 1982, in the absence of a review of the policy, these were to become part of Community waters.

An appreciation of the fishery problem also requires us to note that, although the Third United Nations Conference on the Law of the Sea (1974–6) did not lead to agreement on the extension of national fishing limits to 200 miles, a number of countries indicated that they nevertheless intended to extend their waters. The Community followed suit and in so doing was spurred on by threats of unilateral action on the part of the UK. When the new national 200 mile limits were aggregated, the Community Pond about which there has been so much bitter dispute was formed.

Problems have arisen in connection with sharing up and conservation within the new area. The UK has emphasised the idea of generous exclusive coastal belts but this has met with considerable opposition. The Commission for its part opted for minimal national fishing zones and for a carving up by national quotas of the catch within the Pond. This the UK did not like because she would be contributing half the area in question (amounting to 60% of the fish stocks) but was promised only one-quarter of the Community catch in return. At the time of writing (December 1979) deadlock still exists.

The UK has also been concerned by what it regards as the casual attitude of continental fishermen to the conservation problem. There is indeed scientific evidence of severe depletion and the fact that prices have not reflected this has been caused by the pressure of imports. The UK has acted unilaterally (i.e. without Commission authorisation) in order to protect stocks. It has, for example, set minimum mesh sizes in certain UK waters. These unilateral actions have led the Commission to institute four cases at the Court of Justice. At the time of writing (December 1979) these have not been concluded.

Note

1. The Heads of State and of Government meeting as the European Council can define new areas of action not expressly authorised in the treaties. Article 235 of the Rome (EEC) Treaty provides a mechanism for new policy areas to be opened up.

References

Armstrong, H. [1978], 'Community Regional Policy: A Survey and Critique', *Regional Studies*, Vol. 12, pp. 511–28.

Bayliss, B. T. [1979], 'Transport in the European Communities', *Journal of Transport Economics and Policy*, January 1979, pp. 28–43.

Button, K. J. [1979], 'Recent Developments in EEC Transport Policy', *Three Banks Review*, September 1979, pp. 52–73.

Cmnd 4630 [1971], *Reform of Corporation Tax*. London: HMSO.

Cmnd 7512 [1979], *A Review of Restrictive Trade Practices Policy*. London: HMSO.

Dashwood, A. and Sharpe, T. [1978], 'The Industry Acts 1972 and 1975 and European Community Law', *Common Market Law Review*, Vol. 15, pp. 9–34.

Dennis, G. E. J. [1980a], 'European Monetary Co-operation', in Twitchett, K. J. (ed.), *European Cooperation Today*. London: European Publications.

Dennis, G. E. J. [1980b], 'The Harmonisation of Non-Tariff Barriers' in Cosgrove-Twitchett, C. (ed.), *Harmonisation between Britain and the European Community*. London: Macmillan.

Department of Trade [1979], *Guide to EEC Action Against Dumped or Subsidised Imports*.

EEC [1971], *Bulletin of the European Communities*, Vol. 11. Brussels.

EEC [1972], *First Report on Competition Policy*. Brussels.

EEC [1976], *Fifth Report on Competition Policy*. Brussels.

EEC [1977], *Sixth Report on Competition Policy*. Brussels.

EEC [1978], *Seventh Report on Competition Policy*. Brussels.

EEC [1979a], *Eighth Report on Competition Policy*. Brussels.

EEC [1979b], *Bulletin of the European Communities*, Vol. 6. Brussels.

EEC [1979c], *Twelfth General Report on the Activities of the Communities*. Brussels.

HCP 622 [1971], *Select Committee on Corporation Tax*.

MacLennan, M. C. [1979], 'Regional Policy in a European Framework', in Maclennan, M. C. and Parr, J. B. (eds.), *Regional Policy Past Experience and New Directions*, pp. 245–71. Oxford: Martin Robertson.

McLachlan, D. L. and Swann, D. [1967], *Competition Policy in the European Community*. London: Oxford University Press.

Official Journal of the European Communities [1978], L98/19, 11 April 1978.

Official Journal of the European Communities [1979], C31/9, 3 February 1979.

Rollo, J. and Warwick, K. [1979], *The CAP and resource flows among EEC member states*. London: Ministry of Agriculture, Fisheries and Food.

Stewart, J. Allan and Begg, H. M. [1976], 'Towards a European Regional Policy', *National Westminster Bank Quarterly Review*, May 1976, pp. 34–44.

Swann, D. [1978], *The Economics of the Common Market*, 4th edn. Harmondsworth: Penguin.

Swann, D. [1979], 'The Common Market after Twenty Years' in Bowers, J. K. (ed.), *Inflation Development and Integration*. Leeds: Leeds University Press.

The Economist [1977], 'The trials and tribulations of making up nine minds', 3 September 1977, pp. 49, 53–4.

Tsoukalis, L. [1977], *The Politics and Economics of European Monetary Integration*. London: Allen and Unwin.

Index